Don't Drop the Mic

Don't Drop the Mic

The Power of Your Words
Can Change the World

T. D. JAKES

WITH DR. FRANK THOMAS

Faith Words

New York Nashville

Cover design by Dexter Jakes
Cover photograph by Kathy Tran Photography

FaithWords
Hachette Book Group
1290 Avenue of the Americas, New York, NY 10104
faithwords.com
twitter.com/faithwords

First edition: April 2021

FaithWords is a division of Hachette Book Group, Inc. The FaithWords name and logo are trademarks of Hachette Book Group, Inc.

The publisher is not responsible for websites (or their content) that are not owned by the publisher.

The Hachette Speakers Bureau provides a wide range of authors for speaking events. To find out more, go to www.hachettespeakersbureau.com or call (866) 376-6591.

Library of Congress Cataloging-in-Publication Data

Names: Jakes, T. D., author.
Title: Don't drop the mic : the power of your words can change the world / T. D. Jakes with Dr. Frank Thomas.
Description: First edition. | New York, NY : Faith Words, [2021] | Includes bibliographical references.
Identifiers: LCCN 2020053580 | ISBN 9781455595358 (hardcover) | ISBN 9781546015895 (large print) | ISBN 9781455595341 (ebook)
Subjects: LCSH: Communication—Religious aspects—Christianity.
Classification: LCC BV4597.53.C64 J35 2021 | DDC 230.01/4—dc23
LC record available at https://lccn.loc.gov/2020053580

ISBNs: 978-1-4555-9535-8 (hardcover), 978-1-4555-9534-1 (ebook), 978-1-5460-4166-5 (international edition), 978-1-5460-1589-5 (large print)

Printed in the United States of America

LSC-C

10 9 8 7 6 5 4 3 2 1

Contents

PART 5
The Meal in the Message

PART I

Introduction: The Voice of Hope

In the beginning was the Word, and the Word was with God, and the Word was God. . . . And the Word was made flesh, and dwelt among us, full of grace and truth.

—John 1:1,14 KJV

The book you're now reading is not the one I first envisioned.

In fact, I was a bit reluctant to write a book about communication at all because I consider myself much more a practitioner than a professor, more preacher than a pedagogue, and more personal than professional in my approach. Throughout the years, though, I have been asked many times by younger men and women for advice, counsel, and wisdom on how to communicate effectively. Many of these requests referred to preaching, which is certainly an area of experiential expertise, but as my ministry expanded and new opportunities led me into speaking, writing, creating, and producing, I was frequently asked for tips on communicating in a variety of media.

Then my friend Dr. Frank Thomas, both a seminary professor and a pastor, urged me to share the wisdom I've gleaned from my own experiences, along with my observations and practical suggestions about how to maximize your message at the microphone. With his help, which I'll explain in Chapter 1, I grew excited about considering how I do what I do and how this knowledge can help others. Thinking of my overall concept for this book, I was taken by the duality and paradox of what it means to "drop the mic."

On the one hand, having a mic-drop moment conveys the powerful, resonant impact virtually every communicator desires to have with his or her audience. While you may not literally drop the mic after you speak at the city council meeting, school fundraiser, board of directors' retreat, or church event, you definitely want to make the most of those opportunities when you're required to impart a message. You want to leave listeners impressed and inspired, informed and intrigued, by what you have shared.

On the other hand, dropping the mic can also mean fumbling those same opportunities, either out of fear, a lack of experience, unfamiliarity with your audience, a lack of preparation, or other barriers we will discuss. This kind of mic drop costs you more than you realize and results in misunderstanding, confusion, ambiguity, and diminished confidence in your own abilities to communicate. While every time you speak may not be an earth-shattering, standing-ovation, mic-drop moment, it can be a completed connection of contextual conversation between you and your audience.

Every speaker either creates more distance between himself and his audience, or closes the gap and bridges those differences. My desire is to help you make the most of your mic, whatever it may be, and connect with those receiving your message. Along the way I hope you will realize the unparalleled power of successful communication even as you practice it more productively, passionately, and potently. And let me assure you, I will be learning right along with you!

You see, for the past few months, I have been preaching in an empty church sanctuary due to the need to limit human contact and shelter at home in order to prevent the perpetuation of the COVID-19 virus. Just as the global pandemic has touched and altered all facets of human life, so, too, has it required church to marry technology with tenacity in order to create connections, facilitate corporate worship across countless screens, lift up one another in prayer, and experience sermons intended to empower, equip, and enhance our faith during these calamitous times.

Prior to the pandemic, at the Potter's House we would often stream live services and provide video archives of past services and sermons for our global online congregation. In many ways, though, our electronic capabilities and Internet offerings seemed ancillary, if not peripheral, to in-person participation for the thriving community actively involved in our main church and affiliated sister churches. Then our awareness of the virus descended and changed everything. We maximized our technical capacity for reaching out, connecting, and communicating as a church body. Small groups began meeting with Zoom for their Bible studies, and social media became the method of reaching out to those in need. Overnight, our online audience increased by 200 percent.

The coronavirus amplified the power of the microphone, and I was not about to let it drop. I was bombarded with requests for interviews, overwhelmed by personal calls and texts from people wanting my opinions on how to function in the pandemic, and sought by pastors and ministry leaders for counsel on conducting their services and meetings.

All that sustained us was our words. We had no vaccine or distribution plans for vaccinations. No one knew what to do, where to turn, or exactly what to believe. A reporter interviewing me from a well-known conservative station asked how I prayed for our nation. Another journalist from a liberal news outlet engaging me on the pandemic asked if I would pray for our nation and our world on the spot.

Feeling a responsibility to use my platform to combat the contagion, I invited doctors, scientists, medical experts, and the surgeon general from our state to address my online viewers with critical information about how to prevent the spread of the virus and how to proceed if they had been exposed or were experiencing symptoms. I also asked psychologists, counselors, and therapists to advise us on how to maintain our mental health by keeping depression, anxiety, fear, and anger at bay. Financial advisors and employment coaches also participated.

Words were our most powerful weapons as we sought to educate ourselves and each other about the scientific specifics of this unprecedented virus. Words became our lifelines against loneliness and isolation as we endured separation from loved ones, coworkers, community members, and church family.

This crisis left our nation more separated than ever before. We could not leave our homes, shake hands, or hug loved ones and friends. We grieved alone, struggled alone, died alone. Working from home, we had to learn to command an audience online while our kids cried for more cereal, the cat attacked the sofa, and the doorbell rang with our order of groceries.

Like so many of us, I was stuck at home but never busier. While I was not traveling as usual, I communicated with more people in more venues around the world than I had ever done. I joined my voice with those of other faith leaders in hopes of easing the anguish and angst of us all, knowing our greatest offering was simply hope itself. The Potter's House did what we could to safely meet the needs of our members, our neighbors, and our global ministry community.

We helped feed the hungry, providing more than three thousand meals to third-shift hospital workers who found food outlets and carry-out restaurants often closed when they got off work. This seemed just as important as disseminating trustworthy information about the virus as well as praying for the spiritual needs of individual souls. When Jesus was preaching and people got hungry, he fed the five thousand before trying to impart his teaching. Following his example, we tried to lead using the power of our global mic, supporting the ecosystem and sustaining connection.

Logging in to connect with people from all over the world while wearing my pajama bottoms and T-shirt, I offered whatever words of wisdom, of encouragement, of hope I could. I spoke with Neil Caputo on Fox News, Gayle King on *CBS This Morning*, my friends on *Good Morning America*, TBN—conservative and liberal without discrimination. I was bombarded by pastors calling from Nigeria, the United Kingdom, Australia, and around the world, all seeking to learn and share best practices for how to serve in the midst of a phenomenon without precedent in our lifetimes.

Regardless of the different demographics we served, we shared a common enemy and faced a common crisis. We needed the synergism of different cultures, ideologies, and practices in order to find a sustainable cure to ensure our individual and collective survival. Everywhere imaginable, I continued speaking, teaching, sharing, and dispelling myths that were killing us. I didn't hesitate and was one of the first pastors to speak out against keeping church open during the pandemic. No matter what the consequences, I did not want our services to become a petri dish for the coronavirus.

Every day I talked to pastors who are now on respirators or suffering through the symptoms of the virus because they continued to operate as usual until it was too late. Statistically, African Americans comprise roughly half of all casualties of the coronavirus in our country. The Latinx community has also been hit hard.

All the more reason to communicate truth. We could not afford to buy into cultural myths about drinking hot water or holding our breath. We had to disseminate what was medically and scientifically known. I am probably the least qualified person to talk about the virus. I am not a doctor, scientist, political leader, or surgeon general, but my people trust me! They know I will never compromise the truth. They know I am fully committed to their health and well-being, regardless of whether we agree on all social, political, or theological issues.

At the time the pandemic gripped us all, I had more than eleven thousand people registered to attend my annual leadership conference, but I didn't think twice about canceling it. I would never use my platform to perpetuate anything that puts others' health and well-being at risk. Using your power of communication to address the people within your network of relationships means knowing when to say no and when to say yes.

Even as it felt like we were sinking on the *Titanic*, we pooled our resources to keep our communities afloat. With relatives battling the virus and close friends dying, so many pastors continued to preach in front of empty pews in order to offer words of hope and spiritual power to those they serve. From megachurch founders to storefront pastors, we all collaborated on how to be relevant in serving the needs of their congregations and the world at large.

Why? Because the words of a leader are never more important than during a crisis. Local officials asked our church counselors to talk with first responders over the phone. Through it all, we didn't miss a service—in fact, I added more online services! I know how important it is to have a calming voice say, "I'm in it with you. You're not alone!" We worship together to remind us that God is still with us, in our midst, at work in us and through us.

Even those of us blessed with resources, income, and relationships have experienced trauma from the collective, cumulative, and comprehensive losses all around us. There's hardly a black person in America who doesn't know someone who has died from the virus. We saw bodies stacked in hotel rooms, eighteen-wheelers, and industrial storage freezers. We watched government leaders contradicting one another or competing for resources as if we were vying for a spot in the Olympics rather than fighting to stay alive on a daily basis. We did everything imaginable to keep ourselves and others from freaking out, but the emotional fallout, the effects of trauma, and PTSD are going to last beyond my lifetime.

Through all the uncertainty, fear, anxiety, anger, death, and grief, our words continue to give us life. They give us strength and courage, faith and hope. Our words matter now more than ever. Communication is as vital to human existence as air, water, food, and shelter. Using the power of written and spoken language, we can express our love, defend our rights, attain our education, persuade an opponent, defeat an adversary, and entertain millions of readers and listeners. Thanks to social media and online methodology, we can connect with millions of other people around the world.

As long as we can speak, we have hope.

Communication converts ideas into words and words into actions. From the moment an infant learns to associate the comfort of his mother's embrace with crying out in distress, human beings learn to communicate. Hearing sounds repeated forms patterns. Patterns become languages even as they retain distinct and colorful dialects.

It's no coincidence that the sacred gift of God's Son is expressed as "Word...made flesh" (John 1:14 KJV). Because words of truth always have the power to save us and set us free. We make a sacred offering when we're willing to speak the truth. We receive a sacred gift when we're willing to listen.

Sometimes the best way to beat an invisible enemy is with an invisible weapon. The coronavirus pandemic and everything in its wake remind us that language is surely one of our greatest resources. Our words form the strongest defense and provide the most effective tool. They equip us, empower us, entertain us, and enlighten us.

No, this is not the book I first envisioned.

Instead, I pray it is more relevant, more powerful, and more helpful to you as you accept the mic on the platform you've been given.

Your voice is needed.

Don't drop the mic!

CHAPTER I

The Gift of Speech

First learn the meaning of what you say, and then speak.

—Epictetus

Our words vibrate with the power of possibility. Just as circuits channel the crackle of electric currents, words form messages, whether written or spoken, that have changed the course of history countless times. I first felt the sparks of the charge they could carry as a boy clustered with my family around our television set. Our little house was the last house on the left at the end of a dead-end street, paved now but then just a dirt road, in Charleston, West Virginia. I can still see the ragged couch we all perched on to watch a console filled with tubes in the back and a screen in front made of glass as thick as my grandmother's bifocals.

It was the early sixties and our country was fractured by the Vietnam War, the Woodstock era, and the growing civil rights movement. Willie Mays was playing ball and the Supremes were as popular as Beyoncé is today. Lucy was eating more candy than she could pass down the factory assembly line, Aunt Bee was baking pies in Mayberry, and Lassie was the dog every child wanted!

One night, however, stands out more than all the rest. On the *Six O'Clock News*, we watched as a young man in a black suit enthralled a large crowd of listeners then called colored people. We soon learned he was a Baptist preacher named Dr. Martin Luther King, and never in my young life had I heard a speaker with such a melodious voice deliver tones with the cadence of a song.

As captivating as his speech was, I remember becoming distracted by an even more impressive revelation: My father was sitting with us and watching Dr. King. Through weary, heavy-lidded eyes, my father gazed so intently, his admiration for the man on the small screen unmistakable. Seldom did my father get to sit and watch TV with the rest of us. He was far too busy working to keep the electric bill paid to enjoy the frivolity of television programing. But watching Dr. King with the rest of us, my father had never seemed so engrossed in anything that I could recall.

Dr. King's controversial message of nonviolent resistance to the injustice of the times was as amazing to me as it was to my father. Against barking dogs and fire hoses spewing a deluge of hate, in an atmosphere of unbridled violence aimed at innocent people merely exercising their First Amendment rights, Dr. King stood firm with no weapons, no army tanks, nothing but the passionate elocution electrifying his audience with the sound of his voice and a message of hope.

No matter what his adversaries did to him, he just kept on speaking! His courage was remarkable. His cadence was legendary. It was then that I first realized the power of a man with a microphone. I'm not sure how to quantify the level of his impression on me as a child. Was it his message that moved me? Or maybe it was my father's rapt gaze at him? Whatever the allure, that night left me with one unforgettable takeaway: *A man with a microphone could change the world!*

Power of Life and Death

Dr. King's example illustrates the power of communication to accomplish what wars, weapons, and web wizardry cannot achieve. He ignited an awareness in me, along with millions of others, that what we say can divert devastation and unify those willing to listen with understanding. Dr. King illustrated and amplified the timeless truth I had learned in Sunday school that the tongue has the power over life and death (Proverbs 18:21).

This wisdom remains as timely as ever. Now more than ever, the power of communication commands our public attention as well as our personal interactions. Simply put, the sharper our array of communication skills, the more successful we become in virtually every endeavor.

Who among us can honestly say that their lives, loves, and even their livelihood won't benefit from developing and maintaining better communication skills? Whether they're used for conflict resolution in a tempestuous personal relationship with someone we love or whether we are interviewing for a career change that could affect the level to which we live, work, and play, we have a much better chance at success if we can communicate effectively.

As I embark upon the task of sharing about the significance of speaking and the powerful gift of communication we have been given, I hope you will find my humble offering beneficial in a variety of settings. While I have become a lifelong student and practitioner of communications, I do not write this book in an attitude of arrogance or superiority. Rather, my intent is to enhance our respect for the art of speaking and to enhance our eloquence as preachers, presenters, politicians, performers, poets, and entrepreneurs.

By sharing the ever-evolving journey of my own linguistic development, I hope my pitfalls can divert the direction of your own discourse, providing you with a clearer understanding of what's involved when we share language to convey meaning. Being a communicator myself, I understand its significance within the human experience, the importance of it in our relationships, our emotional equilibrium, and our creative expressions, as well as its vital significance as a lens outside ourselves into other lifestyles, cultures, communities, and businesses.

History would be vandalized if we lost the great speeches and founding documents that have developed, defined, and deepened the human condition. Great men and women have opened their mouths and changed the world. Writers have picked up their pens never knowing of the countless readers their missives would inspire, instruct, and entertain beyond their intended recipients.

You and I wield this same kind of power today.

Method of the Message

While technology gives us the ability to converse with people around the world with split-second speed and impeccable accuracy, it is not the power source of our communication. Now, I will try to avoid the propensity often exhibited among my generation to bemoan the development of technology—in part because it is this very innovation that enables me to pen these words in a cohesive, comprehensive manner as efficiently and effectively as possible! You and I have access to spell-check, grammar correction, auto-fill, and other linguistic conveniences that Shakespeare could never have imagined, not to mention methods such as e-mail, texts, tweets, and other social media.

Interestingly enough, we now live in an era when computerized voices guide us through prompts whenever we call for customer service assistance from major corporations. Other companies employ international troubleshooters to address domestic questions and concerns, which we may notice from the accented voice responding to our inquiry.

Listening devices such as Siri and Alexa, coupled with audio activation of autotype, record our speech patterns and repeated phrasing in order to program around our patterns. Key words on Instagram have replaced blog sites, and the convenience of tweets has replaced heartfelt talks on virtually every topic. I often wonder if our memories have shrunk as our phones have become smarter than their buyers!

Before you scoff at the notion of artificial intelligence robbing your brain of its old job, let me ask you, how many phone numbers do you remember? How many poems, Bible verses, and sports stats can you recite? Before we had such powerful cyber capabilities, we relied on our memories, emoting speeches and conversations that led our nation, solved our conflicts, united our families, and educated our children. For the most part, text and tweets have replaced much of the personal nature of communication. Minds groping for the right word have been replaced by our fingers looking for the right button!

While the Internet and language-interfacing

technology have provided a way for us to conduct meetings without having to travel, to inform others without invading their personal space, to celebrate family milestones without traveling any miles, they have also impaired the way we correspond. When limits of time, screen space, and character quantity dictate our directives, we lose more than eloquence in the details. Artful statements become archaic as personal styles of expressing ourselves to the fullest degree have become less central to cultural modes of communication.

I'm sure you realize that communication invites all the senses from the human eye to the listening ear. Authentic communication, however, isn't just audio, but it is also audiovisual if not multisensory. Communication for us as humans is an interesting mix of subliminal signals as well as audible sounds. A pause, a raised eyebrow, the hint of a smile—they convey just as much as our diction, tone, and style of speech.

Effective communication allows our body language and voice inflection to unite with our linguistics. The connection of all these modes creates a symphonic experience of expression that crescendos into a more elaborate concerto of sensory impressions received by our listeners. Looking back, I've reflected many times on how Dr. King mastered this fusion of speaker and speech, language and listener, method and message. I suspect all the great communicators that have made an impression on you similarly reflect this same rhetorical radiance.

Technology has increased the size of our potential audience, but have we compromised the unspoken intimacy of reading between the lines? Of feeling a message deep in our bones before our minds even have time to process it? Like a flood spilling across the plains, our online communication may cover more surface area but lacks the depth to create a current. Without diminishing the benefits of technology, we must consider how to maximize the quality of our communication, how to retain the rhetorical rhythms and lyrical linguistics that penetrate our hearts and minds, not just our eyes and ears.

Successful communication requires an exchange of understanding that transcends the syllables we hear or the sentences we see. Successful communication requires mastering the art of translation.

Lost in Translation

Communication, no matter how eloquent or effusive it may be, is incomplete if understanding isn't achieved.

Connecting with the recipient of your message is an essential element of successful communication because being understood is the ultimate objective. Words may be exchanged in a common language, but without understanding both the methods and the manners, the message is usually incomplete.

Understanding serves as the glue of effective communication. Being understood and understanding others require shared consideration of context, motive, intention, and culture. Understanding leads to shared space where common values emerge, along with goals of mutual benefit. Your emotional seedbed flourishes in an environment where you are understood. Your economic fortitude is enhanced; your value to the team accrues when you are able both to understand others and to be understood; and your ability to lead grows proportionately.

If the goal of communication is understanding, then it involves sharing more than the same established alphabet, language, and vocabulary. Speakers of the same language must still translate one another's messages within a cultural context and familiarity. We see this across historical periods, generational slang, and regional figures of speech.

For example, I have a friend from the rural South who often expresses his suspicion or doubt about something by declaring, "Something in that milk ain't clean!" The first few times I heard his colloquialism, I chuckled at the homespun wisdom of this memorable metaphor. Such phrasing had a freshness that caught my attention and conjured up a specific image. Over time, the expression began penetrating my thoughts, taking up residence in my head, until—guess what?—I started saying it, too! While I didn't intentionally decide to adopt it, subconsciously I became influenced by the speech of another person!

Is this not how we all learn to communicate when as infants we appropriate language from our parents? From simple vocabulary words and names to phrases and complete thoughts, we formulate our messaging by memorizing alphabetic and linguistic constructions. Sheer repetition establishes the most basic foundation of communication until we master other aspects of language and expression. While using the same letters and language is essential at first, we often overlook the idiosyncrasies of our mother tongue. We rarely consider that something that comes as naturally as speaking could be enhanced or endangered depending on what we do with what we have been given.

Speaking seems and feels natural, though, only because our first language, in my case English, isn't spoken merely because we studied it. We assimilate it because our parents or family members modeled it in their speech to us. Not just their vernacular or vocabulary, but also their intensity of tone, implementation of humor, or overall tenor conveyed consistently in our home and early environments. Like handheld mirrors, we reflect what's closest to us, or where we've been, and who we listen to, without even being aware that they are programming our speech through the filters of our sensory and neurological experiences.

Think of it this way: If a Chinese family had taken me home from the hospital, I would have grown up speaking Mandarin. I would've adopted the tone and timing that fit into the atmosphere and culture of my upbringing. If a family from Paris had taken me across the Atlantic Ocean at birth, I would likely be speaking French and regularly ordering croissants! So then the language we were first exposed to can often become our primary means of communication, complete with a twang, a staccato delivery, or a Southern drawl.

Because speech is reflective and reflexive, when you speak, you are telling me more than the sentences you construct. I am gathering information from both what's spoken and what's suggested by the way in which you speak. This kind of interpretation often gets labeled an impression, as in, the good kind you want to make on a prospective employer, an attractive date, or a new neighbor. Many times, we may not realize how much we convey beyond what we actually say!

Message Received

Where did we learn these nuanced ways of communicating? Those early exposures we had are like zip codes in that they identify general locations as to where we are in life, social status, generational phrasing, cultural colloquialisms, sense of humor, and intelligence. Early sights and sounds can leave us enunciating phrases with a British crispness or the rapid-fire, slurred speech of a street thug. Both speak English but can communicate very different messages even when speaking the same words!

We are influenced and often evaluated with early categorizations and often-permanent assumptions based on the tenor and texture of our speech. I know it's not fair, and I know it's not a completely accurate assessment. I'm just acknowledging that people do it every day! Shouldn't we know the full message we're sending?

Seeing, then, that our early and even later associations, experiences, and exposures can morph into a particular style as different as hip hop is from country music, we must master as many facets of our communication as possible, both to be understood and to understand others. Through these earliest influences we adopted dialects, shaped our accents, increased the use of certain colloquialisms, and established our euphemisms. Greater awareness of the language we speak, as well as how and why we say what we say the way we say it, is our first step toward more effective communication.

You aren't just a result of what you say. You are a result of who you listen to most often, engage with consistently, and spend time around socially! Who are you listening to? And did you ever realize that simply listening to them and dialoging consistently with them is programming you even after you walk away?

Sitting in counsel with those who communicate the way we wish we could can often improve our speaking styles. This sharpening can ultimately improve your economic bottom line, result in invitations to new opportunities, and enhance the number and quality of your relationships. Just as dogs hear high-pitched whistles that fall silent on human ears, our communication style will attract some and be ignored by others. All the more reason to be heard by those whose success you wish to emulate!

Let me ask you again: *Who* are you listening to?

More important, who is listening to *you*?

Power in Presence

My mother wisely said that no one knows how intelligent or ignorant you are until you open your mouth. The moment we start to speak, we learn more than the words formed. We listen to diction, articulation, and accents. We garner further insight from the intensity of pitch and tone, all partnering together to convey more than mere words alone could do. Emotions slip through our tone like sand through an hourglass!

Gifted performers learn to master these nuances. One of my favorite actors has always been Denzel Washington. Like all iconic masters of the craft, he can carry a scene that has no words at all. His facial expressions can speak an entire story arc in a matter of moments, expressing more with a glare, a shudder, or a snarl than any words in the script could achieve. There's a scene in *Safe House* when Denzel's character is dying, and he controls the entire event without saying a word. It is gripping and quite intense. And when he has lines, this Academy Award winner uses both the power of what he says and how he delivers the lines to convey the essence of the character he is portraying.

We often call this quality "presence," that intangible

force that Denzel, along with so many other expert communicators, possesses and wields so judiciously. I maintain that presence, or whatever we choose to call it, emerges anytime our message and our methods unite to reinforce one another. In fact, it is virtually impossible to ascertain how a person feels about what is being said without hearing their voice and reading their body language. This is why texts, e-mails, letters, and transcripts may be open to misunderstanding or misinterpretation more frequently than personal delivery.

Who would want an attorney who couldn't bring himself to stand before the scrutiny of a perplexed jury and passionately deliver a compelling closing statement? Or how does a commissioned sales representative overcome the reluctance of a prospective customer if she doesn't have the ability to use the pageantry of language to close the deal? What would teachers do without the capacity for reframing, restating, and rearranging the words required for their students to absorb new concepts?

Everyone from the politician to the pulpiteer to the parent to the panelist relies on the sheer art of communication to compel transformative decisions every day. The use of language has transformed strangers into lovers, fueling the vehicle that transports them to the altar of a sacred sanctuary to share vows formalizing their union in holy matrimony. The eloquence of language was used to dissuade hostage takers and would-be assailants from igniting the violence of genocide in Rwanda and the atrocities of apartheid in South Africa. Powerful speech abolished the once-accepted societal plight of the South's Jim Crow laws, persuading the Supreme Court to purge our country from the hideous sin of slavery.

We have achieved milestones in human history because someone somewhere appreciated the power of the microphone, not the bullets of an AK47, the intimidation of an army tank, or the barking dogs on the side of nervous police. Counselors have used language to prevent suicides by talking those in despair away from the edge while mothers communicate to calm an agitated baby from hysteria to a slumbering rest. The vocal cords, coupled with tongue and teeth, have been as powerful as any weapon known to us. The Bible tells us even God used "the foolishness of what was preached to save those who believe" (1 Corinthians 1:21 NIV).

Indeed, speech is a powerful tool!

Speak from Your Soul

Down through the years, I've become best known for my communication as a preacher and public speaker. In addition to preaching and public speaking, however, I've also learned to adapt my communication methods and modalities through the movies I've produced, the television work I've done, and the many books I've written. Regardless of the medium, my communication style is a mix of all the previous men and women in the little world that I grew up in. It was born from an instinctive place, influenced by hearing many models.

My style comes from my soul because so much of what I communicate is some form of ministry. My speech and the style of my delivery began outside the camp of any academic training and beyond the doors of any seminary. Instead, I've relied on spirit and spunk, wind and warmth, compassion and conversation—all seasoned with a passionate and often poetic fusion of ancestry, heritage, and the power of a listening ear and open heart.

Nonetheless, I've always appreciated the academic perspective—theological, hermeneutical, and linguistic—showcased by many other preachers and ministry leaders. Which brings me back to my friend Dr. Frank Thomas and the catalyst for this book. Dr. Thomas and I met a number of years ago at an annual ministerial conference when he introduced himself and we began chatting about each other's presentations. I was immediately impressed with his credentials as well as his grounded, practical manner of discussing the more academic facets of preaching. A renowned scholar currently serving as the Director of the PhD Program in African American Preaching and Sacred Rhetoric at Christian Theological Seminary, Indianapolis, Indiana, Dr. Thomas also teaches homiletics there and has frequently published on his findings.

I soon discovered his balanced approach resulted from being a pastor for many years in addition to his education and expertise as a seminary professor. From my experience, the best teachers are also practitioners in their areas of expertise, and such is the case with Dr. Thomas. As we got better acquainted, we realized just how much we had in common despite the different paths taken in answering the call to ministry. He not only enjoyed my preaching over the years but began providing insight and analysis that left me stunned and humbled. Listening to Frank explain some of the sermons for which I'm best known, I felt like I was listening to halftime commentary by a veteran sports broadcaster reviewing highlights of his favorite ball games.

Intrigued as I was, I also felt intimidated and confessed that I had never considered the way I did what I do in the ways he described. Dr. Thomas then urged me to write a book in which I did just that—shared the wisdom I've gleaned about communication and analyzed it in ways that others would find helpful. He stressed the need to create a linguistic legacy for future generations studying preaching and my place in the historical canon of black preachers.

I chuckled at the lofty aspirations he wished to ignite in me, and I explained that I could never write such a book. Frankly, the very idea was both intimidating and intrusive! Such scrutiny of my communication style felt like a violation of the personal, intimate process of creation, a granular autopsy of what begins in the abstract birthing of an idea. It was like asking your grandmother to pass on a recipe that has become part of who she is, instinctively consisting of a dab of this and a smidgen of that.

"All the more reason to ask for the recipe while you can!" Dr. Thomas responded. The more I resisted, the more he persisted, until finally I told him I was willing to consider such an endeavor on one condition:

that he actively participate by sharing some analytical insight afforded by his academic training. I knew that my attempts to explore the facets of the communication process would be limited without the unique perspective provided by the various lenses Dr. Thomas could provide. Intrigued by the creative challenge, he and I continued having conversations about the power of communication in our culture.

The result is this book you're now reading! As you will see, I often include Dr. Thomas's insight in my expository exploration of eloquence, drawing from both his vast historical knowledge as well as his own experience as a gifted communicator. In fact, I was so impressed by his overview of my preaching within a larger historical and theological perspective, I asked him to author his own chapters, which are collected in Part 5, "The Meal in the Message." There, Dr. Thomas runs with our cooking metaphor and unpacks it with a brilliance I trust you will find every bit as delicious and nourishing as a Sunday dinner!

My goal, as well as his, is not to promote my way of communication as the only or best way. We merely hope to challenge you to consider the forces and factors shaping your own style of communication even as you adapt, adjust, and aspire to new forms of self-expression. As we share the ways I often transform my thoughts into words to be shared with various audiences, I hope you can learn from what works for me as well as from the mistakes I've made along the way.

Sometimes we learn the most when our communication falls flat. In fact, I've heard some scholars suggest that I break every rule that they teach about preaching! While I apologize in advance for those broken rules, I do so without shame, because what I do works for me. So let's now discover what works best for you, even if we have to break some rules along the way. Let's learn the unspoken alphabet inside you waiting to unleash the language of your soul!

If nothing else, I hope to spark your passion for language, elevate its significance beyond the formalized rules of grammatical correctness into the lavish coloring of mundane moments, and inspire you to use all the hues and shades available as you wield your paintbrush of speech. Language is a gift and it's time you unwrapped it fully and maximized its potential to influence your life.

Many have been the pallbearers of their dreams simply because they didn't understand that enhancing their communication skills could be the conduit to reaching those dreams. The ability to speak can aid in helping people, serving the disenfranchised, increasing sales, reaching the masses, stopping wars, and gaining untold, boundless advancement, simply by commanding and channeling the constructive, creative force of language.

The more adept we become at using all available resources to convey our message, the greater our impact. From lovers to litigators, entrepreneurs to entertainers, and bloggers to board members, we all want to communicate more effectively, intimately, and efficiently. Whether you're interviewing for a new position, proposing a new business plan, auditioning for a performance, delivering a report for your committee, teaching Sunday school, or sharing your heart with a loved one, this book is for you!

Let's get started, shall we?

CHAPTER 2

Own the Fear Factor

What the mind doesn't understand, it worships or fears.

—Alice Walker

The first time I preached, or at least the first time I recall standing in the pulpit of a small country church in West Virginia, I was a teenager with more energy than eloquence, more ambition than experience. I'll never forget feeling as if my legs might give way and collapse like the accordion file my mother used to collect coupons. My mouth remained as dry as a desert while my heart felt like an anchor sinking into the depths of anxious uncertainty. The butterflies in my stomach morphed into frantic bees buzzing up into my brain in a swarm of colliding thoughts. I had prepared, rehearsed, prayed, asked others to pray, and rehearsed some more.

I doubt there were more than a hundred congregants gazing back at me that Sunday, but I might as well have been addressing crowds in a stadium on that first momentous occasion. Momentous, not necessarily for those in attendance—although I hope they received some spiritual nourishment from my delivery of God's Word that day—but momentous because I pushed through my fears. I refused to let my nerves rule my rhetoric and my doubts sabotage my sermon. I'm sure I stuttered, stammered, paused, and lost my place in the mental outline I had memorized so diligently and the notes I had written out so carefully.

But like David slaying Goliath, I loaded my words into the slingshot of faith and did what I sensed God might be calling me to do. I gave voice to expressions and ideas larger than myself and my understanding of the world. It was far from perfect, but it was a small victory that has had enormous consequences in my life. Since then, I have preached in churches before thousands of people, spoken on stages before world dignitaries, and prayed with presidents, but none of those occasions would have occurred if I had never stood in that pulpit as a young man determined to share what I had to say.

Fear must never be the obstacle that blocks your development, growth, and maturity as a communicator. Fear of failing, fear of succeeding, fear of what others will think, fear of what your mama will think, fear of making a fool of yourself, fear of being misunderstood, criticized, and taken out of context—as with any area of personal growth, fear is likely to be part of the equation. When it comes to communicating, however, fear is but one variable among many, not the limitation that prevents you from being heard by those around you.

Owning your fear is the first step in facing it, and facing it to overcoming it.

The Sound of Your Voice

I'm often amazed that people rank speaking in public near the top of their list of worst fears. Known by the clinical word *glossophobia*, fear of public speaking terrifies some people more than death, divorce, cancer, unemployment, spiders, and snakes! Now all of those certainly frighten me, especially those last two, but allowing any of my fears to prevent me from doing what I'm made to do may be my greatest fear of all.

It's not that I no longer get nervous, anxious, or

even fearful, prior to stepping onstage or standing in the pulpit. It's not that I can't relate to the stress of wanting to have other people understand the layered ideas that seem so clear in my mind yet often get tangled when I attempt to weave my words together. My amazement is because people who refuse to face their fear of communicating before crowds, corporate gatherings, or congregations lose more than they save by avoiding such opportunities. With communication, the old adage of "Nothing ventured, nothing gained" becomes "Nothing ventured, something lost."

For when we allow others to speak for us, when we step away from the mic thrust in front of us by circumstances, then we relinquish power and defer our dreams. Ultimately, I cannot speak for you and your experience, no matter how much we may have in common or how many times we've shared meaningful moments. Consider how people often experience the same event in the same place at the same time and come away with very different interpretations, understandings, and experiences.

You only have to reflect on certain family stories from growing up to realize how differently each relative viewed the incident at the time it happened and how they've interpreted it since. What one of your siblings recalls as a fond incident in which you were teasing one another, you may consider a traumatic event that shifted your relationship into one of fearful antagonism. The same holds true for parents and children. I'm always amazed when one of my sons or daughters remembers a family event in radically different ways than I recall it.

Psychologists and neurologists tell us that not only do we experience the same events distinctly from one another, but our memories also color those events in unique shades and hues, both positively and negatively. Our personality, temperament, other experiences, and circumstances create individual viewpoints as distinct as our fingerprints. While there's nothing new under the sun, there are infinite ways to filter its light through the lens of your unique perspective!

My point is that if you're not willing to face whatever fears and apprehensions you may have about communicating in public, then you lose out and those around you lose as well. You may have the critical input that inspires your team to innovate new solutions to old problems. You might be the teacher capable of addressing students in variations of their own vernacular, revealing the relevancy of information others were not able to impart. You could be the next stand-up comic bringing laughter to millions of people. Or the next mediator facilitating peace among conflicted stakeholders. The next leader bringing communities together to foster change.

But if you're not willing to risk letting others hear the sound of your voice, then none of those will be possible. If you have a dream, if you feel called, if you're inspired to pursue your best life, then you must be willing to speak. You must be willing to communicate before you can hope to realize your full potential. Excuses will always pop up like weeds in the sidewalk cracks, but you must never let them keep you from moving forward and letting your voice be heard.

Giant Obstacles

As you muster courage and find your voice, take comfort in knowing that the fear of communicating publicly is nothing new. In fact, we see several notable examples of inexperienced, reluctant speakers in the Bible, including Moses, Gideon, and Esther. When I reflect on the various leaders God chose to call and anoint to serve his people, I'm struck by the fact that he never went with the obvious choice, at least from a human perspective.

Just consider the scenario when God sent his prophet Samuel to anoint Saul's successor as the next king of Israel. Samuel was sent to a little rural town called Bethlehem, important as the birthplace of not only this king but the King of Kings. Once in Bethlehem, Samuel followed the Lord's direction to the home of Jesse, where the prophet began going from son to son only to have God indicate that this was not the man: "Do not consider his appearance or his height, for I have rejected him. The LORD does not look at the things people look at. People look at the outward appearance, but the LORD looks at the heart" (1 Samuel 16:7 NIV).

Running out of prospects, Samuel asked Jesse if there was anyone else in his household and discovered that the youngest son, David, a mere teenager, was out tending sheep. Surely, he could not be the one God had chosen as the next king! Yet, of course, he was indeed God's choice, a legendary leader later described as a man after God's own heart (1 Samuel 13:14; Acts 13:22).

While David waited and matured into his position of royal authority, he gained plenty of experience in public speaking. He was certainly a gifted poet and lyricist, which we know from ample evidence in the many Psalms authored by him. But writing poems on a hillside while the sheep graze in green pastures is not the same thing as finding the right words in the heat of the moment, when those words have the potential to matter most.

We see young David in this kind of situation not long after Samuel had anointed him, most likely. As Israel fought off the invading Philistines, most able-bodied young men were conscripted into the king's army, including three of David's older brothers: Eliab, Abinadab, and Shammah (1 Samuel 17:13). Left at home to help with chores and tend his father's sheep, David finally got to see the front lines of battle when his father sent him to take food and supplies to his brothers there (1 Samuel 17:17–19).

Upon arrival, David discovered a huge obstacle loomed over the Hebrew soldiers: a giant warrior named Goliath. The warring armies had reached a standoff, with each positioned on a hillside separated by a valley between them. Blocking the Israelites' advancement to defend their borders, Goliath relished his role as merciless marauder and had quite a reputation even before creating this impasse. Specific details about this adversary explain why Saul and his men were "dismayed and terrified" (1 Samuel 17:11 NIV) and "fled from him in great fear" (1 Samuel 17:24 NIV).

Goliath was almost 10 feet tall, and his armor alone weighed about 150 pounds! Not only did he look the part of the snarling, militant mercenary, but this giant loved using the platform so many bullies create for themselves, using the microphone his size and military victories had given him to taunt his rivals (1 Samuel 17:4–10). The Philistine was so confident of his immense power in battle that he offered to distill the entire war into one man-to-man fight between himself and any of Saul's men willing to take him on, winner take all. For good measure, Goliath added, "This day I defy the armies of Israel! Give me a man and let us fight each other." This stalemate continued for 40 days, with the giant yelling his taunts every morning and evening.

Despite the centuries separating us in time, the giant's jibes are remarkably similar to those of the trolls and haters on our social media today. Bullies will always brag, boast, and belittle those who oppose them or call them out on their abuse of power, position, or passion. In our virtual world of immediate, ubiquitous connectivity, everyone can have a voice, which unfortunately includes those who use their communication for intimidation. Ignoring them is sometimes the better part of wisdom, but there are occasions when you absolutely cannot avoid confronting someone who postures like Goliath, either online or in person. Especially if they are terrorizing those who are defenseless or trash-talking that which is sacred to you.

Which is exactly why David was so upset! He heard Goliath mocking the God of Israel, whose soldiers refused to even attempt to engage in battle with the giant. Despite his youth, inexperience, and lack of proper equipment for battle, David knew he had to speak up and step out in faith by accepting the Philistine's challenge. Some occasions demand that you speak up and express the undiluted truth of an injustice that has transpired or make known the heinous offense perpetrated by those in authority.

You see, giants still exist today.

They go by names like Prejudice, Racism, Brutality, Inequality, and Oppression.

A Time to Speak

We have recently experienced an egregious trauma that necessitated not just one but millions of voices joining together in a chorus of outrage, grief, and pent-up anger that had been festering for untold generations. When George Perry Floyd Jr. was tragically and senselessly killed by a Minneapolis police officer before countless witnesses, millions more reached the tipping point of their silence. No longer could they weep in isolation or rage behind closed doors.

No longer could they simply turn away or limit their anger to a singular text or isolated e-mail to others who they knew felt the same way.

No, on May 25, 2020, recognition of the other pandemic afflicting our nation reached a critical level in public awareness. There was no mistaking the blatant brutality and arrogant authority behind the merciless murder occurring before our eyes as the police officer's knee pinned his full weight along the neck of a defenseless man lying on the ground. For more than eight minutes, the unbearable weight pressed into the top of George Floyd's spine, squeezing life-giving air from his lungs as he hoarsely cried, "I can't breathe!"

There is too much to say—books and books long after I am gone—about the intersection of issues and collision of political, social, racial, and cultural variables in that scene. With tears in my eyes as I write this, I will limit my focus to the absolute necessity of overcoming the fear of silence in order to vocalize the unmitigated outrage of such assaults. While many, many others—including Breonna Taylor, Eric Garner, Michael Brown, Freddie Gray, Tamir Rice, and Atatiana Jefferson, just to name a recent few—have needlessly perished in fatal encounters with those supposedly dedicated and paid to serve and protect, the death of George Floyd opened a floodgate of voices protesting the undeniable assault and systemic racism within our society.

Millions of people rose up to speak, to tweet, to text, to e-mail, to cry and shout and demand reform, recognition, and restitution. They marched together, wept together, comforted one another, and demanded that others listen to their message, that Black lives matter just as much as those of any other human beings. In the midst of a global, uncontained viral pandemic, people risked coming together in a chorus of courage rather than suffer in silence or turn blind eyes away from the horror.

And I must say, it was the diversity of people I saw marching, speaking, and carrying signs that ignited sparks of hope in my soul. Yes, I was proud of my community and our willingness to protest with the same peaceful, passionate power as Dr. King's march from Selma to Montgomery in 1965. And I would expect no less from my people who have suffered, endured, and persevered through generations of slavery, savagery, and segregation in order to attain the same basic human freedoms due every citizen in these United States of America.

What heartened me in the protests I observed following the death of George Floyd was the number of Caucasian men, women, and children I saw marching in lockstep with neighbors, friends, relatives, and strangers, showing they refused to be included in the passive privilege of their parentage. They showed that they were with us and would not remain silent, indifferent, or detached from this egregious pattern of injustice, violence, and brutality ripping apart the fabric of our nation.

Many of these people, both black and white, obviously overcame whatever fears and trepidations lurked inside because they could no longer endure the abuse of power and senseless killings outside. Suffering people have always found a way to communicate, from Lamentations and the Psalms of lament we see in Scripture to the gospel songs sung by slaves to liberate their spirits despite the captivity of their bodies. This form of communication is essential to human survival. Even in the midst of utter hopelessness, the kind experienced by captives during the Holocaust, people have dared to carve words of hope into floorboards or scribble prayers on scraps of trash. Human survival relies on our willingness to communicate, especially in the face of trauma.

We're told in Ecclesiastes that everything has a time and that timing is everything, including a time to speak and a time to be silent (Ecclesiastes 3:7). There are indeed times when we learn that our best contribution to a conversation is to keep quiet, but we must never allow fear to gag the truth when we know we must speak. Even when you feel like you don't have a microphone or any kind of platform from which others will hear the sound of your voice, you must still speak up, knowing that there will be opposition and attempts to silence you.

The Right Fit

David certainly faced opposition even as he valiantly chose to do what no one else, including the king, was willing to do—face the giant in a showdown to the death. Not surprising but disappointing nonetheless, the courageous shepherd got little support from his brothers, his comrades, and his king. His own brother apparently misinterpreted David's motive as ego rather than the conviction to stand up for his faith. Eliab basically accused David of being just like Goliath, boastful and arrogant: "I know how conceited you are and how wicked your heart is; you came down only to watch the battle" (1 Samuel 17:28 NIV).

When you use your voice to speak out, there will always be others who misinterpret your motives. Communicators with conviction will always make some people, particularly those who justify their own silence and inaction, uncomfortable and angry. These destructive discouragers either lack the courage required to speak into the microphone placed before them or fear the consequences of others just like them waiting to pounce and pulverize their message. When you know you are doing what God compels you to do, when you know the truth of what motivates you, then you must not be deterred by your detractors.

Nor should you be intimidated by would-be instructors, those people who, whether well intended or jealously skeptical, tell you not only what to say but how to say it! After David told King Saul, "Don't worry about this Philistine—I'll go fight him!" (1 Samuel 17:32 NLT), the king immediately dismissed him: "Don't be ridiculous! There's no way you can fight this Philistine and possibly win! You're only a boy, and he's been a man of war since his youth" (1 Samuel 17:33 NLT).

David, however, would not be stopped from communicating in both word and deed his faith-fueled fearlessness. He explained to Saul that he had killed lions and bears while protecting his sheep and believed that God would empower him to slay Goliath just as easily. It wasn't the kind of experience the king or anyone else expected, but in David's thinking, his past conquests required the same level of courage, determination, and skill.

Resigning himself to what he perceived as the young man's naïve determination, King Saul then tried to equip David with his own royal armor and sword. He not only offered his sword, helmet, and armor to the young man, but Saul actually dressed David in his own tunic (1 Samuel 17:32). Such an action by the king was bold as well as humbling.

Perhaps his offer was made out of pity or to relieve the cowardice whispering within his own conscience. Many times when you speak up and display leadership in the face of adversity, others will try to compel you to use their platforms and microphones. Their motives ultimately cannot be discerned, but they are often a mixture of guilt over their own cowardice, admiration of your courage, and obligation to make a token gesture for the watching eyes of other stakeholders. While you should weigh the benefits of accepting the mic someone else lends you, you should also be unafraid to politely decline.

Saul made an astounding gesture—kings don't offer their personal sword and armor to just anyone, and to David's credit, he tried on the royal weaponry. But then the young shepherd did something almost as courageous as facing Goliath—David declined the king's gift: "I cannot go in these," he said to Saul, "because I am not used to them" (1 Samuel 17:39 NIV). This was not the politically correct, socially expedient response to make to the king!

But David knew this was not the time to be thinking about social etiquette and political correctness because the threat posed by Goliath loomed over all of them. Such a dangerous obstacle eclipsed any hurt feelings or royal breach of protocol Saul might have experienced.

When you have a God-given message to deliver, it may require you to risk stepping on a few toes, declining what others offer, disappointing them, and potentially hurting their feelings and losing their support. You certainly don't want to rush in and leave collateral damage in the wake of your communication unnecessarily, but at the same time you must not allow fear of what others may think to stifle your voice or censor your message.

Like David, you use what you know and sling your message!

And let your words land where they land.

Keep It Real

After rejecting Saul's armor and sword, David took up his shepherd's staff and slingshot and reached into the nearby stream for five smooth stones (1 Samuel 17:40). He used what he felt comfortable using rather than the cumbersome, ill-fitting items offered by the king. David was a shepherd from a small, rural town with no military training or experience in battle. While others might be too embarrassed to use such crude weapons, especially when he could've used the finest available, David knew he had to rely on his strengths, the past experiences he did have, and familiar tools with which he was comfortable.

Instead of posturing like Goliath or the king, David brought himself and no one else to the microphone. If you want to overcome your fears of speaking in front of others, if you want to gain experience in order to develop as a communicator, then *start where you are.* And *be who you are*! Be true to who you are, where you came from, and what you know. Don't try to be anyone else. Don't try to use words with eight syllables just to impress! Don't act like you know what your audience has been through if you don't.

Be yourself and be real.

I cannot tell you how many times I've heard young preachers deliver a sermon that fit them like a cheap suit two sizes too small! Why? Because they're trying to preach like me or Joel Osteen or Jesse Jackson or Billy Graham or the pastor who mentored them. One of the hardest lessons to learn as you overcome your fears, self-consciousness, and anxiety is to find your own groove, your own lane, and your own voice. Of course, you will display certain traits and qualities of the men and women who have influenced you and your message. But there's a big difference between implementation and imitation! Don't try to imitate someone else, but do implement aspects of what you admire, appreciate, and adore about them.

When the moment came for David to step up to the mic and deliver his message, he spoke the truth before following through and defeating the giant. Knowing you can back up your words with actions is crucial if you want to be heard, respected, and valued as a leader. As you and I know all too well, many people say what they believe others want to hear without the ability to follow through and transform their words into deeds. The temptation is great, whether leading a family, a classroom, a small group at church, your team at work, a board meeting, or government office.

As he stepped up to his mic, David also had to

contend with major trash-talking from his opponent. Seeing the shepherd's staff in his young challenger's hand, Goliath taunted, "Am I a dog, that you come at me with sticks?" (1 Samuel 17:43 NIV). He didn't stop there either: "And the Philistine cursed David by his gods. 'Come here,' he said, 'and I'll give your flesh to the birds and wild animals!'" (1 Samuel 17:44 NIV).

If Goliath expected to receive the same kind of insults and threats from David, then I wonder how he received David's response, which reveals a radically different perspective than the giant's trivial trash-talking:

> David said to the Philistine, "You come against me with sword and spear and javelin, but I come against you in the name of the LORD Almighty, the God of the armies of Israel, whom you have defied. This day the LORD will deliver you into my hands, and I'll strike you down and cut off your head. This very day I will give the carcasses of the Philistine army to the birds and the wild animals, and the whole world will know that there is a God in Israel. All those gathered here will know that it is not by sword or spear that the LORD saves; for the battle is the

> LORD's, and he will give all of you into our hands." (1 Samuel 17:45–47 NIV)

Before David defeated Goliath with his slingshot, he said what no one else had dared to say. He reframed the situation into something larger and more significant than a warrior bullying terrified soldiers or even than a battle determining Israel's fate. Saying David distilled the showdown into good versus evil oversimplifies the cultural and spiritual layers inherent in his viewpoint. In David's eyes, the Philistine giant represented more than merely an arrogant blowhard or undefeated adversary in battle—Goliath defied all that David held most sacred, his faith, his beliefs, and the power of God. In light of all that was at stake, David delivered his message by describing what he was about to do and why he was doing it.

Then he did it—with one stone, he toppled the giant!

Speak to Silence Your Fears

I pray you never have to face a ten-foot giant blocking your path, but if you do, I hope you will not allow your fear to prevent you from delivering the message only you can deliver. Most of the giants we encounter only appear to be bigger because of the stress of the situation and our limited vantage point. We allow our imagination to dwell on worst-case scenarios and second-guess what others will think about what we know we need to say.

Consequently, our fears and anxieties amplify and inflate the ways we see and hear those people and positions opposing us. By fixating on our fears, we compound potential obstacles in our path and subjectively increase the size of potential barriers. Fear is never insurmountable, however. You may always feel a little nervous or excited prior to speaking in front of a group, but you don't have to be held hostage by fear. So let's consider four different kinds of fearful reactions you may experience when speaking and how to overcome them.

The first is simply the physical and physiological responses your body produces under duress. When faced with a threatening situation, your autonomic nervous system cannot discern between a prowler, a python, and a podium! Mentally, you know the difference and the level of potential danger posed by each, but your body goes into red-alert mode and prepares for flight, fight, or freeze. Your blood pressure rises, your heart rate increases, and your breathing grows rapid and shallow. At the extreme end, you have a panic attack that incapacitates your ability to function. On a more moderate scale, you may feel weak, experience slight nausea, a dry mouth, and a tight throat.

Overcoming your physiological reaction to the fear of speaking requires hitting the pause button on your body's natural response and countering with a physical habit, practice, or routine that helps you relax. It could be something as simple as closing your eyes and breathing deeply while counting to ten. You might sip some water and focus on the sensation of the cool liquid gliding down your throat and into your body. Visualization is often effective to calm both your body and your mind, with some people imagining a tranquil scene of natural beauty and serenity such as the ocean, a mountaintop, or a lakeshore.

Many people, myself included, will pray silently for a few moments before they say their first words into the microphone. The key is to discover a practice that helps your body break out of the stress mode and into a more relaxed state of focus. This practice then becomes a strategy for handling this kind of fearful anxiety every time you speak, which hopefully decreases as you gain experience.

The mental and psychological aspects of fear must also be addressed before you step up to the mic. Assessing and expressing your fears often helps alleviate them. Recognizing that you're afraid of embarrassing yourself in front of your coworkers can help you avoid doing just that. Acknowledging that you become self-conscious and critical of yourself may reveal the need to recall or recite affirmations, particularly past positive responses from others as well as encouraging truths about your abilities.

Many people feel shameful about the prospect of public speaking because of past times when they didn't perform their best or felt embarrassed by mistakes they made. While there's no magic formula to dispel your past-performance shame, it can be addressed and diminished. Identify what elements of past incidents make you feel this shame and then come up with tactics to avoid them happening again. Control the environment as much as possible by making sure you have a place to put your notes, that the tech portion of your presentation works, and that you have water nearby.

These mental variables may be closely intertwined with the emotional dimension of your fears. While many speakers obviously are afraid of faltering when handed the mic, they may also fear succeeding just as much or more. Preparation, research, and rehearsal can aid in overcoming a fear of failure, but dazzling your audience can be as daunting as disappointing them! Because when you engage them with meaningful content delivered in an appealing manner, you create expectations—essentially your brand.

This is, of course, a good thing, but also can add pressure and generate stress. This fear of sustaining success is something most people in creative endeavors often experience. Performers are only as good as their latest performance, singers as hot as their last song, writers as in-demand as their last bestseller, and speakers as sought-out as their last sold-out event. The key to dealing with a fear of success is staying true to who you were that first time you spoke. Remember, David had no reservations about using a slingshot to slay a giant!

Finally, you may discover your fears also include a spiritual dimension, especially if you're ministering, preaching, teaching the Bible, and wanting to inspire and encourage your audience. You may worry that you have nothing new or worthwhile to offer. You may fret over whether your message will make a difference or, even worse, inadvertently have a negative impact in some way. These are valid concerns, but I would challenge you to go back to what inspires, uplifts, and ministers to you. What have you learned that is worth passing on? How have you seen God at work in your life recently?

Believe that God is the one who has placed you in

this opportunity and trust that he will provide you with his message. When you look around and wonder why no one else is addressing the elephant in the room—especially if he's named Goliath—don't wait for someone else to speak! As David told his adversary, the battle belongs to the Lord. The same is true for us today. You have what it takes to overcome your fears and let your voice be heard.

Your time has come—so speak up!

CHAPTER 3

Preach but Don't *Preach*

I have come to believe over and over again that what is most important to me must be spoken, made verbal and shared, even at the risk of having it bruised or misunderstood.

—Audre Lorde

Whether it's a presentation to your team at work, a speech to accept a community service award, a monologue for open-mic night, or your next sermon, how you construct your message determines its impact. In the parlance of pastors, your congregation expects you to preach, so you want to exceed their expectations and preach with power, passion, and purpose like no one else. They want you to bring it, with "it" being everything you have it in you to communicate. They need you to be their voice even as you are the divine messenger for the transcendent voice of love. Preaching becomes a platform for acknowledging the depths of personal suffering of everyone in the room as well as offering insight, information, encouragement, and inspiration for moving through pain and reclaiming personal power.

It's important to note, however, that the word *preach* sometimes carries a pejorative connotation. In this usage, preaching is directive, prescriptive, often authoritarian, and frequently self-righteous. People might say, "Don't preach at me!" or "Keep your preaching in the pulpit!" They're referencing times when they've experienced preaching as a monologue, not a dialogue, as a way of overwhelming others with certain beliefs that must be accepted.

This kind of preaching rarely goes down well, though. None of us likes to be hammered by the harsh harangue of someone on their high horse! This kind of preaching is not limited to the pulpit but found in the classroom, in the boardroom, and on the campaign trail. It assumes a barrier rather than a bridge between the speaker and the listeners, a boundary that needs reinforcing rather than being reevaluated.

Growing up and experiencing a variety of different preachers and teachers, I quickly realized that the ones who tried to elevate themselves above their audiences created a barrier that only got in the way of the efficacy of their message. These were the teachers who delighted in humiliating students' ignorance in the classroom rather than igniting their curiosity for learning. These were the preachers spewing fire and brimstone from their pulpits who failed to see how scarred and scorched their congregants were from life's circumstances.

The key to preaching like an artist and not an antagonist begins with your attitude. As we have touched on and will explore in chapters to come, identifying and connecting with your audience is essential. Even when you and those receiving your communication have nothing in common except your humanity and a common language—and sometimes not even that, which means you need a good translator—you build from there. You consider what you have to offer those receiving your message and then construct it for maximum impact.

If you want to preach in the best sense and not the worst, then you must align your attitude with your architecture.

Excavation before Exclamation

Just as a blueprint helps a contractor bring the architect's vision to life, an outline or structural overview of your message provides you with a visual for navigating its contents. While you don't want to read from a script or forgo an outline altogether and simply wing it, you will find that having a blueprint opens up the middle ground in between those extremes. Outlines keep you grounded, focused, and centered on the primary points of your communication. They give you a skeleton, scaffold, and structure to support the ideas, examples, and anecdotes of your message.

I use the term *outline* for lack of a better one, but I realize an outline often varies in our associations. Some of us inwardly groan when we hear or see the word because it takes us back to English class or past public speaking opportunities, assignments, and situations where outlines were required and part of our assessment. We felt forced to contrive an artificial order with a prescribed number of points and supporting subpoints based on someone else's predetermined formula.

While using someone else's formula for outlining your message can sometimes help you get started, rarely does it permit you the room you need. In other words, use others' formulas for outlines as launching pads, not constricting containers. This enables you to discover a system of outlining that works best for you. The best borrowed outlines can give you the security of a place from which to build and the freedom to grow organically as your ideas take shape.

If you're not compelled to use a prescribed outline format, then you have the luxury of crafting your own. Some people may find this easy enough and have a natural talent for what they want to say and how best to say it. These people are often logical, analytical thinkers who see how sequences of ideas fit together.

Most of us, I suspect, find the early stages of forming our message a bit intimidating and overwhelming. Perhaps you have a vague idea of the kind of message you want to deliver for your particular audience at your event or occasion but don't know how to start actual construction. This place is often where I find myself when I'm invited to preach, speak, or deliver an address of some kind. Sometimes, I will quickly see how my ideas connect and can come up with a tentative outline.

Most times, though, I need to do some excavation before my exclamation! I call this process "digging for bones." While some topics or messages may lend themselves to outlining before researching, most messages benefit from collecting the parts and pieces that you can then order and arrange to put flesh and breathe life into those bones. Archaeologists dig and excavate for artifacts like pottery, coins, and jewelry as well as the bones of past civilizations. From the evidence uncovered, they begin to form a description and hypothesis about this culture, its customs, and systems. Putting together your message casts you in the same kind of role!

Your research includes looking at the big picture as well as the small details related to your topic, theme, subject matter, and main points. You're playing detective as well as archaeologist, looking for clues that reveal the heart of what it is you want to say. You want to know who the main experts are in your field of study and look at facts, figures, and data, depending on their relevance. Memorable quotations, surprising stats, and historical analyses often provide the hues and shades necessary to color your vivid style of delivery. Make notes for yourself, flagging sources or statements you want to reflect upon or return to later.

Collect more bones than you need so you can see which ones fit together in the best, most organic way. When our children were small, I recall many Christmas Eves spent with screwdrivers and wrenches in hand as my wife and I assembled tricycles, wagons, and bicycles. We would tighten the last screw or adjust the final bolt, and then Serita would point to a handful of nuts, bolts, washers, and assorted hardware and say, "What about these?"

I'd look at her with wide, sleep-deprived eyes and silently communicate, "Are you kidding me? But we followed the directions!" Then we would both laugh and give our newly constructed vehicle another safety check. Following the instructions, we had assembled it soundly but still had pieces left over. My point being, those trikes and bikes worked just fine without them—and so will your message!

Once you feel like you have plenty of bones, then it's time to assemble them into a skeleton for your message, a spinal column that will support the body of the message you're birthing. At this stage, you often sort topics and points that relate to one another, grouping them together based on similarities or on their distinct relationships. You decide what makes the cut and what doesn't, what illuminates and supports versus what detracts, distracts, or diverts your audience's attention. You consider the amount of time you have and eliminate points that ultimately don't justify their inclusion within the bounds of your limitations.

As the bones fall into place, don't be surprised if you discover you have enough for two messages!

The Best Sermon I've Never Preached

It's important at this stage to be very objective and honest with yourself. Several of my writer friends have told me the importance of the adage to "kill your little darlings," a turn of phrase attributed to a variety of authors including Oscar Wilde, T. S. Eliot, and William Faulkner. Regardless of its origin, the harsh wisdom of this editorial edict withstands the test of time. No one is advocating murder or violence of any kind but simply the courage to curate your communication. And it's more difficult than it sounds!

Because your "little darlings" are often your favorite parts of a message, the personal story that means so much to you, the startling research study's findings, or the historical and cultural context of the passage chosen for study. But they're ultimately unnecessary and run the risk of being indulgent, tangential, distracting, or irrelevant. No matter how beautifully phrased or emotionally moving they may be, they have to fit into the body of the message you're birthing. Bodies don't need more than one heart!

You might even be inspired and create an entire message only to discover that it does not serve the needs of your constituents. Perhaps the best sermon

I've never preached was inspired by one of my trips to Africa. If you know me at all, then you know I have a deep, abiding love for the people, culture, and landscapes of this fascinating continent. It's a transcendent, spiritual connection and affinity that ultimately defies my ability to define its many facets.

So after returning from a visit of several African nations, I became drawn to the variety of languages and tribal dialects. Many linguists and historians believe more than two thousand languages were spoken on the continent prior to colonialism. Once Europeans arrived to conquer and exploit resources, new languages and cultural expressions infused the many dialects already in use across the enormous and diverse native peoples. These layers of white supremacy, empirical rule, and tribal oppression, including slavery and servitude, only exacerbated the challenge of inter-tribal communication.

Even today, many African cultures continue to untangle the knotted skein of linguistic threads woven into their history. Many nations are relatively new in gaining independence from colonization and struggle to understand the essence of their identity, including tribal and cultural languages. "Who am I?" and "Where do I belong?" remain essential questions for many individuals as well as entire tribes, cultures, and nations.

With all of this information in mind, I naturally

thought of Nimrod in the Bible (Genesis 10). Noah's great-grandson Nimrod is thought by some scholars to have feared that another flood might wipe out the earth so he decided to build a tower high enough to withstand the flood. His plan coincides with what we're told about the Tower of Babel, which resulted from the whole world having one language and common speech (Genesis 11:1). Harnessing this capacity for such comprehensive communication, the people decided to build a tower reaching to the heavens to demonstrate their abilities. The Lord, however, knew the incredible pride that would result from such a feat and "confused the language of the whole world" (Genesis 11:9 NIV), presumably to keep people humble.

So I began to compile parallels between the challenges of communication in African cultures and the biblical story of the Tower of Babel. I saw all kinds of similarities in the dynamic between the conformity of colonialism and the hubris of people in Nimrod's time, along with the resulting catastrophe of communication after both fell apart. I conducted all this historical research about the Tower of Babel and how different experts interpret and apply it. With an excuse to dive deeper into the languages and cultures of African peoples, I compared forms of communication among tribes and famous examples of miscommunication.

Then, just as it all came together in my mind as this brilliant, perfect sermon, I asked myself a question that leveled my own tower: *What difference does this make?* There I was birthing a message that had come together so naturally and easily, born of my passion, curiosity, and fascination as two of my greatest loves, Africa and the Bible, intersected and briefly united. With all of this information and insight for a sermon, I stepped back and looked at all the bones...and I couldn't figure out my point!

How would my message, for all its self-congratulatory brilliance, inspire and encourage the single mother with three kids in my congregation? How would it speak to the prominent leader in the church struggling with how to love his adult children in the midst of their addictions? What practical value would my message have for the family scraping by from month to month who couldn't pay next month's rent, let alone the medical cost of their baby's surgery?

Because I could not answer these questions, I never preached that sermon! As much as I loved it, I realized it didn't fit my brand because it didn't deliver the promise I'm dedicated to delivering. As the body of your message takes shape, you identify its heartbeat. I think of a sermon like a company thinks about its brand because I want to deliver on the promise established by my message and methods of presentation. My sermons must have spiritual relevancy, inspirational encouragement, and action-worthy application. This one, for all its worth, did not meet these criteria.

No matter how much you like it, make sure those receiving your message will find it valuable, practical, and personally relevant. I could talk about what theologians think of Nimrod all day, but how did that transfer to takeaway benefits for those I was there to minister to and serve? I could tell stories of many indelible, vivid moments from my latest visit to Africa, but other than perhaps entertaining my listeners, what would they take away to help them in their lives? To help their faith grow?

You will have your own brand to fulfill, but as you assemble any message, it's good to keep in mind two foundational pillars: *Who cares?* and *So what?* A friend of mine is an English professor who often teaches writing classes to college students, and these are the two succinct, guiding questions he instills in all his developing writers. "Identifying your audience and keeping them in mind"—*Who cares?*—"is paramount for impact," he told me. "But there must also be something worth saying, the heart of your message that makes some kind of difference to that very audience"—*So what?*

If your message doesn't make a difference that makes your listeners' lives better, then don't bother. Put the bones aside and start again.

Bones and Bends

After you have assembled your bones into the body of your message, then you must bring it to life. One of the best ways to make your communication dynamic is to follow the energy of your topic, passage, or story. When you read a text from an exegetical perspective, the passage or story has bends in it, often as conflicts form, get addressed, and then resolved. These bends may be as subtle as a wink based on a curious word choice or as explosive as a land mine erupting from the text.

Take, for example, the parable Jesus told about the prodigal son (Luke 15:11–32). The drama begins when a certain son, the younger of two, as it turns out, asks for his inheritance before his father dies. He wants to see the world and enjoy himself without having to wait on events beyond his control. So he takes matters into his own hands, and his father grants him his inheritance, which sets up the first major bend as the son gets what he asked for. He enjoys his newfound freedom and the lavish lifestyle he can afford for a brief while.

Then the next major bend in the story occurs when a famine strikes the land. We can all relate to the tumultuous, painful, unexpected consequences this young man experiences when the unimaginable envelops his homeland. None of us imagined the size or the shape or the ongoing impact the COVID-19 pandemic would have on our lives, but it has indeed bent everyone's story in unexpected directions. So the prodigal son does what he has to do in order to survive: work as a field hand for a farmer.

Then as the young man is slopping the hogs, as we used to call it in West Virginia, where I grew up, he has an epiphany—another bend in the story. He realizes that there he is, so hungry that he envies the pigs their scraps of pods, husks, and rinds that he's feeding them, when he recalls that even the lowliest of hired hands were well fed back at his father's house.

The prodigal returns home to discover that his father not only welcomes him but throws a party like no other to celebrate his return, which might seem like the final bend in this story. Only, there's one last revelation: The elder son resents the father's loving forgiveness toward his brother and begrudges him the spectacular party. To which his father replies, "My son, you are always with me, and everything I have is yours. But we had to celebrate and be glad, because this brother of yours was dead and is alive again; he was lost and is found" (Luke 15:31–32 NIV). All the strands come together to reinforce what it means to be lost and found.

Finding the bends and beats in your message isn't limited to Bible passages. Whatever you're talking about, whatever examples and illustrations and anecdotes you choose to include, will all have twists and turns that you must maneuver and maximize for your methods. Sometimes the canvas for your material is a larger-than-life mural while other times it's an exquisite scene distilled to its essence. And you may use one to inform the other!

If you want to provide historical context with dates and documents, don't forget to think about the impact on actual human lives during those iconic moments. If you're showing a tight close-up of an individual's transformational event, you will also want to paint broad strokes in the background. It's one thing to talk about civil rights during the 1960s and another to describe the swollen, aching feet of Rosa Parks boarding a bus home and making an impactful, historic decision.

You can talk about at-risk youth mentoring or

transitional programs for those released from incarceration and include shocking data to make your point. But there is simply no substitute for the angry tears rolling down a child's face as she comes to terms with the devastating pain in her heart after losing a parent in the crossfire of gang wars in her neighborhood. No statistic can compare with the contemptuous glances and slammed doors in the face of a man who has served his time and now seeks employment. Pain always has a face, and your job as a communicator is to place your listeners front and center to hear the stifled cries, taste the tears, and smell the human sweat of those whose story you are privileged to share.

Joy also has a face. The Bible tells us, "Weeping may endure for a night, but joy cometh in the morning" (Psalm 30:5 KJV). For the joy, peace, comfort, and hope you wish to offer your audience to have power, you must frame it with the sorrows from which it was born. The messages infused with supernatural power to inspire, uplift, and encourage never shirk from the harsh, ragged edges of human pain.

In order to appreciate the discovery of Jesus' resurrection on the third day, you must show the bitter tears of his grieving mother at the foot of the cross on the day of his death. You must not flinch from the searing pain of nails piercing his hands and feet, the throbbing pain from the sword that had pierced his side, the blood dripping down his forehead into his eyes from the crown of thorns. Only when you know that Christ suffered the ultimate injustice and made the ultimate sacrifice can his resurrection and gift of salvation have power to speak to our experience.

Obviously, I'm getting close to preaching here myself, but I hope you recognize my point. Whether you're discussing last quarter's budget report, delivering a speech for your women's group, or preaching at your church this week, you still want to identify and follow the bends in your message in order to take your audience with you to a destination where you have gifted them with something they did not have, know, understand, or care about prior to your address.

Know the Needs

One of the keys to making sure you deliver on your promise as you put together your message is knowing the needs of your audience prior to delivery. After I was established as a pastor and had gained some experience in the pulpit, I began to be invited to speak at non-church-related events. While I knew that the city leaders did not intend for me to preach a sermon, I had to make sure I knew what they did expect from me. When human resources executives reached out with an invitation to address an auditorium filled with employees, I wanted to make sure I spoke to the issues that had prompted their invitation.

I quickly learned the importance of a pre-event conversation to discern and refine the purpose of my message for their constituents. Did they want me to motivate high school students to continue their education by attending college? Was I invited to help small business owners weather the challenges of new growth and potential expansion? Were city planners wanting my insight on how to anticipate growth patterns for urban development in the metro area? Answering these questions before I put the bones into the body of my address became paramount to bringing it to life. Meeting before your moment at the mic gives you clarity about your message.

Recently, I was asked to speak at a meeting of the National Association of Minority Auto Dealers (NAMAD). They asked me to address entrepreneurial strategies for marketing to consumers as broadly as possible. Other than my ability to drive and appreciate cars, I have no experience with their product or selling vehicles in any economic climate, let alone the changing times in which we live. They obviously knew this was outside my expertise and instead wanted me to talk about how I have remained true to my brand for a diverse, multiethnic audience. Once I realized what they expected based on my brand identity, I enjoyed preparing my message for them. Like a pharmacist preparing the prescription provided by a doctor for the patients they both serve, I gleaned the wisdom from NAMAD's leaders to provide medicinal insight for all their participating members.

Sometimes a group, company, institution, or event has a predetermined theme or message. When they invite me to participate, usually as one of several keynote communicators, they trust that I will take into account the larger, overarching focus and build my message to dovetail with it accordingly. For example, when I recently agreed to speak at the Global Leadership Summit (GLS), I spent three hours on the phone with their team to help shape my message for the thematic issues promised by their brand for that year's Summit. I had to understand their motivation, the need being addressed, by this large brand promise and then see what I had to offer and how best to share it. The focus for that Summit was on helping leaders address and practice inclusivity and diversity in their own communication styles!

Both the GLS team and I agreed I wanted to do

more than deliver the kind of message many of these participants would expect from me. Those in attendance usually have large platforms of their own as well as experience with effective communication. They needed something fresh, honest, and practical in facing the challenges presented by our current cultural climate of political division and systemic racism. These leaders needed more than just a summary of what they were already doing. Again, I focused on the "So what?" factor for this audience to make sure they would care and find my communication valuable while also fulfilling the larger brand promise made by the GLS.

Knowing the kind of frontline battles many of these leaders were facing, I chose something I suspected every one of them had faced and would continue to face: how to handle haters. I'm no more immune to critics than anyone, and in fact have attracted more as my platform and visibility have increased. So for the leaders at the GLS, I shared about a young man from Chicago who consistently bullied me on social media. No matter what I posted, tweeted, or shared online, this outspoken critic condemned me and my message. He showed no compassion or attempt at kindness or constructive criticism in his profanity-laced diatribes against me.

With the leaders at the Summit, I shared as vulnerably as I could about how angry this online outlaw made me feel, how he deliberately baited me and tried to hurt me with mean-spirited barbs and street-thug epithets. I told them my honest reaction to this critic: "How dare you! Who do you think you are to express so much personal vitriol when you don't even know me?" Then I revealed how something inside me shifted when I let go of my anger and tried to practice what I preach—namely, compassion, acceptance, and understanding.

I realized that just because this young man and I were both black and had experienced poverty during our childhood, I assumed he should see us as having more in common. But then I got to thinking about all of his life experiences that were different and alien to me: the crime, the gang violence in urban 'hoods, the drugs, the police brutality, and the general lack of justice and protection. I had to admit to myself that until I looked at the world through his lenses, I would never see how to bridge the gulf between us.

With kinder vision and more understanding glasses, I considered how his profanity was simply street language to him, not even necessarily profane from his perspective. I saw that in his own way he was attempting to have a conversation with me! He was sending out a cry for help, and yet all I could do was focus on how he didn't know me or understand me, when in fact, I was doing the same to him. I was too busy being angry to see a young man with no father crying out to connect.

After this example and how it initiated an ongoing conversation with someone I once viewed as an online assailant, I shared observations of the same dynamic when counseling couples. My role has always been to help each individual see their spouse's point of view and use different language in order that true dialogic communication could take place. When there is conflict, it's so tempting to resort to the safety of our default scripts, but true understanding only occurs when we risk listening to one another between the lines.

Pivot to the Power

My homework for leaders at the GLS challenged them to experience an environment with people different from themselves, one with a diversity level that forced them out of their comfort zone. Their goal was simply to observe, listen, and learn to see and hear in new ways. I encourage you to engage in the same exercise regarding new audiences and constituencies you wish to reach. Think about what those individuals will see and hear when they look at you and hear the message you're delivering.

Remember, preaching is not about preaching at someone but conversing, expressing, sharing, and listening to those you wish to reach. Spend time preparing, digging up bones, assembling the body, and use the spark between you and your audience to infuse life into your message. Preparation gives you the freedom to be spontaneous. The more you know your material and all the bends in the narrative, the more attuned you can be to your audience.

Many times, I develop an outline or skeleton of a message that I change in the dynamic moment of delivery. I may have prepared three main points from a passage but in the pulpit sensed my audience's reaction to point number two necessitated spending the rest of our time together exploring that second point and why it hit a nerve. If I rushed on to make sure I finished where I planned to finish, I would have lost the opportunity to meet the greatest needs of my listeners.

It's good to cover all the material you researched, explored, and prepared, but if you're present in the moment and sense the need to pivot to where there's more power, then do so! Remember, for all your advance research and preparation, the communication between you and your audience is still a live event! Actors and performers on the stage know that sometimes the greatest moments come from improvising and making spontaneous changes.

Technology may not cooperate and your PowerPoint presentation may freeze on the screen behind you, but such glitches cannot change the impact of your message unless you allow them to do so. In fact, when PowerPoint and nascent technology were first introduced into meetings, sermons, and performances, the message was often eclipsed by the novelty of the new electronic media. Now balance has been restored so that most speakers use tech tricks or PowerPoint slides to enhance their message, not to convey their most important points. The data, images, and pictures projected are more symbolic than instructive.

You are the messenger for the message you're delivering, not your computer! Your phone, tablet, or laptop is your tool, not your crutch, understudy, or surrogate. Your audience wants to hear what you have to say relevant to the occasion, context, and circumstances that have brought you together. Master your message so that you never drop the mic—at least, not unless deliberately at the end of your delivery!

PART 2

The Legacy of Language

Despite the immense power of language to produce change, I can't help but worry that the art of communication has started to erode in our world today. Diplomacy is now seen as weakness. Negotiation has given way to a polarization of an "us against them" mentality. Words lose power before our very eyes and ears as leaders make denials, revise meanings, and manipulate statements made by those who oppose them. One need only listen to political pundits to see that our political discourse—once considered the hallmark of democracy—has eroded to a street brawl.

Consequently, those in authority and those they serve often fail to communicate because of the acrimony and distrust coloring their exchanges. From the hallowed halls of Congress to the electrifying energy of church pulpits, we seem to have lost a vital part of the process of communication. The transformative sounds once delivered by Smith Wigglesworth, Aimee Semple McPherson, Dr. Gardner Taylor, Dr. Charles Adams, and Dr. E. V. Hill have become sound bites with little substance. Where are our great orators like Socrates, Lincoln, Churchill, and countless others?

Of course we still find remnants of such resonant rhetoric in gifted communicators such as President Barack Obama, who succeeded in talking American citizens from both parties into casting votes in historic numbers. Few can deny that the silky smooth Arkansas twang of President Bill Clinton has an artful way of wooing a crowd that has become legendary. The soothing tones of Max Lucado's carefully choreographed expressions also come to mind. I remember being in the city of Detroit at Rosa Parks's funeral services when this crisply coifed woman rose to the microphone and charged the atmosphere, bedazzling the crowd. I later learned that these empowered, passionate words belonged to the former governor of Michigan, Jennifer Grandholm.

You can likely think of your own exceptional examples, but I suspect you will agree that these superb orators are few and far between. We might be tempted to blame our school systems, but they are not entirely at fault when we consider overcrowded classrooms and underfunded educational programs. No, it's not simply the lack of oral reports and public debates in our school. We lack the conversational connectivity in our homes that was once an assumed part of our personal relationships.

Most dinner tables have gone silent as family members scroll, type, and text with others around the world. Today, the only sound we hear above the clinking sound of cutlery is the occasional ping acknowledging a text has been sent or received. This assumes that families even bother to go through the motions of gathering together for meals knowing that each other's online proclivities rarely intersect. Family life chatter that once anchored our home life has given way to a societal silence, leaving us untethered.

Before there was gaming or Nintendo, streaming and Netflix, even poor families like the one I grew up in entertained ourselves with homemade talent shows and makeshift stages with curtains made of bedspreads where my brother, my sister, and I performed for an audience of our mother and father. My sister and I spent a great deal of time getting ready for these simple shows. My brother occasionally joined in, but seldom did he do so without protest! Every now and then he might dance to a record or recite some piece of art. My mother was quite good at quoting James

Weldon Johnson, moving with ease from that to Edgar Allan Poe. It was her recitations that made me as a child appreciate Walt Whitman, Langston Hughes, and Nikki Giovanni.

I admit we entertained ourselves this way because in part we lacked the resources to do much else. But poverty might have been a blessing because it developed and honed a creativity that automation now threatens to take away. The swelling speeches that once inspired us to the armed services and united us in our shared humanity have been reduced to 280 characters of pithy commentary.

Yet, we have an obligation to hear as much as we speak, to think before we rant, to allow what connects us to overcome what divides us. I fear that public discourse has in some ways been diminished while data acquisition has become more refined and algorithms have become a part of our daily speech. Has it done so to the chagrin of human decency? I hope not! Before we get too caught up in the riptides of 5G coverage, let's not allow the power of speech to be diluted into a perfunctory dribble of monosyllabic responses void of the artful inclusion of human expression along with the mutual respect shared by opposing ideologies!

Perhaps I sound like an alarmist, but it is possible to lose this great gift of language, or at least watch it erode into some other, lesser form of communication. While the number seems to fluctuate, it appears that more than seven thousand living languages are active in the world today. This number changes because within each language, many derivatives emerge even as some dialects and variations expire, often unnoticed by speakers of other languages. Apparently, about 40 percent of these languages are in danger of extinction because only a thousand or fewer people speak and write them. You see, about half of the world's population relies on less than two dozen languages.

Many other ancient languages have now expired as they were replaced, outdated, or simply weren't passed down from generation to generation. Asia and Africa seem to have the largest diversity of language. I'm amazed at the wide array of languages on these continents and how users often rely on tribal language as well as more widely used languages necessary to compete in a global market for job opportunities and a sense of inclusion. It is clear that any unused language is eventually lost.

Unfortunately, there is neither a graveyard nor a mortuary that holds these entombed languages. Some of these once vibrant languages have been reduced to mysterious etchings on a wall preserved in a museum, while others are like unclaimed baggage on the carousel of contemporary culture, awaiting speakers and writers who will never return. Their only hope at resurrection comes from the forensics of astute scholars sifting the decaying bones of what was once a vibrant and frequently used vernacular.

The frailty of language can lead to an epidemic of indifference or cultural evolution toward extinction. Anything can replace language, not just new words or surviving alphabets. From tactile forms like Braille to the gestures of sign language, there are always new ways to connect and communicate. Which brings me back to my concern about technology dramatically changing what we communicate as much as how we communicate.

When our machines start to do all the talking, who is becoming more human? And who is becoming more robotically synthesized? I must admit that my smartphone is so smart that sometimes it offers me my next word while I'm still thinking it. For someone of my generation, this is like a scene from *Invasion of the Body Snatchers*! In order to utilize technology for better communication, we must first focus on what we have to say and how we want to say it.

CHAPTER 4

Find the Joint!

From whom the whole body fitly joined together by that which every joint supplieth, according to the effectual working in the measure of every part, maketh increase of the body unto the edifying of itself in love.

—Ephesians 4:16 KJV

I understand that the title of this chapter might mean different things to different people. To the cook, it conjures images of cutting chicken quarters apart. To the surgeon, it might mean examining an x-ray to research the tissue surrounding a patient's kneecap. To the street thug, it may mean finding a supplier who has marijuana for sale by the joint! If he's arrested, he will be incarcerated in "the joint," street slang for prison.

Obviously, none of these meanings conveys what the apostle who wrote these words had in mind. Instead, he alleges that the Body of Christ is edified through the power of *connectivity*. So let's focus on his meaning and leave the rest for others to explore.

No matter the venue or occasion, all communicators want connection with their audience. Every great comedian knows this. Every public speaker seeks it. Everyone, from talk show hosts to YouTube entertainers, TED talkers to life coaches, political pundits to romance novelists, seeks to connect with the broadest array of people. You never want to miss opportunities for the kind of personal alignment required to bond with your audience. In fact, every preacher knows the sinking, gut-wrenching, nauseating feeling that drops to the pit of your stomach when, ten minutes into your presentation, you realize that you're not connecting with your audience. Those sermons seem to last twice as long for everyone present!

Context of Conversation

My connection to my listeners reflects the intersection of where I've been and where they're going. I'm aware that my perspective reflects my experience, ethnicity, the Appalachian mountain culture that incubated me, my posture in my home as a patriarch, and my gender through which I've experienced the world. I was raised in the Baptist church, which also influenced me as a communicator, both as an observer and as a participant. While this church shares theological similarities with the Southern Baptist denomination and other predominantly white evangelical movements, it isn't wise to see them as totally homogeneous. There is a great deal of difference in focus, form, and priorities.

Coupled with the fact that my early years of preaching were shaped and trained by Pentecostal icons, my religious and spiritual experiences deposited an understanding of the Scriptures as well as the objective of the preaching moment. Both the African American experience along with the oppression of Pentecostal people affects the tenor and tone of how we speak about preaching in general. African American pastors often rely on a call-and-response method that takes the preaching moment from a monologue of truth expounded to a dialogue of truth shared and experienced.

How is any of this related? The answer speaks to what I think of as the communicative context of conversation. To comprehend the milieu of preaching as I know and practice it, you must understand the social, cultural, economic, and spiritual dynamics of the African Americans who made their brutal passage from East Africa to the shores of this great country. Simply put, we entered into the American dream while still in the deep sleep of an African nightmare. All that we are and all that we have experienced are all that we have to bring to the podium. It is the lens through which we see a text or an issue. We all endeavor to be objective, but people inevitably, irrepressibly bring all that they are to how and what they communicate. The shaded lenses of our background and history color all that we bring to our study.

Whether you are talking hip hop or poetry, comedy or the novelization of a saga told over generations, all that we have to bring is the sum total of all that we are or have experienced. To separate someone's history from their ideas and approach is nearly impossible! Ultimately, such separation would sanitize the delivery from all that would make us unique from those who only seek to influence the convictions of the crowd rather than to impart truth from the relationship that elicits the call and response of our African background.

Let me say it another way: It isn't uncommon to get spontaneous commentary from the pews.

"Say it, preacher!" and "Amen, brother!" and "Come

on with it..." are merely representatives of all the other reactions blurted out during the preaching moment when a connection exists. These comments are more than emotional outbursts; they are the results of the journey we took that leads us into a deeper understanding of shared truths. Such responses and all other auditory moments from the hearer to the speaker acknowledge our connectivity to that audience.

This background reflecting ministry and its message as both theologist and therapist of a traumatized constituency colors the way we understand the experience of, and with, the microphone. For almost four hundred years, we survived in a sociological construct that stabilized, and often anesthetized, the pain of an oppressed people, which explains why the principles espoused are coequal with the needs of the people we serve. So then, from our cultural perspective, the messenger is responsible for the spiritual and emotional well-being of those listening. To deny this part of our discussion is to ignore the intent of the message and the origin of the purpose of preaching.

Your Secret Weapon

The late comedian and actor Bernie Mac in his book *Maybe You Never Cry Again* explains that he became a comedian because he witnessed at an early age how comedy could have such a powerful impact. He watched his mother go from crying about her life to laughing hysterically at the comedic delivery of then-popular Bill Cosby. Bernie Mac's attraction wasn't fortune or fame. Instead, his attraction to comedy was the power that the mic gave, the realization that it was indeed possible for comedy to alleviate the weeping souls of people by providing lighthearted relief.

Intent, then, at least in this example, shaped the perceived objective of the comedian. Much like preaching, at least for Bernie, was the power to alleviate the pain of life with the power of laughter. All other factors centered around the delivery synchronize in the underlying motive of being medicinal by creating an experience that tranquilizes pain with hope and laughter. If applied to speaking in general, we discover the essential relationship between experience and relevance: *It is nearly impossible to move an audience with something that you are not moved by yourself.*

Love is the secret weapon of great speaking!

Since I am a son and a father, a husband and a brother, most of who I am is predicated upon my relationships. I suggest to you that personal connections are the greatest resource to the speaker. Relationships offer something more akin to cross-pollination than just impartation, which in turn affects the outcome of how we define success. Additionally, the role of clergy has a different objective when communicating to a people who had never had a president who looked like them until the last decade.

Instead, we had the sage voices of the preachers who were seen as professionals and community leaders at the time. This is also true of how we saw teachers. They were seen as professionals at a level that they should be but sometimes are not so regarded today. Our teachers' communication styles often became the catalyst for more than just the information assimilated in their lesson plans. They planted seeds of personal development and aspirational growth.

Yes, most teachers had the same textbook, but the truly great ones augmented the cold and sterile facts of each page by engaging the students in unique and abstract ways to make the subject more salient in different settings for different age groups. I can remember my mother working as a teacher, and she often spent long hours developing lesson plans to engage and stimulate her students. Her focus on reaching them informed her selection of teaching tools, and these, too, harmonized with her awareness of the demographics of her classrooms.

Compass for Community

Throughout our nation's history, the sermon has been the compass that guided our community at large to enlightenment. From voices like the Reverend Jesse Jackson, Dr. Martin Luther King, from Frederick Douglass to Harriet Tubman, who, while not a preacher, was believed to receive messages from God that led her through her fight as an abolitionist. Her example illustrates the multiple facets of a gifted communicator. Almost without exception, the voices that led us were the same voices that fed us on Sunday morning. Therefore, there is an expectation in our community for those who rise to prominence to be called of God in order to achieve impact. Their voices transcend their individual personalities and amplify the internal message of the people for whom they wield the microphone.

This phenomenon does not dissipate but creatively evolves. Consider how the birth of hip hop was widely received as the clergy of the streets, speaking to, and often speaking *for*, the world that informed their perspective. The language was crass and often shocking. But it was often as true as the account of any journalist on the scene, reporting what happened, what it means, and how we should view where we are in life at any given moment. While huge distinctions remain between traditional preaching and performing hip hop, both were and are expected to "tell it like it is" rather than to wax philosophical with feel-good platitudes. Neither group was lauded for espousing principles over people.

Hip hop isn't the only genre reflecting this approach. Countless musicians, songwriters, performers, and producers have often accepted the task to create ground-level works reordering public perception of what's true. The '60s birthed voices like the great James Brown and his bold message, "I'm black and I'm proud!" Marvin Gaye's classic "What's Going On," as relevant now as it was when released in 1971, assumed responsibility for the voiceless while articulating the dissonance felt by generations of people who dared question established illusions.

Along with many other talented artists, they rose to prominence from inside the community in which they were first inspired. They accepted the responsibility, both unspoken and spoken, to use their influence and artistry to further an agenda that included but wasn't limited to speaking up and speaking out for those who propelled them to prominence. Hence, the requisite relationship to the people in the pews, on the dance floor, or in the streets in order to speak for them as much as to them.

It isn't enough to have a relationship with God.

We must also have a relationship with the people.

Our ability to connect with that audience creates trust!

As I traveled to address various audiences, I quickly learned it's not enough to connect with the substance of my message and ignore how my audience will receive it. Without studying my intended audience, I would miss synergistic points of connectivity. Knowing as much as possible about my audience is integral to my delivery. For me, that research begins when I accept the engagement and consider what the letter of invitation reveals about my prospective listeners. It continues by observing who picks me up at the airport, how I am accommodated, as well as all the music, messaging, and speaking that preceded my address. Again, communication is a distillation of relationships.

Your ability to find common ground, points of

connectivity, and illustrations that resonate with the crowd is paramount to your success. To be sure, my voice has gone way beyond my blackness to serve the Venezuelan, the Caucasian, the Hispanic, the African, and the European. With each engagement, the event wasn't only about who I spoke to, but rather where I spoke from. Regardless of the diverse people I address, I must never forget who I speak for and the people who helped me climb the ladder to reach my pulpit.

Oddly enough in a society that loves to find distinctions by focusing on what is unique to us, a good speaker is the antithesis of that ideal. You are looking for what unites us, not what divides us. In speaking with anyone or any group of people, connectivity is everything!

Charisma Connects

All of us have endured those sessions where the person speaking might be knowledgeable about the subject, but listening to them was as interesting as watching paint dry. Charisma, presence, and personality are huge assets when speaking to any group!

I started speaking to groups of largely African American church women through a faith-based empowerment session I called "Woman Thou Art Loosed." These messages were crafted for my specific audience about spiritual and emotional needs I felt called to address. Later, I did a similar session geared toward men called "Manpower." As opportunities to speak increased, I would often have to go from a massive group of women to a room filled with men. Most of the time, connecting with each audience wasn't difficult.

Without a doubt, it's easier to connect with people that you live among rather than people with whom you lack similarities and congruencies. That authentic feeling of connection is invaluable. Many times I was able not only to connect but also to delve deeply into ultrapersonal material once the audience had settled into my style and substance. Having said that, I have had groups with whom it felt quite difficult to connect for whatever reason. Those moments were painful for me and for the crowd because it's impossible to hide when you can't find the joint to connect to your crowd!

Connectivity is built around finding the right metaphors, shared comedy, or a vernacular to which the audience relates. Jesus did it through the telling of simple parables that became conduits of complex concepts. His storytelling unveiled deeper truths in tangible ways his audience could access and apply. He modeled the essence of incarnational connectivity by choosing communication strategies that resonated with his audience.

Such strategies remain essential if you want your audience to remember the meaning of your message. Developing a speaking strategy that enables the audience to find personal and cultural resonance builds bridges between you. It may be something as simple as family scenarios, cultural similarities, culinary skills, technological jargon, or anything that expresses your common background and goals. Personal points of connection align to create a network of engagement with each individual in your audience.

If your past doesn't provide it, your future goals and ambitions might be the joint that connects you with your audience. It could be a common love for country, faith, shared values, or leadership principles that you hold in common. For the most part, understanding the age, the gender, the profession, and political perspectives of those receiving your message helps you deliver it effectively. Seldom do all of those areas provide synergy. But any one of them may be just the thing to break the ice and create a sense of connection and unity with the crowd.

It is a big mistake to spend your entire time

thinking about where you want to take the crowd, or how you want to inspire them, motivate them, or inform them. Those are destination points. But much like using Uber or Lyft or some other transportation service provided through technology, you can't just type in the destination without also including your current location.

Connectivity is all about meeting the audience where they are, and then taking them where you are trying to go. You can't get them to the destination until you locate their current location and estimate the distance between you. How else can you close the gap between where you're starting with them and where you want to go?

Chemistry Lesson

Fundamentally, connectivity is more like a science as it is predicated on knowing. The more you know about them, the better chance you have of locating them. But if connectivity is a science, then your chemistry with an audience is more art. Much like a first impression or first date, chemistry is critical. It's less intellectual and more instinctive, less objective and more subjective.

Chemistry is far more ambiguous. Not all speakers have the right chemistry to connect with all audiences. You can learn to connect through thoroughly researching the crowd, but chemistry isn't something you can discern from research alone. It is like trying to teach a person to have charisma or charm. I'm not sure such qualities can actually be taught, although they can be encouraged.

The science of chemistry relies on chemical reactions, which always results in altered states. When you add one chemical substance to another, one will either alter the color of the other, form a precipitate, form a gas, change the odor, or change the temperature. But when we talk about chemistry between people, the reaction becomes a lot harder to explain. It is more of an experience than an explanation.

When a man and a woman date, they are trying to see if there is chemistry between them. Their appeal to one another isn't merely based on physical attraction, although this can be a contributing factor. You can meet someone who is very attractive but not feel drawn to them because there's no instinctive reaction. But as you get to know them, your view of them may change, either confirming that there's absolutely no interest in knowing more about them or tilting toward a revised impression that piques curiosity. People who may not attract you at first glance may end up relating to you in a way that compels you to them magnetically.

On the other hand, if the chemistry is not there, you can't fake it. Some people just don't do it for us. It's not merely a matter of sex appeal or positive energy. It also includes how their presence creates a feeling, a change, a comfortability, and a sense of excitement. Few can predict it. Even fewer can explain it. But we all know when it is there and when it is not!

Chemistry with your audience often works in similar fashion. Certain types of people resonate better with certain types of groups more than others. Sometimes chemistry can seem mysterious and even arbitrary. Other times, you can identify reasons why you're drawn to certain people just as your audience understands why they enjoy engaging with you, your message, and your style of delivery.

I've noticed that chemistry matters a great deal in political campaigns. A candidate's charisma and appeal to her constituents matters. The nature of our electoral process often gains momentum by the charisma of the candidate and how well she communicates. Often, we elect who the people like the most, without considering that it is possible to be good at campaigning but not good at leading. This aspect of any democratic political process leaves margin for misappropriation by the charismatic over the competent and qualified. One can be a strong leader but not be telegenic, gregarious, or authoritative in demeanor.

In fact, some of the most brilliant leaders, CEOs, doctors, and managers don't always interview well or campaign well. Since the end game isn't the interview or the campaign, we lose chances to have great leaders or employees simply because they don't always have immediate chemistry with the crowd. This loss occurs when communication relies solely on charisma and chemistry.

I remember when my mother was suffering from an illness, one of her doctors had the personality of a doorknob. His bedside manner was blunt and insensitive. He wasn't rude but simply matter-of-fact, which resulted in a lack of chemistry with the family. We found him disengaged with how we felt as a family and insensitive to my mother as a person.

While he lacked the reassuring, compassionate persona we craved, he was a brilliant surgeon who excelled in the operating room. We nearly replaced him, but after much discussion and some investigation, we decided to keep him in charge of my mother's surgery because we realized that his manner with the family wasn't why he was there. He was there because he was a great surgeon.

If you're a speaker, communicator, or performer, however, you must consider chemistry. While doctors and political leaders communicate in order to perform their roles, a communicator's job is to communicate. If you don't have good chemistry with an audience, you can't overlook that and say, "But I can do the job!" Speaking *is* the job.

In full and candid disclosure, I must admit that I have occasionally addressed a crowd and sensed that I completely lacked the right chemistry for that group! My style, my demeanor, my approach just underscored that I wasn't the right person for them in that setting at that time. It doesn't mean that I wasn't valuable or didn't have something worthwhile to impart to them. It does mean, as my mother would say, I wasn't their cup of tea. You cannot be all things to all people, especially if it means that you have to pretend to be something that you are not. Simply put, you can't be prepared to win until you can live with the possibility of losing.

Testing the waters is better than drowning in the pool!

Delivering on Your Brand

No speaker is good in every setting. This is where branding is important. It is important that a speaker not think of themselves in generalized terms of being a speaker. It is important to understand what kind of speaker you are. Like doctors or lawyers, comedians or even politicians, there has to be a deeper analysis to determine with more specificity the kind of speaker you really are. This self-awareness helps you determine so many other decisions related to how, when, why, and to whom you will communicate.

Brand development is at its core a promise. People want to know, "What do we get when we invite you? What will those in attendance take away from what you communicate?" There are some settings where you may not be the best choice for that crowd. The information is there. The interest and compassion are there. But the chemistry may still be off.

Like a couple that starts dating, sometimes you don't discover this deficit until you're in the situation. Don't allow that to make you feel defeated. Make the best of it in the moment and learn all you can from the experience. Let those moments help you find your best audience!

Think of it like you would agriculture. Not all plants grow well in all climates. Sometimes the soil isn't conducive. Other times the climate isn't right for that type of plant. It's not that either of them is wrong or needs to change. It's simply a matter of them not being good together! Awareness of your brand, your setting, and your audience can help you plant the right seeds to yield a thriving harvest.

My range of speaking has been extremely diverse. I've spoken to many variations of the faith-based crowd. I've spoken before entertainment crowds about various aspects of faith-based films, though the audience may not have been faith-based. I've spoken before various American presidents. And I've had the distinguished honor of speaking for the Congressional Black Caucus. I've also spoken in many corporate settings from the Kenyan National Bank to the good folks at Toyota's corporate office. I've addressed leaders at Microsoft.

I've been interviewed on *All Things Considered* on NPR and have enjoyed more relaxed fireside-type chats with icons such as Oprah Winfrey. I've had the privilege on many occasions to sit with Larry King on *Larry King Live* as well as to address a live audience on Dr. Phil's show. In terms of diversity, I've spoken for groups ranging from Pat Robertson's CBN revivals to Operation PUSH for the Reverend Jesse Jackson.

In every case, I sought to add value to the formats I was afforded. I'm not sure what level of impact I actually had in many cases, but my goal was to add value to the opportunity. I sought to contribute perspective and to be true to who I was, while understanding the range of opinions and institutions for which I spoke. While those audiences were quite diverse, their differences did not require putting guardrails on my capabilities. Like all communicators, I am flawed and limited, but those flaws and limitations do not diminish my value when I'm in my element!

Lanes and Limitations

In order to find your best fit, you must consider: What is your element? Every speaker is constrained to varying degrees by the range of their versatility. While we all want to be as versatile as possible, the truth is, we all have some limitations. Acknowledging those limitations is the conduit through which we have focus. It is impossible to extend yourself beyond your ability without compromising your authenticity.

If you try to be everything, you end up not being anything!

How does one determine his or her range? I think that the range of your versatility comes from an honest critique of each experience. It also is derived by exposure to varied settings and attending events beyond your normal gravitational pull to that which is familiar and comfortable. If you want to expand your brand or ignite more dynamic chemistry, then you must do more than preach to your own choir.

Self-analysis coupled with general consensus helps us to determine range of influence. While I absolutely believe any communicator can grow and improve, an awareness of your strengths and weaknesses often aids in strategic cultivation of those areas where you have the greatest potential for improvement. Such awareness also helps you avoid wasting time and energy in areas with little return for your investment. Accepting your limitations provides containment for potential calamity while accentuating your strengths reinforces your brand.

There are some settings that I prefer to do in an interview format rather than a direct address from the platform, while others I simply decline, either because I have no passion for the subject or recognize the request is beyond my brand. It simply isn't my thing.

Sometimes, I may care about the subject and still not be the best choice to lead the conversation. Authenticity is something that I simply refuse to compromise. Without always realizing that's what I was doing at the time, I learned the hard way that conformity not only sabotages my message but also results in regret.

Several years ago, I had a dear friend who had an intense and meaningful ministry to teenagers. His passion was infectious and the stats reflected his powerful impact in reaching this significant demographic. My problem was that I allowed his passion to move me away from my own. He was sure that I would have a huge impact on this stadium filled with these young people. So I agreed to go.

Unfortunately, though, I was not well versed in speaking to their demographic. Because I agreed they were an important audience to reach, I accepted my friend's invitation. Even before I stepped on the stage, though, I knew the audience was beyond my bandwidth. They were gracious and polite, but I could not access the points of connection required for compelling communication. I got through it and hope there was some value for those in attendance, but I learned to listen to my gut more than anyone else's passionate persuasion.

As I drove back to my hotel feeling like a dog with

his tail tucked between his hind legs, I knew I would not be accepting similar engagements again. The lesson was clear: Just because you believe in a cause doesn't always mean that you are the best person to lead the discussion. Knowing your limitations is indeed a strength in itself!

Challenging Cultural Conventions

In order to understand how to connect with your audience, you must recognize cultural differences and consider how they affect your style and delivery. We frequently identify cultural differences and assume they are stationary boundaries or defensive walls that cannot be climbed. One of my favorite examples has nothing to do with ethnicity or demographics but simply contextual, cultural conditioning in a microcosm.

Have you ever stepped into a crowded elevator and noticed everyone is looking up at the descent of the illuminated floor numbers as if they were waiting for some potential revelation to occur? It's always funny to me because our staring up is really an attempt to avoid the risk of speaking to strangers who prefer to seem oblivious to our presence. Sometimes I play the game and look up, too, staring upward like the disciples waiting for Jesus to go up on a cloud!

Other times, I feel compelled to break the ice with a warm smile and a simple greeting, perhaps "Good evening!" or "Beautiful day, isn't it?" Most of the time in those instances, I've witnessed the entire tight cubicle of culture relax after holding its collective breath into a pleasant sigh of cheerful exchanges. I'm often amazed to watch how more times than not, people quickly chime in with equal levels of brightness, dismissing their mannequin-like grimace for a much warmer, more personal expression simply because someone had the courage to speak up!

Sometimes, we perceive certain cultural conditions existing with our prospective audience and assume we can't connect. But please understand that labeling audiences and understanding them purely by cultural labels can be deceptive. I'm often stunned by the false assumptions people make based on labels. Generalities and stereotypes replace actualities and individuals. Not all black people, or white people, or Christians, or Republicans or Democrats are monolithic.

There are so many subsets and sociological constructs that exist within the broad applications of people groups, and relying on labels will leave you ill prepared to understand the unique nuances of these subsets within our audience. We are often influenced to think of certain people certain ways without ever allowing for the individual group nuances.

It is important to understand that not all churches think the same, even within the same denominations. It is equally important to understand that regions affect the culture of an organization as much as any label. Ages and other demographic considerations contribute to the way an entity functions and feels when you are speaking to its constituents. While they often share core beliefs, within those core beliefs are other strong distinctions worth considering.

If you want to find the joint in your speaking opportunity, then know yourself, know your message, know your limitations, and most important, know your audience!

CHAPTER 5

The Process of Preaching

Quality is not an act, it is a habit.

—Aristotle

In an ideal world, you would have all the time you wanted to brainstorm, reflect, pray, research, study, outline, draft, and rehearse before you deliver your message or give your performance. In the real world, you often have to condense and combine those elements, use the specific research you can access, and make the most of what you have. The process of preaching—or communicating publicly in almost any medium, for that matter—reminds me of the quotation attributed to iconic inventor Thomas Edison: "Genius is one percent inspiration and ninety-nine percent perspiration."

While I might be tempted to alter Edison's ratio as applied specifically to preaching, I love the recognition that preparation, hard work, and effort tend to determine how well the creative sparks of inspiration catch fire. How they come together, though, in different combinations with different ingredients at different times makes analyzing the process of creation quite challenging.

As I shared earlier, I was reluctant at first to write this book because I wasn't sure how to dissect the ways I communicate and study my own process in order to describe it. After many decades of preaching, speaking, performing, teaching, and writing, I rely on my instincts and experiences to fuel my creativity. Each person has their own style of communication in their respective lanes, just as I have mine, and I didn't want to encourage anyone to imitate me or believe I could reduce what I do to a transferable formula.

So in order to discuss the process of preaching, we must consider how the wisdom of experience often makes the crucial difference. Just as the experienced chef produces delicious meals more consistently, communicators with experience learn how to adapt their process to meet the requirements of their opportunity more successfully as well. Experience is not merely repeating your sermon, speech, or performance a certain number of times until it reaches perfection. Experience is the icing that holds your cake together!

Control, Curate, Convey

The wisdom of experience allows you to adapt, pivot, and connect your message as you put it together for each particular audience. That's why early in my ministry, I accepted almost every invitation to preach. Not only was I eager and excited to use my gifts, but I wanted to have another experience from which to base the next sermon I gave somewhere else.

The gifts of experience cannot be underestimated. Many talented young adults have sought me for counsel about using their abilities to launch and sustain a ministry or artistic career. A number of them are exceptionally gifted with a stunning ability to preach, paint, perform, or produce—a few even do all of these well!

Based on our conversations, I suspect most of these aspiring individuals want me to reveal some secret about marketing on social media or changing the nuances of their current delivery. They've seen something go viral and catapult a peer into the stratosphere of success overnight. They see how quickly a social media post, pic, or tweet can make or break someone's career. While those are certainly factors in today's world, aspiring talents must not overlook the hard work of rehearsal, repetition, and revision.

More times than not, when someone asks me for advice on how to preach better or perform with greater impact, I simply emphasize the importance of experience. "Keep doing what you're doing," I'll tell them. "Pay attention to the feedback you get from people you trust. But ultimately, listen to your instincts as you learn from your experiences."

If my advice disappoints them or seems too obvious to repeat, they are too polite to tell me. The ones I've witnessed going on to ascend great heights of success and acclaim repeatedly illustrate my point. They discover what is unique about what they've been given and then they perfect their ability to control it, curate it, and convey it.

Using our metaphor of cooking, these young chefs take the recipes passed down to them, make them their own, and then seize every opportunity to serve the results to others. They learn quickly that if you don't recognize the ingredients you have at your disposal, then you miss opportunities to maximize your potential. Expressed another way, don't overlook what you have in order to be something you're not!

If you spent years working as an electrician, use what you know to explain your message to your audience or congregation. If you have considerable experience as a hairdresser and cosmetologist, share the natural comparisons you see to the message you're delivering to your group or conference participants. Especially as you're getting started, it can be tempting to adopt a persona of what you think you should be. You know, the solemn, serious professional with the perfect uniform for the occasion, glasses to make you look smart, and a new leather briefcase. I'm exaggerating but not by much!

If you want your audience to be comfortable with you, you have to be comfortable with you! Don't try to be who you think they want at the expense of who you are. Of course, there's definitely a time and a place to acclimate to local cultural customs and expectations, certainly regarding etiquette and respect toward your hosts and listeners, but most of the time, they're interested in who you are. Use your opportunities to speak or preach as moments to be as authentic as appropriate to the occasion.

Many times I've been asked to offer an invocation at an event, conference, or banquet. Sometimes these are familiar settings with familiar faces, but often they're new venues with people I may know about but do not know personally. For example, I'll never forget attending a once-in-a-lifetime event where I felt overwhelmed by greatness. I was intimidated to say the least, which tells you something about it because I'm not easily intimidated!

Spirit of the Event

My friend Tyler Perry was hosting the grand opening of his new film and TV studio in Southwest Atlanta. Occupying 330 acres, the $250 million facility features 12 sound stages, with each one named for an iconic black actor, including Cicely Tyson, Sidney Poitier, Diahann Carroll, Denzel Washington, Will Smith, and Whoopi Goldberg—all of whom would be honored at the gala in moving tributes to the entertainment trails they had blazed.

Tyler was determined for this event, which some referred to as the "Black Met Gala," to be worthy of the groundbreaking facility it officially inaugurated. Merging past and present in the culmination of one man's dreams, it is the only major film studio in the nation owned by an African American. It features a replica White House, airport terminal, hospital, jail, trailer park, and suburban neighborhood. The studio incudes six-lane freeways for car chases along with sets depicting major cityscapes in both the United States and Europe. The place literally has every kind of scene, both exterior and interior, a filmmaker or producer might want! The fact that this facility is built on property once used as a training base for Confederate soldiers during the Civil War called Fort McPherson makes it even more amazing.

So needless to say, Tyler pulled out all the stops and created some starts no one knew existed for this spectacular event! And he had asked me to pray an invocation at the beginning of the evening's program, which simultaneously left me honored and humbled at a level few events have ever reached. I knew that my role would be short and delivered before a literal who's who of superstars from every major arena—including movies and TV, music, sports, and politics.

Standing up in front of not just a few but hundreds of famous faces left me breathless! Bill and Hillary Clinton sat at a table, smiling up at me. I saw the honorees, many of whom I'd been privileged to meet or work with but also many iconic individuals that left me starstruck. There was Oprah, of course, whispering to her best friend, Gayle King. Scanning the crowd, I noted Halle Berry and Viola Davis, Jennifer Hudson and Patti LaBelle, Usher, Ludacris, Beyoncé and Jay-Z. To my right I glimpsed political powerhouses including Atlanta Mayor Keisha Lance Bottoms, Rep. Maxine Waters, Rep. John Lewis (less than a year before his own passing), Stacey Abrams, and many more. Honestly, I hate to sound like a namedropper, especially because there are hundreds more I'm leaving out!

Simply put, it was a gathering unlike any other before or since. And there I was with a mic wondering if what I had prepared to say and pray was elevated and grounded, celebratory and reverent enough for this esteemed audience. I couldn't tell you exactly what I said, but I basically tried to recognize the achievements of those we were honoring, including the astounding vision and vicissitude of our host himself. I kept in mind that while we had plenty of Protestant Christians in attendance, there were also numerous attendees in the Catholic, Muslim, and Jewish faith traditions along with some atheists and agnostics. With such diversity in mind, I focused on the accomplishments we were there to celebrate and how the creative arts united us all. I tried to express the spirit of the event as a voice for all the spiritual power in the room!

Flavor of the Favor

When you've assessed where you will be speaking or performing and the stakeholders in attendance, you can then choose the ingredients you want to include. While the topics, issues, or event etiquette may dictate your approach, you still have many options on how to combine them, connect them, and communicate them. We can all follow the same recipe, but that doesn't mean we will all produce the same dish!

Sometimes having limitations or being asked to address a specific topic even works in our favor. You've probably seen those cooking shows where participants are given hampers filled with an eclectic, if not seemingly random, assortment of edible ingredients from which they must prepare a culinary masterpiece for the judges. It's a deliberate form of the same game my mother and countless other cooks have used when confronted with the dreaded question "What's for supper?"

Mama would go to the cupboard and see what she had on hand, check the refrigerator or freezer, and unleash her creativity and resourcefulness. Soups, stews, and casseroles could be assembled quickly from a wide array of whatever we had. She was also inventive with leftovers and could transform them into a meal distinct from its predecessor, magically waving her spatula like a wand to make last night's pork roast and vegetables into that night's pulled-pork barbeque and potato salad. Growing up in a frugal home herself, my mother learned at an early age to make the most of what she had.

The best communicators do the same. They know that the process determines the quality of their delivery. And even when you're presenting the same material or message, each time will have its own unique flavor. I can't tell you how many times I've preached the sermon I've prepared in our first service and have it land one way only to preach it again in the following service and have it catch fire! Not to mention when I've preached on the same Bible passage but taken a slightly different approach for different audiences.

Part of the process for delivering your best sermon is discernment. It's not expecting every sermon to conform to the same three-point outline or flow in a linear, consecutive manner. This is where you have to allow your creativity to serve as a catalyst in your communication. Creativity tends to follow its own direction and follow its own sense of timing. From my experience, you can cultivate creativity but you cannot force inspiration on command. You have to prepare your sermon openhandedly and adapt to the needs of your audience.

Just as a good cook knows when to add another dash of salt or teaspoon of milk, good communicators know when to add a bit of humor or allow silence to speak (more on this in Chapter 9). One size does not fit all, but this doesn't mean you don't begin with some kind of pattern in mind. Your process must be strong enough to support the substance of your ideas and supple enough to bend to the unique and distinct needs of your audience.

If you find yourself stuck or in a rut when it comes to your process, then you likely need to nourish the creative wellspring within. You may need to read some authors and books that you haven't encountered before. Talking to stakeholders with diverse points of view can stimulate your understanding of how they see the issues at hand. Considering how other communicators have channeled their message with fresh insight might also inspire you. Move beyond communication and your particular medium. Getting acquainted with artists, sculptors, dancers, actors, musicians, poets, and songwriters can give you new perspectives and sensory experiences of your subject matter.

I love to learn how other creative individuals work

and often find transferable principles and parallels to my own experiences. Legendary singer/songwriter Tom Waits said, "Some songs don't want to be recorded. You can't wrestle with them or you'll only scare them off more." He compares it to "trying to trap birds" rather than ones that he discovers fully formed like "digging potatoes out of the ground." Some are unique and messy, "gum found under an old table," while others don't work but can be "cut up as bait" and used to "catch other songs." He describes the very best songs as "dreams taken through a straw."[1]

The same is true for preaching!

Time Out

While we would all like to have ample time for our messages to percolate, simmer, and ferment, necessity often forces us to produce what we can in the time available to us. As a young man early in my ministry, I received several late-night phone calls on Saturdays from pastors suddenly needing someone to preach for them the next morning. Most had just experienced some kind of loss or faced a family emergency. Sometimes these calls created a domino effect because if I accepted their request, then I would need someone to fill in for me at my church. Nonetheless, I did my best to help out and serve them.

The first few times I faced the pressure to preach in just a few hours, I felt too nervous to be spontaneous and lacked the confidence to "wing it." Instead, I either relied on the sermon I had already prepared for my own congregation or pulled one from my files to dust off. While I would like to think those sermons spoke to the hearts of those in attendance and ministered to their needs, I suspect those early offerings were more likely polite placeholders. Looking back, I see I was more concerned with being in control and trying to make a good impression than ministering to the flock briefly entrusted to my care.

My response was understandable, but as I grew in experience and confidence, I began to rely more on prayer, divine inspiration, and gut instinct. If I knew anything about what was going on in the church where I filled in, then I would try to use that knowledge. If I was acquainted with elders, deacons, or other members of their fellowship, then I might place a call or two for insight and encouragement. Sometimes I went back through previous sermons I had preached and pulled parts and pieces, but I no longer needed the security of serving a prefabricated message.

I'd like to think those last-minute sermons were as

powerful as any I've ever preached. In the last couple of decades, I've been more likely to be the one calling on another pastor or evangelist to fill in for me when something has come up to pull me away. I usually have a shortlist of candidates in mind simply based on who has impressed me, spoken to me, or ministered to me in their preaching.

Out of love and respect, they rarely say no when I call them only a few hours before they're needed in the pulpit. But I can still hear the fear and uncertainty in their nervous voices. Some even ask, "Are you sure you want me to do this, Bishop?" as if I had dialed them unintentionally! Although they know the logical answer, they need to hear me say, "Yes, I know you have it in you or I wouldn't have asked. You will deliver exactly what people need!"

Like Moses making excuses about why he could not lead the Israelites out of Egypt, or Gideon wondering if God had made a mistake in choosing him as the least qualified, we all experience this kind of fear, anxiety, and dread at times. We want to help a friend or serve another leader in need, but we also feel panicked at the prospect of accelerating—or forgoing altogether—our usual process.

That's when you must remember that the creative process is always in play! Every thought and feeling, observation and experience, memory and message you've absorbed all contribute to your unique ability to craft the communication required. While deliberate, devoted time to your process is important and vital to your success, you probably do not need as much time as you think.

Many studies show that crafting a speech or writing an essay in a short amount of time versus having weeks to prepare often makes no difference in its quality. In fact, when you have a long lead time, you may be tempted to procrastinate and still wait until the last minute to get started. When your schedule is jam-packed and you know you have only a brief window in which to craft your communication, then you're forced to come up with something. It may not be your best, but then again, it might!

On the other hand, I would encourage you to avoid the phenomenon a writer friend told me he had developed but didn't recognize until he was in college. Working well under pressure, my friend said he usually waited until the night before to write the required essays, speeches, and other assignments. He received good grades and positive feedback from this method, but then one day his teacher returned a research paper he had written in record time with only a C.

"Well, getting a C isn't so bad on a paper I wrote

in a few hours the night before," he thought. Then he realized how he had allowed himself to have a built-in excuse for not maximizing his talents and seeing how far his skills could take him. Rather than pacing himself and using his time more consistently and judiciously, he had conditioned himself to see how well he could do without adequate preparation.

Whether you have more than plenty of time or get put on the spot to speak extemporaneously, make the most of the opportunity!

Driving Lessons

Regardless of how much preparation time you have, the engine of your message needs a transmission. You want to glide smoothly even as you accelerate to the climax of your communication before concluding and bringing your listeners to a gentle stop. You are the driver, the pilot, the conductor controlling both the speed and the route to your destination, the major point you want listeners to take with them and use in their lives.

Accordingly, you must plan the best course and know where the twists and turns are located. Just as when you're driving a car, you don't want to pass the turn you need to take in order to make your next crossroads. When we fly, we often discover there is no direct flight to our desired destination, which means we must use a connecting flight. If our first flight is delayed, then we might miss our connection and lose the opportunity to reach our destination on time.

Connections and transitions often make the difference between a great speech and a good one. While shifting from one point to another sounds straightforward and easy enough, rarely is the direct route the one that takes in all the sights you want to see along the way. You must remember that many people in your audience have already visited your loquacious locale. They know the story of Jonah and the whale. They've already read about the risks involved in launching a new start-up. They've heard others talk about how to overcome depression.

With the Internet at our fingertips 24-7, most content is available in some form online. Your audience is trusting you to filter it, fortify it, and frame it in ways they probably haven't considered. With so many sound bites and scrolling-screen messages bombarding us all the time, you have to compete for attention from distracted, often overwhelmed minds. You want listeners as fully engaged as possible with you and your message. You want your substance and style to synchronize in ways that satisfy and exceed their expectations.

So when you're putting your message together, think about how you will drive to get your passengers where you want to take them.

I remember an old six-speed manual Cutlass I drove shortly after Serita and I married. The clutch would stick sometimes, which made it hard to know when you had shifted successfully. The gearshift also had a propensity to skip from second into fourth, resulting in an abrupt stop-stall-start-try-again sequence of shifting. It was reliable but more stubborn in its idiosyncrasies than a mule pulling a farmer's plow!

After a year or two, however, I knew I had to drive that car without having to think about every shift, every acceleration, and every glitch. I would hold the stick shift tighter and carefully make sure we hit third gear. I would apply just enough pressure to the clutch to keep it from sticking. I knew how to tap the brakes just enough to decelerate and downshift. I was aware of what the car could and could not do based on my experiences with it.

The same holds true for the message you're driving home to your audience. You want to avoid unintentional quirks, distractions, and pauses that might jerk them out of their engagement with you and your message. As you move from point to point and example to application, you want them to track with you. Sometimes noticing the raised eyebrows or confused expressions on faces in the congregation signals you to slow down, to back up and make a clearer, cleaner connection. If those faces looking back at you seem restless, anxious, or heaven forbid—bored!—then you may want to pick up the pace or move on quickly to the next mile marker.

The last thing you want to do is panic and floor it. Racing through your speech as well as your material may get their attention but leave them wishing your pews had seat belts. So much of the process is about anticipating how your message will be received. Again, the more practice you have in shifting smoothly, as well as reading the responses of your passengers, the easier it becomes to reach your intended destination.

Delivery by Design

While I've already shared my trepidation about relying on templates and formulas, I generally do follow a process in the practice of my preaching: Study yourself full, think yourself clear, pray yourself hot, and let yourself go. This organic process begins with discerning the text for my sermon. While some passages, stories, and themes emerge naturally due to the season, such as Easter and Christmas, others emerge as I consider the needs of the congregation as well as the relevance and applicability of the text to a broader universal audience. Beginning with prayer and immersing the entire process in prayer is a given. I try to listen and pay attention to the movement of the Holy Spirit upon my heart. All these factors shape how and why I'm drawn to a particular text in the Bible.

Once I feel confident in the text, I begin by thinking as broadly as possible about its meaning and relevance for all people. In this regard, I must consider it not as a black text or a white text, not as a text for old or young, gay or straight, rich or poor, but a text that transcends demographic and prejudicial perspectives. I believe the Bible inherently applies to all human beings so therefore I want my sermon to do the same. I don't want to preach a message that only speaks to women in their thirties who vote Republican, because then I leave out the rest of my listeners in the room.

In addition to its universal appeal and applicability, the text has rules based on its original context. It was written for a specific audience, in a particular time and place, so before I establish my message for a contemporary audience, I must get a handle on the meaning of the text in light of the ancient audience for which it was written.

Only after discerning the original intent do I feel prepared to bring the depth and power of that original meaning to the situation and circumstances of my current audience.

I must also gather all the relatives of the text. Just as virtually everyone has relatives—mother, father, siblings, aunts, uncles, cousins, on and on—every text has relatives of its own, the other verses, passages, stories, and history that intersect in whatever way to form some kind of relationship. It's essential to consider as many relatives as I can find in order to appreciate all dimensions of the text. Just as knowing something about your family helps others know you, I want to know my text's family in order to better understand how and why its message was first born.

From there, I try to think myself clear in finding ways to connect with my audience and provide an experience emerging from the text. Basically, I want to convey the wisdom of the passage being preached, which I know in part relies on the wisdom I've gathered and experienced in my own life. All of life can provide malleable experience that can be shaped into wisdom if the preacher knows how to carve experience into a usable shape for the sermon.

I believe the grace of God through Jesus Christ is what saves people, which is reflected in countless ways throughout the biblical text. Therefore, the preacher's experience should point audiences to the text, or the sermon will become about the preacher—what the preacher thinks and feels, and not about what the God revealed in the Bible thinks and feels. I try to be a conduit, a facilitator, a bridge between the truth of the Scripture and the needs of my congregation.

Once I have the context, the theme sentence, the wisdom of the text, and life experience as a window into the text, I carefully consider the images and metaphors that seem most accurate, compelling, memorable, and powerful. I'm convinced images and metaphors are vehicles and containers that route profound wisdom and theological content into the hearts of people based upon familiar objects. Visualizing a concept and engaging it with one's senses, even if only imagined based on my choice of words, makes that concept much more memorable and relatable.

I suspect my reliance on images and metaphors once again goes back to my mother, who was a teacher, and as such always used object lessons, both in the classroom or at home, to teach principles by tangible tokens. She often cited the perfect example of Jesus and the way he taught by providing familiar images and scenarios—building a house, making wine, planting seeds—to create metaphors with maximum impact.

Choosing the best images and metaphors for a sermon also relies on their arrangement. There's nothing worse in preaching than to give an answer without establishing or clearly identifying the problem! Without a context of knowing the layers of a specific need or issue, it's virtually impossible to share an accessible solution. The power of the answer is the result of the complexity of the problem. So if the preacher solves the problem before the creation of the complexity in the head and heart of the listener, the sermon is in crisis.

This is where suspense can be so crucial in the arrangement of what's presented. Really, any good story, anecdote, joke, or lesson creates expectations in listeners that becomes a kind of suspense. The audience expects to be taken somewhere and for that destination to be worthwhile in some way. I believe suspense is why people listen. If I'm not building suspense, often in various ways that run parallel to one another, then I'm probably not holding the attention of most people. Why keep listening if you already know the answer? Most people won't, so be mindful of ways to pique their curiosity as you design your delivery.

Let Yourself Go

Finally, once the other stages have been successfully assembled and negotiated, it's time to let yourself go! While this sounds simple enough, this can be one of the most challenging parts of preaching and speaking. If you're shy, reserved, and inhibited, it's difficult to preach effectively because your self-consciousness works against the freedom to deliver your message. Ideally, you want your voice to be like a finely tuned instrument being played by a virtuoso. There's a musicality when preaching that must flow naturally and often instinctively. It can be taught just as a metronome helps a musician keep time, but yet again, if the speaker or preacher becomes too focused on keeping their voice supple and musical, then other aspects may be neglected.

The voice is the hammer that nails each point home. You want to use it efficiently and rhythmically in a way that appears effortless, or at least free of distraction, for your listeners. Many communicators view their voice as merely a necessary by-product of human speech, but this greatly underestimates its importance. Speakers and pastors struggling with vocal control must find a way to respect their vocal cords as a musical instrument that requires care and maintenance. They may need to practice voice exercises or drink hot tea or another soothing beverage as a way to warm up before they go on.

In conjunction with the voice, the body is also an instrument. Just as some may misunderstand their voice as a by-product of human speech, there may also be a lack of comprehension of the body as an instrument of communication, usually based in some form of speaker inhibition. The body communicates the depth of a preacher's sincerity and truth. Rather than being self-conscious about movements and mannerisms, the preacher has to be God-conscious. Basically, this means you surrender yourself to God so that your entire being is available to deliver his message.

When you fully make your body available, you give your facial expressions, your hands, your chest, your hips, your legs, your feet—all of you. And why not? When you're having a disagreement with your spouse, you bring your body to it. When you're defending your territory, serving dinner, or making love, you bring your body to the delivery as well. This includes whatever imperfections you may have or think you have with your body. If you're too thin or overweight, have long hair or short hair, everything can be used and should contribute to how you speak and move and deliver your message. If you don't have an arm or your leg is broken or you have a prosthetic limb, use it. If you're on a crutch or in a wheelchair, make it part of the message.

I've learned that wherever I'm placed, I'm going to use everything I got! And I encourage you to do the same. Even if you're standing at a podium giving budget reports, your body can help you convey confidence, a comfortability with your part of the proceedings, and a calm sense of relaxed control. On the other hand, if you look so stiff, those in attendance are afraid you might break, or if you're so fidgety and antsy that you can't quit tapping your foot or cracking your knuckles, then your body will get in the way of your message.

Trusting your voice and body to work in tandem also allows you to react in the moment to what you sense your audience needs. This can be especially important as you close your sermon and end the service because there's no one style of closing that's appropriate for every sermon every time. Some sermons are meant to be thought-provoking and some to be decision-making. Some are emotional and others are more educational. It goes back to the text and its relevance and application for your audience.

One thing I have noticed over the years, though, is that you don't want to shift your tone or style dramatically at the end. If you haven't used humor at any time in your sermon, then don't close with a funny story. If you've been dramatic and outspoken in your delivery, it might not work to suddenly go soft and quiet. Of course, these strategies very well could work, too! Any rules I try to point out are bound to be broken because I've certainly broken my share of them.

There are many kinds of sermons and closes, and the preacher must strive, without inhibition, to deliver the close that is natural and organic to the specific kind of sermon that's being preached. Stay true to the sermon just preached rather than veering dramatically or shifting tone or style suddenly at the end. Find a cohesive way to end the delivery so that people know where they are and how they've been changed by what they've just heard and experienced. Imagine that you're a pilot and land the congregation safely and smoothly in a new place where they see new sights and hear new sounds from where you started with them.

Letting yourself go means owning the freedom to align your voice and your body with the message you're delivering!

Planning Your Path

A basic but effective way to shape your listeners' expectations is to tell them up front: This is where we're going and here's how we will get there. You give them a little summary or overview, like a movie trailer or pop-up ad, to tease them with a preview of your coming attractions. At the same time, you don't want to summarize or condense so effectively that they feel like they already know all you're going to share with them. We've all seen movie trailers that show the film's best moments and most dramatic scenes so thoroughly that we feel like we don't need to see that movie at all!

So even as you set expectations for where you're going, create some mystique that will show them they don't know all you know about the journey. Use unexpected words or phrases your listeners may not associate with your topic or message. Choose a surprising metaphor that's not forced or contrived but opens up your points in intriguing ways. Try not to worry about being too clever or cute or dazzling, and keep the focus on providing a service, offering a benefit, and meeting a need.

When in doubt, there is never any shame in the KISS method—Keep It Simple, Stupid! If your time is limited or shared with other peers, if the event or occasion has a certain theme or mood, then a straight route may be the best. I recall being asked to speak with several others at an event at the National Cathedral in Washington following the devastation of Hurricane Katrina. I had only ten minutes and had thought long and hard on how to maximize them. Once I decided to focus on showing why we must always lend a hand to those in need, I brainstormed a dozen reasons—far too many for almost any talk.

Combining some and cutting others, I curated my collection down to five points, still a lot for ten minutes but doable. And all five were important and not necessarily predictable. I felt compelled to keep all five, which meant I then had to figure out the order to address them. Then I noticed a kind of natural progression among the five reasons and knew I had my structural flow. Because I could see how they related from one to another and how they reinforced my key theme, I knew a direct approach was best. There was no time to adorn, embellish, or enhance so I concentrated on the hub of my message and these five spokes.

Sometimes you can bring new life to an old message by changing the vantage point from which it's told. Like changing the key in which a song is played, you can also focus on a different theme, issue, or detail and achieve a new and different sound. This is especially true for the events included in Scripture. It can create an experience for your listeners that draws them into a scene as if they were there instead of merely telling them what you want them to know about it. It's the difference between summarizing the conversation you overheard and letting them eavesdrop and hear it for themselves!

These different methods might arrive at the same destination—what the other parties said—but create very different experiences. From Dallas, where I live, you can get to Los Angeles by taking a plane, driving yourself, riding Amtrak, going Greyhound, or riding sidecar on a Harley! Each will get you to LA, but each journey will vary in numerous ways. Just consider the way flying would take under three hours and make the journey seem quick and effortless. Driving, on the other hand, would take more than twenty hours and be an exhausting journey—but it would also give you a more vivid picture of what's between the two cities.

Miracle in Your Message

Let's consider an example I've used before in sermons, the encounter Jesus had with a blind man named Bartimaeus (Mark 10:46–52). We're told Jesus and his disciples are on their way out of town as a large crowd follows them. By this time in Jesus' ministry, word had gotten out about who he was and the miracles he could do. Sitting beside the road begging, Bartimaeus heard the crowd buzzing about Jesus of Nazareth, which prompted him to call out, "Jesus, Son of David, have mercy on me!" (Mark 10:47 NIV). People around him then told him to keep quiet, perhaps embarrassed at the ruckus he was causing. But Bartimaeus only shouted louder, which worked because Jesus heard him and asked to have him brought forward.

Jesus then asked Bartimaeus, "What do you want me to do for you?" to which the blind man said, "Rabbi, I want to see." This Q&A is the heart of their encounter, very simple and direct on the surface. Jesus told him, "Go, your faith has healed you," and Bartimaeus instantly could see the face of the one who just healed him (Mark 10:51–52 NIV).

Knowing that many in my congregation would be familiar with this story, I wanted to look at it from a different angle. So I chose to focus on what resonated with me in that moment: anxiety! Not surprising, given the tumultuous times we live in, but I see in this scene that anxiety is nothing new. What's not stated explicitly is that Jesus and his disciples, along with the crowd following them, were returning to Jerusalem for the last time before Christ's death. Only Jesus knew what awaited him there, but I can't help but wonder about the unspoken tension in the air, a sense of foreboding.

Then there's the anxiety of Bartimaeus, a blind man begging beside the road. On any given day, he would likely feel the anxiety and dread that come from poverty, from not being able to see and therefore relying on the charity of others who might take pity on him as they went by. I suspect Bartimaeus' normal anxiety was heightened considerably when he heard the crowds approaching. What were they chanting? Who were they following and what was their mission? Would they riot? Harm him?

Sadly enough, when we experience uncertainty now, we tend to jump to worst-case scenarios and brace ourselves. When you've lost so much and experienced trauma in your life, then it's understandable. But it also makes living, hoping, and trusting others that much harder. I wonder if this blind man's anxiety was also raised by what he apparently had already heard about the center of attention now approaching him, Jesus of Nazareth, the carpenter's son, descended from King David.

Again, we don't know what Bartimaeus may have heard, but we can certainly imagine the sensational stories and grandiose gossip wafting toward his heightened sense of hearing from the voices of those rushing past him. Could those sound bites be true? Did Jesus really heal the sick and bring Mary and Martha's brother, Lazarus, back to life? And praying over some boy's lunch with five loaves and a couple of fish, Jesus was able to feed more than five thousand people? Really? Who was he? Could he really be the Messiah, the Son of God? If so, then why were the Jewish religious leaders so angry? And what about those rumors of a conspiracy to kill Jesus? Just idle gossip or inevitable outcome?

Bartimaeus was literally in the dark. Even though he could not see, however, he had faith. He believed that despite all he had heard, Jesus was indeed who he said he was. So then it was just a matter of getting his attention! Which may have been more challenging than Bart first thought because of the noisy crowd, especially when some tried to silence him. What if they dragged him away before Jesus heard him? What if others prevented Jesus from coming to him?

But Bartimaeus knew that it was not the time to remain silent. It was an opportunity that might never come again, a moment with the potential to change the rest of his life, to transform his destiny. To give him sight. So even if he failed, even if he embarrassed himself and those around him, even if Jesus turned out to refuse his request, Bartimaeus had to try. He had to try! To shout louder and longer, to cry out from the depths of his soul, to beg God to do the impossible and restore his sight.

When Bartimaeus heard that Jesus was asking for him, he jumped to his feet and left his cloak behind. This in itself demonstrates complete faith because surely his cloak was a prized possession, a garment for keeping warm and protecting his body from the elements. He did what he could do as fast as he could do it, rising from beggar to seeker, from blind man to 20/20 visionary, from someone in the darkness of anxiety to the light of healing. He no longer had need of the cloak that had been his security blanket in the darkness.

If it could happen to a blind man begging beside the road outside Jericho almost two thousand years ago, then it could happen to you and me! If we keep the faith, listen carefully, and raise our voices, God meets us in our need and does the impossible. He reunites broken families, heals afflicted bodies, restores betrayed relationships, and removes the shackles of addiction. Like Jesus with Bartimaeus, God hears our cries and comes to us and asks us what we want from him. "Cheer up! On your feet! He's calling you," the crowd told Bartimaeus.

That's the message I'm telling you today! Throw off your old cloak and step out of your comfort zone. Look with fresh eyes on your message and how you can help others experience it anew. Whether you're preaching in a pulpit, summarizing quarterly trends, or toasting the bride and groom at their reception, let others experience the miracle in your message!

CHAPTER 6

Where Does It Hurt?

I've learned that people will forget what you said, people will forget what you did, but people will never forget how you made them feel.

—Maya Angelou

"Does it hurt here?" asked the doctor, gently pressing on my wife's abdomen. "Or how about here?"

Serita winced in pain and the answer was clear.

What remained unclear, however, was the internal source of her pain.

This incident occurred several years ago and started with a sharp, severe ache just below my wife's rib cage. Ruling out a stomachache and indigestion, we then thought it might be her appendix rupturing or some other malady requiring immediate attention.

We rushed to the emergency care facility nearest us and went through a battery of examinations and tests only to be told that her appendix had not caused the problem.

But they weren't sure what had. Her pain was not related to her heart, lungs, or kidneys either. Her pain and distress revealed the severity of her suffering but not its cause or remedy. So doctors prescribed medication to dull the pain while we made appointments with her primary care physician. He ran more tests of course but still could not pinpoint the problem. Meanwhile, Serita's pain persisted and increased in its intensity. We were both worried by the unknown.

"Where does it hurt?" was replaced by "*Why* does it hurt?"

Medical Mystery

While Serita pushed through and continued to attend church services and take care of our home, I knew she was in unbearable pain. The worst part was wondering when a doctor would be able to identify the cause of her excruciating anguish and provide a diagnosis to remediate and eliminate it. The situation reminded me of when our children were very young and would get sick. They could capably express their pain and distress in general terms but struggled to describe and locate it so that we, or their pediatrician, could diagnose the problem with precision in order to resolve it. "Where does it hurt?" we would ask the child, following their finger to the tummyache, scratched kneecap, or sore ankle. From there, we could continue our exam until we made progress in providing a solution.

My wife could articulate her suffering in great detail, but the seemingly invisible cause continued to resist detection. Fortunately, after half a dozen appointments with various specialists, along with numerous blood tests, sonograms, and x-rays, an internist determined the source of Serita's pain and scheduled surgery to eradicate it. While the surgery itself could be performed efficiently without requiring hospitalization, the recovery lasted six weeks and included pain that rivaled its predecessor!

My wife has a high pain tolerance, however, and motivated herself through the agonizing weeks following surgery because she knew she was growing stronger and healthier. Recovery pain was therefore easier to bear because it was constructive and healing rather than the destructive, unrelenting pain signaling the internal trauma in her body. Her diagnosis baffled some of the best doctors available, but once the right expert recognized the problem, he could prescribe the requisite remedy.

In terms of diagnosing an invisible, elusive pain, preaching is much like a doctor's medical exam. In fact, most communication requires you to identify the primary need of your audience in order to deliver a targeted message addressing that need. It might be the need for motivation to raise funds for new band uniforms at school. It could be the need for insight into the cause of recent vandalism in the community. Perhaps the need for celebrating a couple's golden wedding anniversary.

Sometimes the need, which is distinct from an audience's expectation but often overlaps, seems obvious and up front. Local entrepreneurs invite you to share your experience and wisdom about launching a successful small business. A church leader asks you to lead your women's Bible study group as you read, discuss, and apply the Book of Ruth. The local TV affiliate wants to interview you about the new nonprofit you're starting. You're asked to preach at a homecoming service for the church where you grew up. Regardless of the venue and viewers, knowing how to diagnose your audience's need accurately is vital to your success as a communicator.

Let the Need Find You

Sometimes you go looking for the need, and sometimes the need finds you.

When I wrote *Woman, Thou Art Loosed!*, I could not imagine the impact it would have on the lives of millions of women. All I knew was that I saw a need, a glaring vacancy in the spiritual resources available to women suffering wounds that would not heal. Many of these women had experienced abuse—physical, sexual, mental, emotional—as children that had left permanent scars on their souls. Others had lost loved ones in what seemed like an ongoing cycle of abandonment and grief—husbands who'd left them, parents lost to dementia and disease, children consumed by addiction.

Some of these women made no attempt to hide the toll their suffering had taken. I could see the pain etched in their faces, leaving them to resemble unfinished sculptures displaying harsh blows from the chisel. Their shoulders slumped and eyes moist with tears, these ladies carried the burden of their afflictions with dignity and refused to pretend otherwise. Because even in the midst of such anguish, they were still standing with an undeniable strength and unwavering faith in God.

Other women looked like the last people you would expect to be falling apart on the inside. Taking great care with their appearance, they appeared to be well informed, well organized, and inherently efficient. Many were young wives and new mothers in the early phases of nurturing their families. Others were consummate achievers on a fast track up corporate ladders, using their gifts, talents, and ambition without apology. Only when I looked closely could I see the flicker of past pains still burning within them despite their best attempts to pretend otherwise.

Many confided in me and my wife when they could no longer bear their suffering in silence. Others had reached a breaking point when their latest crisis could not be contained alone. Some found comfort in our church and heard me preach on the power of God to comfort, heal, restore, and redeem us from the terrors, traumas, and tragedies of life. They wanted to experience spiritual healing in order to facilitate holistic wholeness and restoration in all areas of their lives. With tears in my eyes, I never felt more humbled and honored to be a vessel of God than when preaching, praying, and presenting the Good News to these sisters of faith.

But the more I tried to minister to them, the more my awareness grew about the number of women suffering spiritually and the extent of the agony they carried. Their need overwhelmed me, and as much as I longed to do more, I knew I was only one man in a small church in West Virginia. Although I always had them in mind when I preached, I decided to deliver a series of sermons on a scene in Scripture that distilled the essence of healing available to us all.

Taken from the words spoken by Jesus to heal a crippled woman, this series was called *Woman, Thou Art Loosed!*

Loosed by Love

Found in Luke 13:10–17, this passage reveals an encounter between Jesus and a woman, identified only as a "daughter of Abraham" (v. 16), crippled for eighteen years by a demonic spirit that kept her bent and broken. Jesus noticed her among those listening to him teach in a synagogue on the Sabbath. Even among the many faces staring back at him, he discerned a need in this woman that he knew he could meet.

Perhaps it was the way her neck tilted at an angle or the cringeworthy way her arms flailed from her shoulders. Maybe Jesus could not visibly see her bent body and only recognized the crippling pain transmitted by her eyes. Or maybe it was simply that he detected the demonic shackles binding this woman's spirit so that she could not experience the health and freedom for which she was created. Regardless of what drew the Savior's attention, he saw her need and called her forward.

Then he spoke to her in words conveying both a command and a declaration, an imperative observation of her immediate healing. Jesus called the woman to him and said, "Woman, thou art loosed from thine infirmity" (Luke 13:12 KJV). Other translations use more contemporary language to indicate Christ's message, with all conveying that this woman was free of her affliction and liberated from her liability. But something about the beautiful, archaic simplicity of the King James Version struck a chord in me.

In addressing her as "Woman," Jesus makes her both the specific individual standing before him as well as a representative for all women. He uses the familiar second-person address, which the King James Version renders as "thou" while we would say "you," followed by the life-changing message of instantaneous healing hanging on the unexpected word "loosed."

When we hear "loose" today, it's usually used as an

adjective to describe something separating from what it had been attached to, such as a loose thread or loose wire. Using it as a verb, we might say, "I loosened the screws in the machine" but not "I loosed them." If you're like me, more times than not, I might pause to make sure I wasn't confusing *loose* with *lose*!

Forgive me for playing English teacher, but the word *loosed* describes the liberation this woman experienced so perfectly! She had been bound by a Satanic spirit, as Jesus later explained to the Jewish religious leaders upset that he had healed her on the Sabbath, their traditional day of complete rest requiring everyone to refrain from action as much as possible (Luke 13:16). Calling them hypocrites, Jesus reminds them that they would untie their donkeys or oxen so that their animals could have water to drink but yet they criticized him for untying this poor woman from the oppressive spirit holding her captive.

Loosed is the perfect word here because it conjures an image of letting go, of locks unlocked, chains undone, tight grips unclenched, and bindings unbound. "Loosed" connotes free-and-easy, unlimited, unfettered independence from oppression in a way that is both poetic and powerful. For people whose ancestors were brought to this country as slaves, the word *loosed* describes the sense of exhilaration that must have ignited upon emancipation. For people whose parents and grandparents had marched at Selma or peacefully protested the injustice of segregation, the word *loosed* echoes with rights being wrested from those whose bigotry, prejudice, and systemic racism attempted to maintain oppression.

The fact that Jesus loosed this woman from the dark spirit crippling her for eighteen years speaks to the way suffering can end suddenly, immediately. I'm fascinated by the fact that this dear woman was there in the synagogue on the Sabbath despite how pain reverberated through her twisted body. Her body distorted at angles our joints were never intended to support, this daughter of Abraham could have embraced the role of victim.

She could've remained home in bed. She could've tried to drown her sorrows in wine. She could've been seeking out charlatans selling potions promising to straighten her spine. No, this woman had faith! She refused to allow the demon squeezing her bones to win. She would not give up on God but would faithfully worship in his temple. She would dare to hope that one day she could be free of the adversity crippling her body and gripping her soul.

Healed instantly as Jesus placed his hands on her after speaking, this woman cried out with thanksgiving and praise. Her prayers had been answered. Her faith had been fulfilled. Her body and mind had been restored. She had been loosed by love! In her suffering she embodied every woman who has ever endured abuse, oppression, and crippling of any kind. In her healing she offered hope to us all!

Message before the Movement

The response to my sermons on this woman's healing exceeded anything I had seen up until that point. Those services became sacred times of healing, anointing, and praising in a category all their own. Requests for audio tapes and transcriptions of these services went through the roof! Testimonies from women of every age who had experienced blessing, healing, and anointing flooded our church. This was back in the pre-smartphone era so people could not digitally record on phones or tablets, nor could I post on a church website or social media.

Invitations to preach this message at other churches, conferences, and events poured in—as well as persistent requests to preach it again at my home church! I had hit a raw nerve of ravenous need that had not been addressed by the church as directly before. Women who had experienced forms of abuse from fathers, uncles, brothers, boyfriends, and sadly, even pastors, especially resonated with *Woman, Thou Art Loosed!*

Many told me they had never had the courage to confront their wounds, let alone their abusers, and knew it was holding them back in life. But now they had found the courage to confront the past so that they could ransom their future. Others shared relief that the shame and stigma was being removed from something they endured through no fault of their own. They had been silenced by the darkness crippling their souls, but no longer.

For the first time in their lives, they felt heard and seen as survivors, not victims, as beautiful children of God worthy of respect instead of damaged goods with no value. They refused to keep quiet any longer while others tried to stifle their screams of rage and pain. They had grown weary of being told that it was their problem, that they had imagined the abuse, that they enjoyed being the victim.

Jesus perfectly balanced grace and truth and never compromised one for the other. When the religious leaders tried to condemn him for healing this woman on the Sabbath, Jesus turned it back on them. If I may offer my paraphrase, "Don't tell me to ignore the suffering of a human being because it's the seventh day of the week—not when you're willing to untie your animals and give them water!"

The women being loosed by God's power through my message embraced the freedom that comes from knowing the truth. Their affliction had been diagnosed and the Great Physician allowed me to prescribe his perfect peace that passes all human understanding. Requests became so frequent and demand so great that I made it my mission to reach as many women as possible with this message of hope. So I decided to hold a weekend conference for women so they could experience the same kind of hope and healing as the crippled woman Jesus restored.

The conference allowed me to look at other women who had experienced healing and restoration from their suffering, including Eve, Sarah, Ruth, and Naomi, Mary the mother of Jesus, and Mary Magdalene. The response was overwhelming and requests for conference materials exceeded my resources to fund, print, and distribute typed copies. So I was inspired to write a book, one that I could sell to cover the costs of its production. Working evenings and weekends, I got my wife to help me type up my notes, sermon transcripts, and new material.

Once I had a completed manuscript—and at this time I knew little-to-nothing about the editorial, marketing, and production processes for publishing books—I found a printer willing to run five thousand copies, which I would make available through our church and the next Woman Thou Art Loosed! conference, which was already scheduled with full enrollment. I had barely lifted the boxes of finished books into my basement and the trunk of my car before they disappeared!

Women who had experienced new life from hearing the message or attending the conference wanted copies of their own as well as books to send to their mothers, daughters, sisters, nieces, and best friends. So I printed another five thousand, and then ten thousand, and then it became a race to keep up with the growing demand. Considering my time and labor, I made no real profit from sales and kept reinvesting proceeds to fund larger print runs.

Eventually, my little self-published book landed in the hands of Destiny Image, a traditional publisher of faith-based books, around the same time my preaching and speaking also began to take off. In order to have the professional support and infrastructure, particularly with production and distribution, I partnered with an established publishing company that seemed to understand the significant need my book addressed. Other books addressing other needs followed as I discovered the power of amplifying my messages across an aligned media platform.

Today, we're coming up on the thirtieth anniversary of *Woman, Thou Art Loosed!*'s first publication. That first book I once gave away, sold at cost from my trunk, and mailed to readers has since birthed updated editions, workbooks, devotionals, study Bibles, gift editions, greeting cards, and a Hollywood feature film! I share all this with you not to brag or boast, because I can take credit only for obeying the call God placed on my heart to pay attention to the needs of my flock. He gets all the credit and glory for how he has used it to work in millions of women's lives around the world.

Long before it was a movement, it was simply a message addressing an urgent need.

Terminal Silence

While some urgent needs may seem invisible to others, once you see those needs, they cannot be ignored no matter how large, frightening, or dangerous they may appear. I compare these kinds of needs to the unexpected diagnosis informing a patient of a malignant tumor. They went to see their doctor about the persistent skin rash on their elbow only to discover cancer had invaded their body. They thought they had a minor surface wound, but it turned out to be a symptom of a larger, pervasive condition throughout their entire respiratory system. They assumed they needed a shot and some ointment when they actually required chemotherapy and radiation.

Many times, these needs become the proverbial elephant in the room—an issue, problem, conflict, or crisis that everyone knows exists in their midst but which they try to ignore nonetheless. They consider it impolite, uncomfortable, and messy to acknowledge such needs so they consequently attempt to perpetuate a conspiracy of silence.

Keeping quiet in the face of an urgent, traumatic need, however, makes those who keep silent complicit in its consequences. Silence in the face of trauma becomes terminal. Those who choose silence when handed the mic in these instances, whether it's literal silence or empty messages intended to distract listeners, harm just as much as perpetrators. Feel-good messages and pleasant, benign homilies become salt in the wounds of those bleeding beneath the surface. Ignoring trauma cannot stanch the hemorrhaging of souls or alleviate the actuality of those in anguish. Would you give a gunshot victim bleeding out before you a Band-Aid and vitamin C?

I compare this kind of deadly, complicit silence to what I've observed in the lives of others who carry hidden scars. After counseling hundreds of individuals during the course of my ministry, I've all too frequently witnessed the courage required to confront childhood abuse. It takes strength, faith, and considerable bravery to stare your demons in the eye in order to clear your vision. Working through rage is required for survivors to unpack buried feelings about their abusers.

I've also noticed, however, that these people feel just as furious—if not more—at the silence of those who enabled the abuse. Mothers who turned blind eyes and deaf ears as their husbands exploited stepdaughters. Family members who knew but shamed the victim. Neighbors and church members who denied the clues and symptoms or outright refused to believe the testimony of those who suffered. Teachers, pastors, and coaches who didn't want to get involved or take risks that might result in the scorn or criticism of others. Those who have experienced abuse know that others' willingness to remain silent wounded them just as deeply as the touch of their abusers.

The impact of others' silence is often the same when considering abuse, injustice, and violence on a larger scale in society. I'm thinking particularly of the recent recognition of systemic racism that has plagued our nation since before its founding. Although I've touched on it briefly in previous chapters, allow me to share a few more thoughts about the importance of communication during our culture's ongoing awakening. Because rioting, violent protesting, and looting will never produce the positive change we all long for. Only peaceful protests, civil discourse, and honest conversations can move us forward.

Ghosts in the Castle

Perhaps there have been moments when I should have said more, but rarely have I kept quiet! I have never been one to ignore those elephants tromping around the room. Whether foolish or courageous, I've always believed that my voice can make a difference. I grew up believing that words could change lives, that sermons could convey the power of God's love to save souls, and that conversations could mend marriages and end wars. This belief has fueled virtually every endeavor I've undertaken in my life.

This belief that our words, messages, sermons, and conversations can effect positive change motivates me still. So in the wake of George Floyd's murder, when so many hundreds of other names were finally spoken in acknowledgment of the brutal injustice of their deaths, I did not hesitate to speak. I felt compelled to share my observations and opinions in hopes of guiding our national conversation toward constructive healing. Not that I had definitive answers or adamant ideology to advance but merely a message balancing our harsh truth with divine grace. This is the example Jesus set for all of us, and he alone did it perfectly during his time on earth. But if we seek to follow him, then we are called to step out of the easy safety of our comfortable cubicles and risk living by faith.

In one of my favorite examples of how beautifully he lived from this balance, Jesus was engaged in conversing with a Jewish legal expert who hoped to find fault with his answers (Luke 10:25–37). Baiting Christ by asking what one must do to inherit eternal life, the lawyer was in turn asked about keeping the two most important commandments: "'Love the Lord your God with all your heart and with all your soul and with all your strength and with all your mind'; and, 'Love your neighbor as yourself'" (Luke 10:27 NIV). Undeterred, the crafty lawyer then asked, "And who is my neighbor?" (Luke 10:29 NIV).

Jesus then shared the story that we know as the parable of the Good Samaritan (Luke 10:30–37). A traveler was robbed and beaten and left to die on the side of the road. A priest came by and then a Levite, a religious leader in the temple, and each one saw the wounded man and crossed the street to avoid him. Only a despised foreigner, someone from the pagan land of Samaria, took pity on the poor traveler and bothered to stop. He bound the man's wounds and took him to a nearby inn, paying for a room and asking the innkeeper to keep an eye on the stranger.

It's a story you've likely heard before. Jesus answered the lawyer's question and ours by making it clear that "neighbor" is all inclusive. No one who loves God can ignore the plight of another human being in need, no matter what differences may seem to separate them. The parable is often preached to inspire us to greater service for those in need, which it indeed does. But we must not overlook the fact that the first two passersby, the priest and the Levite, are the very ones who should immediately have stopped to help the man dying at their feet! I fear now, just as then, we're tempted to obey God and show his loving-kindness to others only when convenient.

This deadly hypocrisy represented by the priest and the Levite in Christ's parable reminds me of my visit to Elmina Castle in Ghana a few years ago. Built in 1482 by Portuguese explorers as a trading post, Elmina is the oldest European building in existence south of the Sahara Desert. Today it is a UNESCO World Heritage Site visited by thousands of tourists each year, but for centuries the castle served as one of the regular stops for the Atlantic slave trade.

In the castle's basement, I saw the dungeons where countless slaves were held before being transported in chains to other continents. These crude jail cells were not only dark and dank, but the stench was overpowering. The smell of human bodies—sweat, blood, urine, feces—intermingling decade after decade had distilled into the hard ground. I placed my hands on stones and wooden beams to trace the desperate designs formed by scratch marks, the result of bloody fingers clinging to the fetid walls of their prison rather than leave their homeland, their wives, their parents, their children.

Tears fell from my eyes as I stood there reeling in the moments I imagined and the countless others I could not. I cried not only to commemorate the epic inhumanity in that place but because I knew what was also upstairs, just two flights above me: *a church.* Next to the rooms where human bodies were bartered, bought, and sold; near the areas where enslaved women were washed and bathed only to be raped by their captors; beside the chambers where shackled men screamed out in the unanesthetized agony of castration, there is a beautiful pre-colonial sanctuary, the Chapel of St. George.

Many of the very men who worshipped there, prayed there, sang hymns there also bought and sold human beings who had been violently assaulted and ripped from their homes, their families, their villages. These same men, many who said they were Christians, also raped, castrated, and murdered men, women, and children.

Unbearable.

Unthinkable.

Unimaginable.

But Elmina Castle, like the essence of the parable of the Good Samaritan, contains both the unspeakable truth and the indelible grace of our relationships, with one another and with God. The castle and parable symbolize the same duality being exposed in our country and our world right now. Silence can no longer be endured. Thanks to social media, we each have a mic to make our voice heard. Better yet, we have opportunities to meet, to talk, and most important, to listen to others.

Both those alive today as well as the ghosts in our castles.

Hope Is Contagious

No one can ever balance truth and grace as perfectly or adroitly as Christ, but as believers, and for myself as a pastor, we must always try. Regarding issues of systemic racism and prejudice, I am well acquainted with the ugly realities of the fractured fault lines within our country. Growing up during the '60s, I can remember watching my father go to the back of restaurants to pick up our order, drinking from separate water fountains, and using segregated public restrooms. I saw the division of opportunities—for education, employment, entrepreneurial development, and advancement—be determined by the color of a person's skin.

I also heard the stories and knew the legacy of my enslaved ancestors just a few generations before me. In particular, I knew the horrific details of my grandfather's death at the age of twenty-two. You see, I am named for him and was born many years later on the same day he died a terrible death, June 9.

Coming home from work each evening, he often took the shortest route by swimming across a lake. His routine became familiar in the community, until some local bigots devised a stunningly devious and callous trap for my grandfather. They strung barbed wire back and forth underwater across the route he took, knowing he would become ensnared and drown. While his pregnant wife, later my grandmother, waited at home cooking his supper, my grandfather died an unimaginable death for no reason other than the hatred a handful of white men had for the color of his skin.

But I am also aware of the power of God's love to override human ignorance, bias, fear, anger, and violence. Where I grew up in West Virginia, only about 5 percent of the population was African American so I knew many white people—some good and kind, others mean and nasty, some indifferent, and some just plain old crazy! You know what, though? I also knew just as many black people who could be described that way.

I had then and have now close, dear friends whose skin differs from my own, some white, some tan, some brown, some black. We're not colorblind and don't try to pretend that our skin colors are the same or don't matter. But we also don't judge one another by our races any more than we would try to assess each other's character based on the color of our eyes or the size of our shoes! We try to see the heart beating beneath the skin, to feel each other's pain in all the various sizes and shapes it may take, and to show God's love as Good Samaritans as best we know how.

Whether you have a mic thrust in your face, grab it when given the chance, or create a platform of your own, you must consider the message you are dispensing in light of the needs of your audience. No matter our differences, we share a hunger for hope. No matter your form of contagious communication, you will find that offering hope in one of its many forms satisfies your audience every time. Hope for belonging and being accepted. Hope for respect and kindness. Hope for compassion and understanding. Hope for love and forgiveness.

Hope for a future that shows we have finally learned from the past.

PART 3

The Promise of Practice

No matter how much you know *about* preaching or speaking in public, there is no substitute for experience! Practice does indeed make perfect even if there's always more to learn. One of the reasons I love to preach is because I not only love learning from experts, historians, scholars, and theologians, but also enjoy the creative synergy of how it comes together and gets delivered. Each sermon, even if conceptually or thematically the same as one I just preached at an earlier service, affords a new experience, a different dynamic, a fresh set of variables. The promise of practice is the revelation of what can only be learned by doing, by the experience of growing from your mistakes and honing your triumphs.

With all due respect to Dr. Thomas and other preaching experts, the *practice* of preaching—not the theory of preaching—is at the center of this unique form of communication. Practice comes first, and yet as Dr. Thomas points out so brilliantly, we also need theory—we must make theory explicit in order to improve practice, and also to pass the tradition to the next generations. This perpetuates the history and culture in the oral tradition. It's the catalyst for storytelling and sharing anecdotes with one another, which is in itself a foundation of social interaction.

As I've grown older, the more I've appreciated the incredibly rich tapestry of conversations, stories, family history, cultural traditions, and yes, even neighborhood gossip that I absorbed growing up. They formed a kind of crazy quilt of communication for me, weaving different genres and voices together, setting the pace for suspense, demonstrating the mastery of a punch line expertly delivered, and stitching words together in poetic patterns that made them memorable as well as musical.

I recall as a boy how we would often just sit around and talk—well, I would listen along with the other kids present while the grown-ups talked. It might be after Sunday dinner or on the front porch when our neighbors stopped by, in the backyard on a summer evening or around the picnic table at a church potluck. Without even realizing it at the time, I grew up witnessing how organically stories informed the traditions of the community. We would sit around the kitchen table as Mama poured more coffee or iced tea for everyone. She would ask my cousin Marleen if she had met the new youth pastor at church. My aunt Wiza might be there, because she came down about every fourth Saturday to see Papa, my grandfather, and we'd all gather 'round them on the front porch steps.

Listening to their stories told me who I was and where I came from. It's how I learned that my great-grandmother was a slave and that my mother sang in the choir with Coretta Scott. Our stories passed down in the oral tradition so it's no wonder we birthed the Frederick Douglasses and the Malcolm Xes and the Dr. Kings, because we didn't have anything else that formed so rich an inheritance. Orators echoed the tradition, and the best orators helped the community perform new versions of itself without losing its identity.

Before you begin practicing your own process, pause and consider what you've learned and absorbed from the best practices of others! You might be surprised what you already do, as well as what you may need to do, based on the communication traditions you inherited. Simply put, the promise of practice means using what you already know to discover what you don't!

CHAPTER 7

Every Shot Is the Only One You Have

It usually takes me more than three weeks to prepare a good impromptu speech.

—Mark Twain

In the musical *Hamilton*, Lin-Manuel Miranda's brilliant historical-contemporary, music-genre hybrid about the life of Alexander Hamilton, "My Shot" provides a mantra for anyone given their moment at the microphone. "I am not throwin' away my shot," raps Hamilton, asserting his ambition, passion, and determination for making the most of any and every opportunity he has to share his revolutionary message and overthrow British colonial rule. He identifies with this new land of limitless opportunities, which he considers just as "young, scrappy, and hungry" as himself.

Other patriots echo Hamilton's refrain, including John Laurens, a statesman and abolitionist who dreams of riding into battle with America's first all-black regiment. The song takes an ironic turn by the end of the show when Hamilton duels his nemesis Aaron Burr and intentionally misses, while Burr's fatal bullet finds its target. The double meaning of "shot"—an opportunity as well as firing a bullet—converge with one another to be one and the same.

The musical impresses me on many levels, but I especially enjoy the emphasis on maximizing your message in every possible moment. Words can have the force of bullets without the violence, carnage, and fatalities—which makes them even more powerful in their ability to affect change. Any criminal, dictator, or vigilante can use physical force and firepower to try and control others. But as we have seen from the outrageous loss of black lives at the hands of those entrusted to protect us, bullets cannot kill the truth.

Ultimately, words wield more power than weapons.

Which makes our opportunities for communication all the more important.

Waiting in the Wings

Obviously, every opportunity at the mic does not carry the weight and gravity of those in the Revolutionary War or the Black Lives Matter movement. Nonetheless, I urge you to consider even the humblest situations worthy of giving everything you've got. Whether you're petitioning your local zoning board at a town council meeting, preaching on the parable of the prodigal son, or inspiring business leaders during a live-streaming online event, you never want to waste their time or your own.

You never know when an opportunity will become a threshold of destiny. I'll never forget one of the seminal times in my ministry when I went from audience participant to keynote presenter at the same event the following year. Fortunately, I paid attention to one message in particular when attending, which in turn prepared me to take the microphone when I was invited to preach the following year.

I had been invited to Tulsa, Oklahoma, to attend what's known as the Azusa conference, an annual Pentecostal commemoration and celebration of the powerful revival that occurred back in 1906 at a small Apostolic Faith Mission located at 312 Azusa Street in Los Angeles, California. Led by Bishop William J. Seymour, the fervent experience of God's Spirit led to the birth of the Pentecostal movement as we know it today. Well aware of the dynamic legacy of Azusa, I was thrilled to attend my first anniversary event, a gathering of ten to twelve thousand people, all from different faiths and backgrounds, united by our desire to worship, sing, pray, and praise together.

My first night there, I sat anonymously in the balcony of the auditorium, delighted to be part of this diverse body. The music, worship, and preaching electrified me along with everyone else inside that sacred space. Although I was viewing the stage from a great distance, I relished how close I felt to all in attendance as we enjoyed the bonds of Christian fellowship.

The next evening I experienced the service from a much more intimate point of view—the front row! My friend Sarah Jordan Powell, the legendary gospel singer, invited me to sit with her and her family up front at the edge of the stage. From there, I could observe every blink, smile, wrinkle, and bead of perspiration on those leading, singing, and preaching. The energy was just as powerful, but in a more direct way because I could sense the anticipation, nervous excitement, and emotion just a few feet in front of me.

And I'll never forget how I felt when Bishop Richard

Hinton, a pastor and church leader from Chicago, preached his message on the importance of preparation. It was as if he spoke directly to me when he explained the necessity of doing all we can to be ready for those opportunities God has waiting ahead for us. Bishop Hinton compared this personal preparatory time to the way an actor waits in the wings before she takes her cue to go onstage. Long before the lights go up, the curtains part, and the last ticket holder takes their seat, actors in the company for that show have invested untold hours in their performance.

From the leads to the understudy, the stars of the show to the chorus, each actor has memorized lines, cues, blocking, and depending on the kind of show, songs and choreography. They've rehearsed, fussed with makeup, and adjusted their costumes until everything comes together there in the shadows backstage as they wait in the wings. Ready for their cue, they take their mark and deliver a performance perfected by all that has taken place behind the scenes. The audience often has no idea of the work, dedication, and preparation that go into even the briefest scene between characters.

So, too, Bishop Hinton preached that night in Tulsa that we must do everything in our power to be ready when God shines the spotlight on the stage of our lives. When we are thrust into new roles of leadership, greater positions of authority, and unexpected opportunities for advancement, we should be ready to take our lives to the next level. We must be excellent stewards of all the resources that God has presently entrusted to us if we expect to handle what he wants to give us next. "Whoever can be trusted with very little can also be trusted with much!" Bishop Hinton shouted passionately, quoting Jesus from the Gospel of Luke (16:10 NIV).

Like the echo of a bell long after its last chime, his message resonated within me in the days, weeks, and months that followed. God spoke to me that night and I listened. Taking his words to heart, I invested more time in studying, practicing, praying, and preaching. I gave myself completely to my ministry and used my gifts to the best of my ability. So the following year, I was not entirely surprised—shocked and thrilled but not surprised—when I was invited to preach on the closing night of the Azusa conference. What a difference a year can make!

Ready or Not

Standing on the stage that night, I looked out into the thousands eager to receive the message God had placed on my heart. I was so humbled and so nervous to be there that the butterflies in my stomach felt more like a bees' nest, buzzing and humming with energy to produce something sweet. My nerves reminded me how excited I was, but I didn't mind them because I knew without a doubt that I had done everything possible to prepare. All my late nights and early mornings, my sermons that sometimes went on too long and prayers short and sweet, my failings and my triumphs all converged. I had prepared and waited in the wings. When the mic was handed to me, I knew my shot would count.

I knew it would count, not because it would be a launching pad for the successes and ascent of my ministry that followed, but simply because I knew I had tried to be the best steward of what God had given me. Standing onstage under the white-hot lights that night, feeling the sweat trickle down the back of my neck and beneath my starched shirt collar, I felt on the threshold of the past and the future, of the man I had been the year before and the man I was in the process of becoming.

Not long after I closed the Azusa conference that night, more opportunities began to open before me. The owners of a new faith-based television venture, the Trinity Broadcast Network (TBN), approached me about broadcasting my sermons. At the time I had no fancy equipment, huge church, or extensive staff team. I was just being myself and doing the best I could to fulfill the potential that I knew God had ignited inside me. Was I afraid? Terrified! Afraid of failing, of not knowing what I didn't know, of growing too fast, of not growing at all, of fumbling the opportunity.

But I refused to allow my fears to barricade my baritone from the airwaves! As long as I sensed the Lord's guidance, I would follow and continue learning, growing, and being stretched. And I quickly learned that each step, each new opportunity, prepared me for the next. Because not long after I began airing on TBN, I was offered a regular slot on Black Entertainment Television (BET).

The rest, as they say, is history! Or at least it seems that way looking back more than two decades later. More invitations to speak and preach poured in. Publishing partners asked me to turn my messages into books that could have the same impact. I traveled around the world, preaching in open-air arenas and stadiums before tens of thousands of people. Being interviewed by household-name journalists and appearing on the cover of *Time* magazine.

Forgive me if I sound like I'm bragging and dragging out my highlight reel! My intention is merely to point you to the powerful impact that preparation—mental, emotional, intellectual, physical, and spiritual—can have when it's your turn at the mic. It's been said that failing to prepare is preparing to fail. As clichéd as it sounds, I must agree.

If you're waiting in the wings for your chance in the spotlight, then you better be ready.

Because ready or not, your moment is coming.

Brand Management

When your moment at the mic arrives, your audience has already started their relationship with you before you ever open your mouth to utter the first word. Then, within the first sixty-to-ninety seconds after you begin speaking, they will already be forming conclusions about you and your message to determine if you're worthy of their time—and their attention. Depending on the setting, you may have their time because they feel socially and culturally obligated.

But we all know that even as we sit and nod at the visiting pastor, the principal of our children's school, or the consultant brought into the workplace to motivate us, we still have a choice. We can sit there and politely endure the sermon, school update, or pep talk, or we can fully engage and receive the message being delivered. In light of our recent, necessary changes, many events and meetings that we once attended in person now utilize virtual participation. We can be at home in our pajamas watching, choose to mute the sound if we get bored, or multitask while listening just enough to know the surface of what's being said.

Part of the challenge with engaging our audience also stems from their basis of comparison. When I was growing up, I would compare our pastor with others I occasionally heard, as well as a handful of times when I might hear someone on television. Of course, I was aware of occasionally hearing Dr. King deliver a message or address on TV, but otherwise, it was more likely Walter Cronkite! I suspect it's only human nature to do so, part of the way we're wired in order to form impressions that intersect with other knowledge, which often distills into our instincts.

In the past decades, we've been exposed to more media speakers and personalities who often have the benefit of film editing and reshooting, professional hair and makeup stylists, and teleprompters. At first many of these were probably news anchors or reporters, entertainers and commentators. But as you well know, with the advent of social media, everyone is everywhere talking about everything all the time!

So more than ever, communicators in whatever setting or venue, whether live and in person or virtual and edited, must measure up to an enormous pool of talent that their audience has likely heard and seen. Particularly in our world of sensational sound bites, scintillating social media, and vociferous voices, you have to find some way to make a memorable impression that connects with those receiving your message.

In those first couple of minutes when you're greeting your audience, thanking your hosts, and breaking the ice, the distance between you and those listening will either contract or expand. They will either continue giving you their attention and stay with you, or they will metaphorically take a step back and make your attempt to connect with them incrementally harder. Keep in mind that their expectations also shape how they assess you. Have they heard of you prior to your present encounter? If so, what have they likely heard and therefore expect?

As we have seen, each time you communicate before an audience, you're conveying a message, but also your brand. Everything about you contributes to your brand when you have the mic because you're shaping future expectations as well. With the seemingly infinite reach of the Internet and digital downloads, your message may be available in cyberspace for centuries to come!

We've seen many leaders, speakers, and entertainers say things online that they later regret. Consequently, their brand turns out to be a contrived veneer for the person lurking beneath the persona.

Marketing research consistently shows that people want brands to be clear about their mission and authentic in their messaging. Trying to create a brand that does not reflect the real you rarely takes you to higher ground and greater opportunities. People can sense when someone is not who they're trying to convince you they are. Stand-up comics, talk show hosts, and interviewers often try to appeal to their viewing audience in ways that make it hard for them to stand out from their peers and competitors. Viewers want to be able to relate, to admire, to understand, and to identify with at least some facets of your personality.

Oprah set the untouchable standard for this ability to connect with people in ways that established faithful bonds of trust, admiration, respect, and authority. She refused to treat guests on her show in ways that were hostile, bombastic, antagonistic, spiteful, and sensational. While other hosts tried to shock viewers and embarrass their guests, Oprah stayed true to herself. Her intelligence, poise, compassion, and formidable strength shone through millions of television screens in our country and around the world.

Fans and viewers trusted her. She wasn't just trying to entertain or educate but to empower them with each program. They knew she would not waste their time by pretending to be someone she was not. If her show was going to be fun and lighthearted, she was always the one having the most fun. If she was focusing on heavy, painful, or controversial issues, then her equanimity, courage, compassion, and determination would prevail. Even if viewers didn't always agree with her, they liked her. And if they didn't like her, they still respected her.

Without a doubt, she's a hard act to follow and took public discourse and the powers of communication to new levels. While you and I cannot be Oprah, we don't have to be and shouldn't try. Because we can still share authentically in the means and methods of our message!

Means and Methods

While overthinking your brand message can be paralyzing—after all, you can't please all the people all the time, you should be as shrewd and deliberate as you can without losing time and resources in your assessment and execution. If you work too hard to focus on your brand more than being present in the moment of your message, then your audience may be inclined to view you more as a sales rep or marketing manager. Unless that is indeed your role in an appropriate setting, I don't believe your audience will find it appealing.

When communicators sound overly scripted and seem too polished, the audience's reception may be the opposite of what the speaker had intended. They may view you skeptically and detect a slight detachment between you and your message, which in turn widens the distance between you and them. They might question your sincerity and wonder what you truly believe. Perhaps they will view you as being elevated and above them, which leaves them feeling patronized or pandered.

My recommendation is to make sure you believe in the message you're delivering. If you have areas of doubt, uncertainty, or concern, then share those as well. Because if you've tripped over these rough edges, then members of your audience will as well. I've heard it said that a side benefit of always telling the truth is not having to worry about forgetting which lies you told to whom. The same is true for communicators seeking to discharge their speech or sermon.

Arguably, you are still selling your message and

main ideas rather than a tangible product or specific service, but most people want to believe they're glimpsing something authentic about you and your brand even so. They're looking for your intellect as well as your heart in what you deliver. They want to know if you see them, identify with them, feel them. They also want to know if you have something new, fresh, or innovative to share with them. Audiences often want both familiarity and accessibility as well as elements of surprise.

That feat may seem daunting in light of wanting to be prepared and rehearsed. Granted, it's a balancing act, a skill much like that of an aerialist walking the high wire, combining intensely focused strength with the delicate art of deliberate equilibrium. As I have told many pastors, leaders, and entertainers over the years, you prepare thoroughly enough so that you are comfortable improvising should you be forced to do so. Now I'm not saying learn just enough so that you can wing it—I'm saying overprepare so you could fly if necessary.

The research, study, reflection, and practice become part of you and so integrated into your identity that you don't have to worry so much about notes, outlines, PowerPoint slides, or teleprompters. Those tools are fine to utilize for support and enhancement, but they will never provide the cool confidence, convincing character, and convivial connection that only you can bring to the microphone.

You want to know not only the material supporting your message, but the way you relate to the message. Because how you relate to it will come through and influence how your audience relates to it. You are your own first audience before anyone else hears your message.

Dress Rehearsal

Once you've put in the time to put the bones together into a working skeleton, once you're identified the bends in your story or sermon, then it's time to focus on presentation. Many people find it helpful to write out their entire message beforehand, and use it as either a loose script to follow or a model for memorization. Others rely on detailed outlines with prompts, cues, and reminders of the actual examples, illustrations, and anecdotes that make their points. Some communicators may even appear to deliver their ideas extemporaneously without aid of supplementary tools, making their transmission appear smooth and seamless.

There is no one-size-fits-all recommendation for the kind of props that will best support your presentation. As a viewer and listener, I don't mind if someone uses notes or an outline as a reference point, a kind of compass as they lead us through their ideas toward a conclusory destination. Those notes and props become problematic only if they distract from the speaker's delivery. In other words, if you are too reliant on your notes, outline, or script, then you will devote more energy to what's on the page than to the people looking at your podium.

If you can become familiar enough with the flow and parts of your message, then your outline or notes can become your security blanket—there if you meander too far from your message for whatever reason but not slowing you down or interrupting your delivery. The best way to become comfortable and familiar with the order and parts of your communication, at least from my experience, is threefold: practice, rehearse, and solicit feedback from others whom you trust.

Practice is often as simple as speaking or reading your message aloud, over and over, so that you can hear yourself, practice pronunciation, and smooth out any spots that cause you to slip. When I was first starting out in ministry and feeling God's call to preach, I was terrified! So in addition to research, study, prayer, and reflection, the only thing I knew to do was practice. I would take my Bible and perhaps a few notes I had scribbled in its margins or on a legal pad and go somewhere alone where I could talk aloud without others thinking I was a crazy man.

Sometimes it was outside in the backyard or on the front porch; other times I practiced in my house if I found a rare moment alone or at work when doing a repetitive one-man job such as mixing paint at the hardware store or connecting circuits for the power company.

Talking it out, I would imagine standing in the pulpit with my congregation sitting before me. Then I would just dive in and deliver my sermon, trying to hear myself as my congregation would likely hear me, dividing my attention between being both preacher and listener, and stopping to make changes and take notes along the way if possible. If I had trouble with a certain word or phrase, then I would either say it repeatedly until I didn't have to think twice, or else find another word or phrase!

I would also think about when I wanted to step away from the pulpit—for emphasis or engagement or simply to make sure my legs didn't lock from standing in one position. I would consider which moments in my story required me to express or physically reflect details and descriptions, which we will discuss in more detail in the next chapter. When to refer back to details of Scripture and when to connect those details directly to us today.

When I wanted to raise my voice and allow my passion to amplify my words and when I thought lowering my voice to a whisper would be more effective. And just as important if not more, when to let silence speak in ways more powerfully than anything I could offer. In fact, using silence and the sacred space it creates is so vital to effective communication that I've devoted Chapter 9 to it, as we'll explore shortly.

Practice and thinking through the parts should be followed by at least one rehearsal if possible. Rehearsals differ from practice in two significant ways: A rehearsal involves delivering your message before at least one other person as well as visiting the actual facility where you will be speaking. Ideally, you can combine these two and stand at the podium using the mic while your spouse, family, or a few friends listen. They may even sit in different locations throughout the sanctuary, auditorium, or theater to ensure consistent volume and diction.

I can't tell you how many times Serita would sit in different pews of the church I was pastoring on a Saturday morning, often with our young children racing up and down the aisles, and listen to me rehearse my sermon. As our kids grew older, I began welcoming their feedback as well. Occasionally, I would ask a good friend, often another pastor or mentor, or one of my elders or deacons, to listen and provide suggestions or comments.

Their input often proved invaluable in helping me realize where in my sermon I risked losing them with the progression of points or when they needed more time to absorb my application. But make sure your listeners in rehearsal are trusted supporters willing to offer only constructive criticism and encouragement. The last thing you need just prior to your time is someone who undermines your confidence or criticizes elements beyond your control.

Even if you cannot rehearse in the exact location or venue where you will be delivering your message, I encourage you to at least get a feel for it ahead of time. If you've traveled to a conference or an event, try to attend the night before and hear another speaker solely as a member of the audience, much like I was able to do that first visit to the Azusa conference. If that's not possible, then arrive early enough before your appointed time to survey the stage, podium, or position of your delivery. If possible, test the microphone, slides, Wi-Fi, or whatever technical capabilities you require. Make adjustments, corrections, or changes as necessary.

If physical rehearsals are not feasible, then study photos and videos of the venue online. Notice the layout and design of the facility, the acoustics and staging. Then, mentally rehearse by seeing yourself there and visualizing your successful delivery. Trust that you have everything needed to ignite your audience!

Passion + Practice = Performance

When the mic is in your hands, you want to give it everything you can. No matter what preparation you weren't able to complete, no matter how much more time you wish you'd had, no matter how much more research needed to be done, go with what you've got. Let go of what you don't have or didn't do and take hold of what's in your hand. Just as God instructed Moses to lead the Israelites out of Egypt by using the shepherd's staff in his hand, we must use what's in our hand as well.

I recall a conversation I had with a friend of mine who is a well-known, award-winning actor and entertainer. We were discussing how she started in show business and when she first got her big break. She described how she arrived in L.A. inexperienced and naïve, a young woman from a small town in the rural Southeast with a dream like countless others who come to Hollywood every year.

My friend was fortunate enough to get an agent quickly, one who insisted she audition for any and every part—commercials, television, film, stage plays, and regional theater. "It was exhausting and overwhelming," she told me. "I was doing several auditions a day, and I did get a few gigs, but none of them were significant enough to stop the audition merry-go-round." Still, her agent adamantly believed that quantity was the key to becoming a star. And if not a star, then at least a steadily working actor.

Then one day, my friend auditioned for a part she passionately wanted. It was for a TV series she knew well, one with actors she admired and respected. So she began preparing more thoroughly than usual, even skipping some other auditions to get ready for the one she really wanted. On the day of the audition, she dressed and looked like she knew the character would look because she knew the role so intimately.

She got the part—and she also got a new agent! "I treated that audition like it was the only one I would ever have for the rest of my life. And once I got the part, I realized that my agent didn't have focus and vision for my talent and the kinds of roles I could play best and should be going after. He sent me to audition for anything and everything. When I trusted my gut and followed my heart, I narrowed my focus for the role I wanted. Getting that role shaped my career and helped me be the kind of performer that's true to who I am."

My friend learned that focusing her talent and leaving everything onstage was the key to her growth and success. She began going after only the parts that suited her best and treating each audition as the only opportunity she would have to ever act again. Her passion fueled her practice which, in turn, produced astounding performances.

I believe the same is true for most communicators. Giving the same speech over and over again becomes tedious if you can't find new dimensions, new insight, new pathways through the material. If you grow bored with your message, I promise your audience will, too. You have to find a way to pour your all into each and every opportunity. Although I've given the same sermon more than once, I would like to believe I've never given the same sermon twice!

Treat your opportunity as if it's the only one you will ever have. To the best of your ability, don't leave any margin for error, for excuses, or for accidents.

Focus on your strengths instead of trying to correct your weaknesses. Motivational icon and author Dale Carnegie once said, "There are always three speeches for every one you actually gave. The one you practiced, the one you gave, and the one you wish you gave."

To the best of your ability, close the gap among these three so that you become more comfortable and confident that what you practice enhances what you perform. Give your all every time there is an opportunity to speak and deliver a message. Learn from each opportunity and use that wisdom to become better next time.

Every shot is the only one you have.

Don't throw away your shot to be the best!

CHAPTER 8

Learn the Grammar of Body Language

People may hear your words, but they feel your attitude.

—John Maxwell

Fidgeting has always been our body's rebellion in the midst of boredom.

I remember being in church as a boy and being required to sit still and, if not engaged with the sermon being preached, then to look attentive. It only took one raised eyebrow from my mother or a quick nudge from my father to remind me to pay attention—or at least pretend to! Most of the time, this was not a problem and I enjoyed listening and learning from the message delivered from the pulpit. Sometimes, however, my mind wandered and my body twitched.

When I couldn't concentrate on the passage from Leviticus or Habakkuk, or some other passage that escaped my interest at the time, I'd think about what Mama was planning for Sunday dinner, how much homework I had to finish before Monday morning, and when I could hang out with my friends later that day. My feet would swing back and forth like twin pendulums or, once they could touch the floor, would bounce as if live wires had been placed inside them.

It wasn't necessarily the pastor's fault, but there was no mistaking my body language. Because I wasn't interested and tracking with his message, I was ready to move on and had to work to contain my restlessness. As I grew older, I soon learned to recognize similar tendencies in the adults around me, including my parents. Although more discreet, their behavior also betrayed their level of engagement.

My father would slowly move his hand to his other wrist and push back his shirt cuff and the edge of his suit jacket sleeve to reveal the face of his watch. Then he'd casually glance down and check the time, assuming no one noticed. The funny thing, at least for my young self, was that almost all the other men in the congregation were doing the same routine! And Lord help us if the pastor kept preaching when my father and others thought the service should have ended. I can remember stomachs growling, babies crying, and adults growing agitated long before the altar call or end of the service.

For my mother, her restless energy and liberated patience would manifest in the way she clutched her Bible more tightly or quietly rummaged through her purse for a tissue or cough drop. The only exception, of course, for her and so many others, was when sitting in the choir loft directly behind the pastor's pulpit. Elevated just enough to be highly visible to those of us in the congregation, choir members had to look like they were enthralled by the sermon or at least reflectively engaged.

Once I was on the other side of this scenario, I realized people's response to my sermon was often more transparent than they realized. When I first began preaching, I struggled not to notice the yawns, the drooping eyes, the discreet and not-so-discreet glances at watches, the fidgeting of children, and the wandering gazes of members who appeared to be somewhere else. I tried not to take it personally, especially once I realized how I influenced these indicators! Because I soon understood that my own body language was often being reflected back to me. If I lacked confidence, lost my way to the point I was making, or rambled to recover from a tangent, then naturally my listeners also struggled to sustain engagement.

On the other hand, if I remained focused, in control, confident, and certain of the message on my heart, the one that had been building in me at least all week if not longer, then I could see our bond displayed in tearful eyes, thoughtful nods, cries of "Amen!" and shouts of "Preach it, Pastor!" If I looked comfortable in my own skin and at least willing to embrace the pulpit I had been privileged to speak from, then my flock would follow my guidance to greener pastures and higher ground. How I felt—about my message, about my life, about my relationship with God, about my church—was on full display.

When you communicate, the same is true for you: Your body language and energy level will largely determine the energy level, engagement, and intensity of your audience.

Punctuation Marks

In those first moments, you will have their attention. But will you keep it? Will you be able to sustain their interest, engagement, and eye contact for the duration of your delivery? While your message and its delivery are central to answering these questions, your appearance, mannerisms, tone, inflection, and body language will be working either for you or against you. You will either be confirming what you're communicating or distracting viewers by the dissonance of your disconnection. Please allow me to give you an example.

Let's say, for instance, that you're attending an event on launching a new business from home. You have lots of creative ideas and great products but struggle with the business knowledge and administrative details requisite for your start-up. Attending this event in hopes of gleaning the information and entrepreneurial education you lack, you plan to hear a speaker address "Organizing Your Launch." You show up in time to grab a seat in the conference room packed with a few hundred other participants. The time comes for the session to begin, but no one's there.

After two or three minutes, the crowd begins to chatter to pass the time, assuming the speaker is running late or the conference schedule has been derailed. Then five, ten, fifteen minutes pass before the speaker finally dashes onstage looking as if he had just finished an Olympic marathon. His appearance is disheveled and he's out of breath. He tries to begin but then discovers he's lost his notes.

Time drags on as the presentation goes from bad to worse. His PowerPoint slides are out of order and seemingly have little to do with his suggestions, which begin to sound random and arbitrary. He stutters and stammers and then apologizes for the tenth time for being so late. He keeps his eyes focused downward and talks much faster than anyone can keep up with in an attempt to make up for lost time. There's nothing about him or his presentation to inspire your confidence in his knowledge and authority.

Yes, I may be exaggerating, but you get my point. Certain details of our speaking situation may be beyond our control, which is all the more reason to possess the power that comes from determining details we can control. Once again, I'm focusing on the unspoken communication taking place based on what your audience sees and the impressions and conclusions they form accordingly. Your words and ideas are only part of the message being transmitted. Because over the course of your presentation, your address will become synonymous with how it's expressed—and how you're dressed!

To deny or ignore what you're communicating aside from the language is to forfeit some of the tools at your disposal. Just consider how challenging it would be to read the words in this book if they were jammed together without punctuation, grammar, or a uniform style. Perhaps you've received—or even sent—texts from someone who forgoes capitalization, punctuation, and the conventions of our standard American English language. I'm guessing that you still managed to communicate at a basic level, but without those regulations, it presented unnecessary problems and distractions.

While omitting standard language conventions, using slang, and inventing your own language of abbreviations, symbols, and emojis may work for texting and online chats, these idiosyncrasies limit your range of reach. If you're texting with your best friend, the shared systems work more effectively than if you're responding to your boss, your child's teacher, or an elder in your church. Why? Because your best friend understands how you're handling language in your particular, unique ways—ways that aren't appropriate or effective in other roles and relationships.

Driving Lessons

My mother was an English teacher so I learned early in life that the rules and regulations exist so that we can communicate as effectively as possible with one another. I recall her comparing grammar and punctuation to the traffic laws and shared cultural customs we follow when driving. She said both systems help us regulate movement among people trying to get from one place—or idea—to another.

For instance, we drive on the right side of the road instead of the left like other countries may choose, just as other cultures have different rules for syntax, grammar, and punctuation for their distinct languages. We slow down for a comma like we do for a caution light, while a period brings us to a full red-light stop. Just consider how crazy and chaotic it would be without any rules and cultural conventions of driving! More accidents would likely occur with every driver going any direction they pleased or behaving according to their own standards.

Punctuation and grammar help us to convey our thoughts, feelings, ideas, and messages in an orderly, comprehensible, uniform method that provides greater likelihood of understanding as long as the rules and conventions are shared among the parties communicating. We learn to read and write in school according to these same or similar language systems that permit us to inform, entertain, describe, instruct, honor, commemorate, compare, agree, and disagree with one another. Language and its conventions are far from perfect, but as one friend, a college English professor, once told me, language is adequate. And depending on how we use it, some people communicate more clearly and carefully than others.

Curiously enough, however, many communicators believe in-person exchanges allow for greater precision, control, and intensity of emotion than written messaging. While we can use all the conventions of standardized language, including grammar and punctuation, the page or screen still has limitations compared to oral delivery and aural reception.

I learned this truth early in my ministry when I wrote my first book. As I shared with you, I had preached a series of sermons that came to be known as *Woman, Thou Art Loosed!*, based on Jesus' words to the woman he was healing. The response was tremendous and overwhelming, but when I looked at transcripts of those sermons, I quickly realized how different they read compared to how they sounded when I had delivered them as sermons in our church. Not only were there many grammatical errors, typos, and sentence fragments, but my emphasis wasn't always clear. Whereas I can raise my voice, change my expression, or pause dramatically when preaching, the page doesn't provide such indicators.

Written language has its own ways of constructing,

conveying, and communicating language that are distinct from spoken-word messages. Obviously, they overlap in many ways, but understanding their distinction can help you be a better speaker. Because you can energize your words with a number of tools and enhancements that writers cannot. Yes, they have their own devices as well, but maximizing your abilities as a speaker often serves you well in both media and their various genres.

Herbs and Spices

The possibilities for misunderstanding, confusion, and obfuscation, although diminished by shared written systems, still remain. We've probably all experienced times when someone sent us a text, e-mail, note, or letter that left us confused or even upset about their missive's intended meaning. Were they angry and trying to sound sarcastic or facetious? Were they trying to manipulate or deceive you by what they shared—and didn't share—in their text? Were they afraid to be direct in making their request so they buried it in the middle of a rambling rant instead?

In those instances, we wish we could see the person convey the message instead. Then, we could ascertain by their tone, expression, volume, inflection, the look in their eyes, and posture a more accurate understanding of the language they selected. When you can hear rage simmering underneath a controlled tone and see the clench of their jaw, you then have a more accurate filter for decoding their message. If they're smiling, relaxed, with twinkling eyes and a lighthearted, even humorous tone, then you have a very different interpretation.

With oral communication, your audience does not have the benefit of the written conventions of language used when we read and write, and instead they rely on your visual and non-language auditory expressions. If your eyes widen and your volume increases, they're going to pay more attention than if you're looking at your notes and talking in a softer, quieter register. If you stare straight ahead and speak in a monotone with a repetitive cadence, your listeners will begin to get very sleepy, gently rocked back and forth by the unintended auditory lullaby you're providing. Talking too fast at record speed like an auctioneer, an infomercial announcer, or a kid giving her first book report, however, is just as deadly to your delivery. They will wonder why you can't slow down or recognize their inability to comprehend your communication at that velocity.

Ironically enough, many communicators believe in-person exchanges allow for greater precision, control, and intensity of emotion than written messaging. While we can use all the conventions of standardized language, including grammar and punctuation, the page or screen still has limitations compared to oral delivery and aural reception. Use this information to your benefit and maximize your speaker's arsenal of advantages.

Your body language, physical presence, voice variations, and speech patterns provide extraordinary opportunities to enhance, reinforce, and embellish your message. In the recipe for cooking up fresh ingredients into delectable communication, these provide your herbs and spices! Similarly, you want to use them sparingly, deliberately, and judiciously. A speaker with too many mannerisms, exaggerated expressions, and vocal modifications runs the risk of becoming an actor in a one-man show. Which is fine if you're Tyler Perry and that's what you're doing, but not if you're preaching on the crucifixion!

That's not to say, however, that you shouldn't dramatize such scenes or infuse them with fresh perspective. Just be sure you're not inadvertently sounding more like a parent reading a bedtime story than an adult speaker addressing an audience in a very different contextual setting. In fact, I have always been fascinated by the way different individuals responded to Jesus' last twenty-four hours before he was nailed to the cross and died, only to be raised on the third day. In particular, I've often been drawn to his mother, Mary, and the trauma and turmoil she must have experienced.

Looking at Calvary from Mary's perspective gives us fresh insight and a different point of view than we may have considered before. It helps us appreciate Jesus as a human being, a man, and a son. I know so many people in my congregation may have lost adult children—to disease, addiction, violence, or racially motivated brutality—so that Mary instantly opens the familiar story of events in new ways. They realize that they are not alone in the depth and gravity of their devastating loss. Even the mother of God's only Son had to endure the same kind of pain in order for his sacrifice to be made on the cross.

Recognizing and identifying with Mary's pain also infuses the incredulous joy of the resurrection with more personal intensity as well. It's one thing for them to hear me repeat, "It may be Friday but Sunday's coming!" but another for them to experience a seed of hope taking root in the bitter ashes of their weary souls. Which is why I'm willing to use my body language and voice as vessels for the emotional experience of my message. Letting my audience see my tears as I imagine myself in Mary's place at the foot of the cross, allowing them to hear my trembling voice and feel the pain of a parent who knows what it means to worry, suffer, and delight in his children. Who can't bear to ever lose them.

My vocal variations and body language communicate in ways more concise, potent, and concentrated than language seems to convey. This is where your unspoken communications can reinforce the ineffable truth of your message, assuming such sublime substance is appropriate to your topic, context, and audience.

Basically, you want to use your body language to season and flavor your communication but also to give your audience an experience they would miss otherwise. To call it your performance as a speaker may overstate it. To ignore it in favor of delivering your sermon or speech at a podium as if you're holding a filibuster on the floor of the Capitol is missing a vital opportunity. So you must discover how to use these other unspoken aspects of your delivery to your audience in the most effective ways possible.

You want them to get you, to think about at least one big idea from your message long after they walk out the door, and to remember you with a sense of gratitude and an eagerness to hear you again. Otherwise, you haven't left everything on the stage. You haven't utilized all the tricks of the trade to teach, reach, beseech, or preach!

While ambiguity or uncertainty may be deliberate as a rhetorical strategy at certain times, generally your goal is precision. You don't want to leave room for doubt, confusion, or misunderstanding. If your audience struggles to hear you clearly, distinctly, and consistently, then they cannot concentrate on what you're saying. If you mumble, stutter, or have some other speech impediment, they may not be able to decipher your message. It's not that your delivery must be perfect or that you can't have occasional missteps or vocal vacillations—it's simply that you want to do everything you can to remove all obstacles to understanding.

Dress for Success

What will your audience experience when they look at you and take in all the unspoken punctuation marks, grammatical guardrails, and critical capitalization that comes from your appearance and the image you project? How can you utilize the grammar of body language to your advantage when speaking?

The answers, in many ways, come down to the visual impression you create in your audience and how this visage relates to the voice at the microphone. If what you see is what you get, then obviously it makes sense to carefully consider what your audience sees! Many people are so self-conscious that they cannot imagine overlooking this consideration. You would be surprised, however, that even when they're mindful of how they look, many communicators mishandle the mic when it comes to visual messaging.

Everyone wants to look their best when they're up in front of a group communicating their message. Once again, we must contend with the ubiquitous exposure of professional speakers, performers, and entertainers with an army of attendants on hand to dress them, style them, and administer attention to their makeup and hair. But just because you don't have these resources or a designer wardrobe doesn't mean you can't look appropriate, impressive, and stylish.

What you choose to wear when you're speaking, preaching, teaching, or performing should be something comfortable, both physically and emotionally. You don't want to feel like you can't breathe because your collar's too tight or your dress is too snug. Shoes that pinch or fail to deliver adequate support will also cause you to be distracted by your distress. So think about what you plan to wear to your event or speaking situation at least a week beforehand in order to give yourself enough time to make suitable choices. Don't assume that your favorite outfit or best suit—you know, the one reserved for special occasions—still fits or looks as good as you remember.

Depending on your sartorial skills, I encourage you to assemble everything you plan to wear and try it all on together. It may feel unnecessary or a waste of time, but you might be surprised how many "wardrobe malfunctions" can be prevented by simply planning ahead with enough adequate time to make adjustments. You want your audience to remember your message for its meaning and your delivery for its eloquence—not your broken zipper or ripped seam!

You will want to consider what flatters your features and figure without being too conspicuous, outrageous, or unexpected. Wearing loud colors with sequins and fringe might hold everyone's attention but for the wrong reason! Unless you have an intentional purpose, such as using them as visual aids or to make a point, you might avoid over-the-top fashions involving capes, trains, sheer panels, feather boas, and exposed skin. That is, unless you're attending the Met Gala, a couture show, or fashion event!

You don't want what you're wearing to get in the

way and become a constant distraction for your viewing audience. On the one hand, what you're wearing should be invisible in that it doesn't call too much attention to itself. You don't want your audience members to find themselves losing focus because they wonder what in the world you're wearing. On the other hand, you want it to be stylish and appealing enough so that it reinforces your credibility, authority, and professionalism. Simply put, your ensemble should reflect something about your style and sensibilities as well as the occasion and dress code expectations of your audience.

When in doubt, consider your location and what members of your audience will be wearing. Think about the season of the year, the predicted weather, and the temperature and lighting in the venue. Ask yourself:

What can I wear that will give me confidence?

That will allow me not to worry about what I look like?

What can I wear that authentically expresses and reflects who I am? Who I want to be?

What will communicate who I am to my audience before I even begin to speak?

If you find yourself struggling with these questions and undecided about what to wear, don't hesitate to seek assistance. Ask for help from your spouse, your savvy adolescent, your best friend, or someone whose style you admire. But don't leave your image to chance—or you'll miss an opportunity to create a more memorable, indelible impression.

Pace Yourself

Once you've considered the visual impression you'll be making, then consider some of the nuances you can control in delivering your speech. Two of the most important aspects are the rhythm and tempo of your delivery, the pace as they're often called. Pace refers not necessarily to the speed of your speech but to the way you move through your message. Generally, the pace of your delivery depends on the length of time you're allocated to speak and the amount of information you wish to disseminate in that time span.

Just because you have a half hour to fill doesn't mean you should cram in as many words as possible. As we will see in the next chapter, which is on the power of silence, pace requires you to balance the ebb and flow and regulate the tide of words and information washing over your audience. The more time you have, the more room you have to segment your message and change the tempo accordingly. If you have a long slot to fill or more than one opportunity to speak at the same event or conference, you may choose the luxury of a more conversational, discursive, personal tone. You and your audience have more time to get acquainted and create a conduit of communication going both ways.

On the other end of the spectrum, if you have a very short amount of time, then focus it as sharply and concisely as possible. Keep it clear and simple by focusing on one point, purpose, or takeaway for your audience. Making an announcement, sharing a five-minute testimony, or introducing the main speaker forces you to focus as tightly as possible, concentrating your entire communication into a succinct selection of speech.

Most speakers and communicators will set their pace somewhere in between, which makes setting the tempo to match our material. The more time you have, the more you must prepare. If your message doesn't require the amount of time you've been given, then you can either expand—not pad—your message or you can make it clear—to your hosts, to your audience—that you will not be using the designated amount of time.

Depending on the purpose or intention of your

message, your pace may not be determined by the time span as much as by making sure your message is received. Winston Churchill, the legendary prime minister of the United Kingdom during much of World War II, said, "If you have an important point to make, don't try to be subtle or clever. Use a pile driver. Hit the point once. Then come back and hit it again. Then hit it a third time—a tremendous whack."

Good advice to consider about making the most of your moment at the mic, particularly when you consider that many communication experts believe that audience members will probably only remember one, or maybe two, points of your speech, sermon, or presentation. Research studies and focus groups confirm that what people take away from your message will likely be your one big idea and how—or if—your big idea affects them personally.

The more relevant your message is to them, the more they're likely to remember. If they don't connect and identify with you, if they don't find your message relevant to their lives, if what you have to say isn't new or fresh, at least in how it's presented, then you will lose them before your opening remarks.

I encourage you to create a kind of relaxed urgency in your delivery. You want to have energy and presence without seeming contrived or melodramatic. You want to keep your central thesis and overall purpose in mind even as you move through your message at a pace your audience can keep up with. Don't belabor points they're likely to already know or assume. Don't skip over brief explanations for words, terms, phrases, or jargon they're unlikely to know or have heard before.

One good exercise for setting your pace is identifying your elevator pitch and then making sure every point, part, or portion connects directly to your big idea. Don't be afraid to connect the dots for your audience or remind them of the relationships you've just covered. You don't want to be so repetitive that they're annoyed, but you also don't want them wondering what they've missed in terms of connecting your points to your big idea.

Using your body language is both art and skill. Like other aspects of communicating, it, too, improves as your experience grows. At the very least, be mindful of the physicality of your presence: what your audience will see when they look at you. Use this visual dimension to engage them in ways that are uniquely your own. Along with your voice, your body is your greatest asset in delivering your message—make the most of it!

CHAPTER 9

The Pregnant Pause

The most important thing in communication is hearing what isn't said.

—Peter Drucker

Silence is the negative space framing the beauty, gravity, and dignity of your message.

Just as an artist may use an empty area or margin—usually referred to as negative space—around an image in a picture, drawing, painting, or work of art, so does a speaker utilize silence. As we will see, the purposes and effects of silence when communicating are indeed similar to the impact artists have with negative space: for emphasis, for expectation, for complicity, and for individual appropriation and application.

Our natural speech patterns incorporate silence,

if even for a split second, to give breathing room between our words so that our listeners may recognize breaks between syllables, words, phrases, and sentences. Speakers also need to breathe as they speak, usually through their noses while their mouths are busy. Silent pauses give them time to catch a breath, swallow, take a sip of water, and keep their mouth from going dry.

You might be tempted to consider silence as marginable or even negligible—after all, your audience is there to hear you communicate, not to watch you meditate! But you will be underestimating its power and efficacy if you overlook both the practicality and the profundity of silence when you deliver your message. American writer Mark Twain observed, "The right word may be effective, but no word was ever as effective as a rightly timed pause." I wholeheartedly agree!

Silence is a language unto itself.

Its alphabet may be based on the absence of language, and its vocabulary may be incredibly limited. But silence lubricates the ideas, examples, and anecdotes shared in communication. Silence can create tension and suspense, provide emphasis and direction, open space for reflection and application, and add value, honor, and respect. Knowing how to maximize silence also enhances your ability to communicate with language as well as without. Silence is a gift, a tool, a frame, a relationship, and an invitation.

In the military and espionage worlds, going dark means someone, often an operative in the field, is temporarily suspending communication with their home base or other team members. In aviation, going dark means the pilot and the crew of a plane or a helicopter are not responding to attempts to communicate from air traffic control or other aircraft. This may be deliberate in order to escape detection by their adversaries, or it may be because of mechanical failure, capture, or even death.

Going dark in the midst of your message is not a good idea unless you're about to turn on the light! In other words, do everything in your power to avoid moments when you forget what you wanted to say, lose your place, or suffer a physical distraction such as a cough or dry mouth. Not that you cannot recover from going dark unintentionally, but usually you want to command the silence utilized in your communication.

For communicators, silence is indeed golden!

The Pause That Refreshes

When I'm preaching, I consider it a conversation between myself and my congregation, although of course I'm doing most of the talking. But I know how invaluable silence can be in helping me punctuate my points and strengthening my relationship with people in the pews. The scale and conversational context may differ, but I use silence when speaking before a crowd in ways similar to when I'm only talking to one other person.

If you and I were sitting outside on the patio enjoying a cup of coffee or cold beverage together, we would converse. You might ask a question and I would answer. There would be a brief pause as we sipped our drinks and settled into our thoughts and this opportunity to dialogue together. I would then ask you a question or comment on a topic of shared interest. Back and forth we would go, not like a tennis match necessarily but more like the net, catching some of the ideas served back and forth, letting others go out of bounds.

Our conversation would not be a competition but a shared experience, a "good visit" as my mother and aunts used to say. I can still hear them talking and laughing together from when I was a boy loitering on the porch as they caught up on family news, traded neighborhood gossip, and shared opinions on everything from last week's sermon to this week's headlines.

In between the laughs and eye rolls and knee slaps and lowered voices, there would be moments when no one talked. We could hear the birds chirping and the dog barking down the block, a child playing or a car turning into a driveway. These intervals helped the women savor the intimacy among them without having to say anything. The bonds were time-honored and enduring. The warmth, the fellowship, the joy, the shared burdens and celebrations—my mother and her sisters and their friends revealed to me the way silence can provide a canvas for a conversational masterpiece.

In the pulpit or at the podium, silence may seem counterintuitive. You're there to fill the silence, not to lead a silent retreat. Going silent might be your worst fear as a speaker, someone who freezes up and can't collect their thoughts or find their voice. If you understand silence, however, it can help you maintain focus and give you room to breathe, both literally and figuratively, as you convey your message.

And of course, you want to use it strategically and not as a way to pass the time or be overly dramatic or drawn out. Depending on your audience and your level of engagement with them, using silence may be a way to draw them in closer. But it can backfire as well if they think you're stalling, patronizing them, or losing your train of thought. You want to control silence and not have it controlling you!

To maximize your control of it, let's consider the four ways to use silence effectively when you speak, beginning with emphasis.

Dinner Is Served!

When I was growing up, I quickly learned that when my parents or other adults were upset with me, they often used silence to underscore their frustration, disappointment, or displeasure. When my mother quietly, slowly called me by my full name, lingering dramatically in between each part, then I knew I was in trouble. Her refusal to voice her constricted emotions worried me more than if she spoke her mind and called me out on my mistake. Self-containment was the way to emphasize the severity of her anger and intensity of her rebuke.

In communication, pausing for a few seconds forces your audience to realize you're placing a silent frame around a particular point, insight, or bend in the story. You're deliberately stopping so they can absorb the impact of your words. When communicating your message, you can stop momentarily right after you reveal your point or insight, or you can go silent briefly *before* your drop-the-mic moment. Each has its own advantages.

If you are preaching, teaching, or speaking and building to a revelation, usually one of several, then you will likely need to pause after each one, particularly your first. Building up to your first silent stop, you will likely have increased your pace and volume. You might be gesturing with animation or striding across the stage so that your body's energy matches your voice's. The pitch and timbre of your voice may even go to a lower or higher register as you relentlessly speak the truth of your message.

As you build and gain momentum, your audience expects you to reach a stopping point. They assume you will let them know when you've arrived. Your energy level will be ascending toward the peak, the summit, the climax of your communication, and once you arrive, you stop. You let your audience take in the view of the vista where you have led them. You pause to catch your breath as participants scrutinize the scenic overlook, realizing the distance you've covered with them from where you started. They each embrace and own the shared experience you've created by taking them to that moment.

Or allow me to return to our cooking metaphor. By the time you serve the entrée of your message—lifting the lid on the serving dish to reveal your punch line, refrain, or thematic revelation, you will have set the table for silence. It's like the big reveal in a luxurious restaurant, as the silver-domed serving piece is lifted by the gloved hand of your waiter and he proclaims, "Dinner is served!" The dome is lifted and your senses take in the sights, sounds, and smells emanating from within.

You will have created a hunger in your audience for the meal you're serving, and once you place your dish on the table, they need a moment! Just as dinner guests need a moment to inhale the delicious aroma, study the colors and textures of the food before them, listen to the soft bubbling or crackling as it cools, and anticipate that first taste, your audience members need time to savor your message.

Continuing with this culinary comparison, you should also consider the way a good meal is paced. People don't just sit at the table and eat continuously until their plates are empty! Or if they do, it's considered rude, impolite, or unpolished. No, when you're having dinner with company, each bite receives adequate time for the diner to enjoy the flavors and textures. There's time to compliment the chef or praise the host and hostess, to chat about the meal and the shared experience you're all enjoying.

The meal proceeds until diners are finished, and then they linger for a while, perhaps over coffee or tea, letting the rich food digest and basking in the after-glow, or the carb coma as one of my sons once called it! No one has rushed or raced to complete the meal. Instead, it unfolded at its own pace, with ample time provided to have a second helping, to sip a beverage, to converse casually with others at the table.

Communication requires the same kind of time for savoring and enjoying the flavors of your sermon, speech, or address. After you lead your audience to each point, they will need a couple moments to grasp your idea and consider its implications. As your delivery continues and you unpack your message and create a shared experience, your listeners and viewers require digestion time. With each course of the meal or new idea presented, recipients need time to integrate it before continuing.

I'm not talking about sixty seconds or even thirty—not unless you sense your audience requires such a duration. Your silent pause or momentary stop will probably be only a second or two. And as you gain experience, you will become more adept at knowing just how long to extend your silence. But you always want to give your audience time within your message to own it, share it, and respond to it.

A Sprinkle of Suspense

You will also want to consider incorporating a sprinkle of silence in serving your message as a way of creating suspense and building anticipation. This shifts silence from an agent of emphasis to one of expectation. While there's a hint of this as you reveal your ideas because you've created a hunger in your listeners, using silence to build suspense shifts its weight toward your audience's expectations.

Using silence this way is what I call the "pregnant pause." You're not only fueling a hunger or desire in your audience, but also creating the shared experience of discovery. You're birthing new life through the gestation of transformative ideas and relevant solutions. You're sharing the intimacy that comes from revealing scars, uncovering old wounds, and seeing one another in the nakedness of vulnerability and transparency. You're telling listeners to be patient as your ideas grow and come to life within them during the experience of being together. You set up an expectation that a birth will occur at the conclusion of the pregnant pause.

Certainly this may not apply to all messages, and once again please keep in mind that most of my experience derives from my preaching. My role as a pastor is to feed my flock, to keep them safe, to help them escape the wolves at their heels, and to provide sanctuary from the storms of life. Depending on your role and the purpose and context of your communication, you may need to be more lighthearted, practical, or entertaining. But even in this case, your audience still values substance and authenticity. The pregnant pause can facilitate both!

In many ways the pregnant pause reminds me of the cliffhangers used at the end of episodic storytelling. Whether it's a bestselling thriller, a binge-worthy series you're streaming, or a narrative podcast, writers and producers know that curiosity sustains consumers' investment in their stories. Perhaps in ancient times, listening to oral historians or watching dramatic performances, it was the suspense of discovering how a journey, battle, or narrative ended.

This continued with the written word, particularly with fiction as novelists and short story writers held readers' attention from page to page and chapter to chapter. Charles Dickens wrote many of his greatest works chapter by chapter for serialization in magazines and periodicals. Publishers sold their weekly or monthly publications and needed to sustain and increase readership to enhance profits. Dickens knew how to leave beloved characters in peril so that readers couldn't wait for the next installment.

We see the cliffhanger perfected in the twentieth century in popular forms such as comic strips, pulp fiction, radio programs, serial dramas, and soap operas. The term *cliffhanger* likely originated from the suspenseful moments of unresolved tension when a character would literally be hanging on for dear life at the edge of a cliff! The villain might be above them stepping on their fingers or a ravenous beast might be waiting below to devour them. Audiences cared about characters left suspended in danger and couldn't wait to find out what happened.

Would Little Orphan Annie ever find her way home? Would Red Ryder catch the bad guys who stole the cattle from the ranch? What would become of Mary Lou now that her husband had joined the army? Who was the mysterious stranger seen running from the scene of the crime? Who shot J.R.? What plot twist would Shonda Rhimes throw at us next? Readers, listeners, and viewers had to wait until the next episode, issue, or broadcast to find out.

While you likely will not utilize your pregnant pause or seconds of suspense quite the same way and certainly not as frequently, it's an important tool for drawing your audience closer. When you hook people's interest and pique their curiosity, they want resolution. They want to know what happened next, how the problem was solved, or who ended up doing what. The key to keep in mind when setting up a pregnant pause is labor and delivery. Once you put in the labor to birth an epiphany for your audience, make sure you deliver it.

Nothing loses an audience faster than an awkward silence of stillborn familiarity. If the disclosure you're building is too predictable, then you've likely disappointed people, who may check out on you. "Oh, she really doesn't have anything new to tell me," they may assume. Whether their assumption is true or not, you've pushed them away. Worse still is when you sustain a pregnant pause and deliver your baby without anyone caring, noticing, or sharing in the experience.

Oh, they may be polite, nodding and smiling, but you will be able to tell if they're with you or not. It's like the people who look at an infant in the carriage and say, "Well, isn't he something! I know you're so happy he's healthy." Any mother who heard that message would also hear what was not said, "How beautiful! He's so cute and adorable. He must get his looks from you and his father." Unveiling your baby provides unique opportunities for bonding with your audience, and you want it to be worth the risk of silence.

Pregnant pauses should surprise, delight, and enthrall your audience with your birth announcement!

Stone-Cold Silence

No one who's ever walked the earth used the pregnant pause more effectively than Jesus when he was placed in the middle of some Jewish religious leaders who had caught a woman in adultery. While Jesus always communicated in ways that captivated those around him, in this instance he was deliberately placed in a moral and legal trap by the Pharisees and other religious leaders threatened by his refusal to conform to their systems and expectations. These legalists despised Christ's message of grace in light of their own strict conformity to the law. Consequently, they frequently tried to paint him into a corner as they do here:

> Jesus returned to the Mount of Olives, but early the next morning he was back again at the Temple. A crowd soon gathered, and he

sat down and taught them. As he was speaking, the teachers of religious law and the Pharisees brought a woman who had been caught in the act of adultery. They put her in front of the crowd.

"Teacher," they said to Jesus, "this woman was caught in the act of adultery. The law of Moses says to stone her. What do you say?"

They were trying to trap him into saying something they could use against him, but Jesus stooped down and wrote in the dust with his finger. They kept demanding an answer, so he stood up again and said, "All right, but let the one who has never sinned throw the first stone!" Then he stooped down again and wrote in the dust.

When the accusers heard this, they slipped away one by one, beginning with the oldest, until only Jesus was left in the middle of the crowd with the woman. Then Jesus stood up again and said to the woman, "Where are your accusers? Didn't even one of them condemn you?"

"No, Lord," she said.

And Jesus said, "Neither do I. Go and sin no more." (John 8:1–11 NLT)

I love the brilliance and compassion Jesus displayed here! Of course, as the Son of God he didn't fall into the Pharisees' trap, but the way he tied them up with their own rope exemplifies the perfect response. The key to his response's power emerged in the way Jesus refused to conform to the expectations of his audience. He sidestepped their trap so gracefully that they never realized the noose was being placed around their own necks!

If you or I were put in the middle of such an ugly dilemma, we might feel flustered and allow our anger to drive our response—which is exactly what the religious leaders wanted. How could Jesus deny the authority of the law of Moses and still claim to be the Messiah? On the other hand, how could he allow them to condemn this woman and stone her to death, as per the law, and still proclaim God's grace and mercy?

Instead of being squeezed by the binary burden of this tension, Jesus gracefully used silence to convey his answer. Finally, he stooped down and wrote something in the dust, but the very fact that we're not told what he wrote indicates that it was not as important as what he did not say. When his accusers refused to accept his silence, Jesus delivered a divine mic-drop moment! "Go ahead then and follow the law," he basically said to the Pharisees, "but only those who have never sinned get to throw stones!"

After answering them, Jesus once again crouched down to write something in the dust, again something undisclosed to us. Whatever it was again does not seem as important as the fact that Jesus did not waste his words trying to argue, explain, defend, or persuade those aligned against him. His stone-cold silence reminds me of David's smooth stone flying from his shepherd's slingshot smack into the middle of the giant Philistine Goliath's head! Jesus knocked down the giant they had schemed to contrive using as few words as possible, in my humble opinion.

Finally, with her accusers slinking away like dogs with their tails between their legs, only the poor woman remained before Jesus. Keep in mind that she had probably been caught in the act, dragged from her lover's bed by the hair on her head, allowed only to cover herself with a robe or blanket grabbed in haste. The trauma of her arrest was surely compounded by the public shame and humiliation her accusers delighted in heaping on her. The woman surely expected to die in one of the most painful, torturous ways possible.

Instead, the silence of Jesus spoke louder than any words against her.

Make 'Em Laugh

As we've seen, silence is an ally in communication to emphasize and to create—or in the case of Jesus upend—your audience's expectations. Pausing for a few moments can also strengthen the complicity of your shared experience, particularly when utilizing humor. Every exceptional comic knows that waiting briefly for your punch line to sink in is essential to the impact of your joke. You want your audience to get the joke and relish it before you move on.

Humor is incredibly tricky when the mic is in front of you. Many people ask me about incorporating jokes, humor, and funny stories into their sermons, speeches, and talks. I tell them it's one of the biggest risks any communicator can take. The payoff can be enormous when it works but equally as deadly when it doesn't. And what works with one audience, context, and situation may not necessarily transfer and work with another audience—even when those audiences are quite similar.

I recall hearing a pastor break the ice by telling a joke involving his wife buying a new dress. He described how broke they were when first starting out in ministry many years ago. Then one day he came home to discover his wife had bought a new dress, a purchase not only unbudgeted but several hundred dollars way over anyone's budget. "How could you do this?" he demanded.

"Well, I was window-shopping when I spotted this dress," she replied, "and it was like the devil whispered in my ear, 'You would look gorgeous in that—go ahead and try it on!' So I went inside and tried it on. Standing in front of the mirror, I heard the devil telling me to buy it."

To which her husband said, "Now you know how we deal with temptation—the same way Jesus did. We say, 'Get thee behind me, Satan!' "

"I did," said the pastor's wife. "But the devil said I looked gorgeous from back there, too!"

Granted, it's an old-fashioned, corny joke, but the first time I heard this pastor use it, he knocked it out of the park. Considering why it was so funny to his congregation, I recognized how well they knew his personality and that of his wife, their First Lady. This pastor was known for being frugal and highly disciplined with his finances. His wife, on the other hand, loved to shop and always looked beautifully put together in her wardrobe. Because the audience knew this information, the setup for their pastor's joke aligned with their expectations. The incident may or may not have happened, but the fact that it very well could have happened made his little story even funnier.

The pastor waited at least ten seconds for the laughter to subside, giving them a big grin and knowing look. They appreciated his risk and enjoyed the mirth it added to his sermon, which turned out to be on overcoming temptations.

I also happened to hear this pastor use this joke again when speaking at a pastors' conference. Although many in attendance likely knew him or respected his reputation, his joke fizzled this time. There were a few polite chuckles, but nothing like the hearty laughter and thorough enjoyment of his home congregation. Nonetheless, he waited just as long before continuing with his sermon, only this time the silence felt awkward and uncomfortable. Those last few seconds felt like hours, and I, along with many there, felt embarrassed for him.

Once again, knowing your audience makes all the difference. With listeners who are familiar with you or know something about you, using humor can be a way to remind them of your relationship. Also, if your joke falls flat with them, they're likely more forgiving.

In new settings, serious situations, and solemn occasions, however, I would be extremely careful about including humor. On the one hand, it may simply be inappropriate. At an event commemorating a tragedy, for example, I'm not sure there's a place for a joke or a one-liner. It's simply not worth the risk because, even if it works, there is no escaping the gravity of why you're all assembled there.

Regardless of the occasion, make sure not to risk anything that could be considered offensive or insulting. That should go without saying, I know, but you would be surprised how many speakers I've heard say things they later regretted. Whether they were improvising and going for a cheap laugh in the moment or simply overlooked the potential for offense, it's hard to recover either way.

Again, depending on the event or occasion, you may find humor effective with a new audience if it helps them see you as human, relatable, and identifiable. Self-deprecation shared appropriately can create instant affection in these situations. When you tell the story about the hole in your sock, the dog breaking the leash, and the flat tire, they relate and find a common bond of sharing those bad days we've all had before.

Allowing for moments of laughter, when you're all in on the joke together, builds tremendous rapport.

Letting Music Speak

The final benefit of incorporating moments of silence when you communicate is to create sacred personal space for your audience. Whether preaching a sermon or not, most communicators can use momentary pauses to enhance their message by giving their listeners the opportunity to absorb, personalize, and apply the message to themselves. In the church such moments often occur at the end of a service. The pastor wants to leave room for God to work in the hearts and minds of the congregation.

In my church tradition, music often fills these moments. While the preacher is silent or lingering between phrases or statements, organ music conveys the climactic emotional soundtrack for the shared experience about to reach its conclusion. All the great preachers I heard when I was growing up incorporated organ music into their sermons. Many used it interspersed throughout, but almost all of them brought in music to speak for them at the end.

I came to the church through music and served as a choir director in my early years of ministry. I know firsthand, as both a leader and a worshipper, the way music expresses and often compresses many emotions, memories, associations, moods, and ideas. When I'm in the pulpit, I often get to the point near the end of my sermon when I'm emotionally spent and have nothing left to say, at least not using spoken words. That's when I pray silently, repeat what I feel compelled to say again, and allow the music to speak for me.

As a movie producer, I also know the impact music has on viewers. If you see Sally coming home from work, going up the steps, unlocking her door, dropping her purse on the table, and hanging her coat in the closet, you likely haven't formed expectations yet. There's no dialogue or narration so how can the filmmaker set the tone and mood? By choosing music that speaks without language. If the scene is about to become suspenseful and tense, then bring in violins or some ominous score. Or perhaps Sally is about to get a phone call from a prospective boyfriend, in which case the music is more lush, romantic, and wistful.

Even when characters are interacting in a scene together, they may have no dialogue but deliver a stunning moment in the film. For example, consider the movie *Antwone Fisher.* Viola Davis plays Antwone's biological mother. When he comes in to see her, she has almost no lines. She's in the ghetto, and now after giving him up at birth, her son has come back.

Antwone tells her who he is, and she says, "That's my firstborn son." All the mixed emotions emerge in her eyes before she gets up and walks out of the room.

The heart of this scene has no words, and yet it's saying everything! In her pained expression and emotional intensity, Antwone's mother silently says, "Don't judge me. I didn't want it to be like this, and here you come after all this time to bring up the past. I don't want to think about what happened and replay the agony I went through in deciding to give you up. I'm glad you're here. I'm scared you're here. I'm worried you're here." All of this and more without a single word. Really great actors, like Viola Davis and Denzel Washington to focus on the stars in that film, can control a scene with saying anything. This talent-driven ability is what separates the masters from the mediocre.

The music playing in the background is also instrumental to the scene's success. Music creates an atmosphere. It's not necessary for every preacher to preach with music behind them or underneath them, but those of the African American preaching tradition clearly understand that, at least at some level, preaching is a collaborative effort between the preacher and the musician.

My go-to musician for more than twenty-five years

participates in creating unspoken emotion and space for the audience to encounter the sacred. Early in my ministry I became very picky about who played for me. I'd rather have no one at all than someone who was into music and showing off their lovely chords and riffs. I need someone who feels me throughout the entire sermon, and that's what my man, Marcus, does at the keyboard. He knows whether I'm going in or coming out. He and I don't have to go over my outline and choreograph when he will play. For him, music is his language of communication. I've seen him play with tears streaming down his face so hard that he can't see the keys. He expresses himself with his fingers while I express myself with my voice. We're both preaching and enhancing the message and the shared experience for those present.

Regardless of whether music plays or you simply allow moments of silence to make room for your audience to ponder, reflect, and take away their share of your message, do not forget to close your communication as gracefully as possible. There should be no doubt when you're done, and those in attendance should feel like they're returning from a journey. A journey in which you blazed a trail with your message while leaving room for them to come alongside you in moments of silence.

PART 4

The Discovery of Delivery

When you draw on the legacy of language and discover the promise of practice, then the discovery of delivery is your reward. There's something so electric and sacred when you're present in the moment, allowing your voice to reach out into the minds and hearts of your audience. The responsibility is immense, which makes the responsibility of your reach more than humbling!

In some ways, preaching inherently includes and requires a delivery that provokes a response from the congregation. If the message I'm delivering is divinely inspired, and I pray every time that it is, then I also hope and pray that my message is divinely received. I love the fact that the Holy Spirit is often identified by the ancient Greek word *pneuma*, which literally means "breath" or "wind." The Holy Spirit is both the rushing, powerful, gale-force wind of Pentecost as well as the gentle, life-giving breath of fresh air beneath our wings. God's Spirit gives us life and also empowers us. The best preachers, and likely the most effective communicators, have the same effect.

When your delivery seamlessly serves up your message, then your audience receives a lift, like the invisible current beneath the wings of an eagle. Ironically enough, though, one problem that often arises, particularly for individuals new to public speaking, is remembering to breathe. Now, obviously, breathing is an involuntary function of a healthy body, which means you don't have to consciously choose to inhale and exhale. Breathing is so essential to our existence that it's automatic.

When you're standing in the pulpit, however, or at the podium or on the stage or wherever you may be speaking, your breathing requires some level of attention you normally don't have to consider. Like a singer finding moments in her song to breathe without disrupting the mood, tempo, and melody of her performance, expert communicators also pay attention to their oxygen intake during their delivery. I don't recall experiencing it myself, but I've witnessed speakers becoming light-headed or even dizzy because they were so nervous, they began to hyperventilate. Their breathing was either so frantic and shallow or overlooked and sporadic that their bodies, including their brains, weren't getting enough oxygen.

Practically speaking, literally, your delivery relies on your breathing, on the ability to inhale adequate oxygen and exhale carbon dioxide, in order for your body to sustain your speaking. You need breath to force sounds and syllables into words and sentences and ideas. Breath gives life and nowhere is that more important than when you are sharing your life and the life of your ideas with other people.

There's much to discover from the discipline of delivering your messages, but I'm convinced it begins—and ends—with the most basic of functions. Just as flight attendants always tell us to fasten our own oxygen mask before assisting someone else with theirs, we must make sure we're breathing deeply in order to be the breath of life for our audience. So take a deep breath as we consider other ways to help your delivery soar to new heights!

CHAPTER 10

Tour Guides and Trailblazers

The tongue is the only instrument that gets sharper with use.

—Washington Irving

Great communicators bridge the legacy of the past with the dreams of a better future.

Dr. Thomas often reminded me that with the art of preaching, practitioners must know the foundational shoulders upon which they stand, honoring and commemorating the contributions of all who have gone before them. But they must also aspire, innovate, and invent, bringing their original and inimitable creative style and methodology to the microphone. Simply put, they must be tour guides as well as trailblazers, pointing out the historical and cultural milestones and turning points but also leading the way into a new, uncharted territory of ideas.

Many of my predecessors have inspired and influenced my preaching style as well as the way I communicate in general. Whether in the pulpit, at the podium, on the stage, or around the boardroom, they not only provided models of merit but, both directly and indirectly, infused me with the confidence to bring my authentic voice to every speaking opportunity. They showed me when to be direct and when to take the long way in order to make my point, how to create and fulfill expectations with my audience, and how to surprise them with unexpected moments of insight, clarity, emotion, or inspiration.

Without the many mentors, exemplars, speakers, and leaders before us, there would be no legacy upon which we could build our own platforms and extend our own dreams. Each time we communicated before an audience would feel like the first time, attempting to guide our listeners with very little illumination from those who went before us. Fortunately, we have the examples of so many men and women who have shown us, both in times of adversity and in times of abundance, how to shine the light of the heart through the power of the voice.

Some provide more historical perspective as guardians of the past while others innovate as they communicate new visions for tomorrow. They are both essential, and the best communicators know how to draw on the skill set of each. With this ambidextrous assumption in mind, let's consider ways to respect the repertoire of tour guides as well as flirt with the ferocious freedom of those who blaze their own trails.

Scrap the Script

My perspective on tour guides changed when I made my first visit to London. I had been invited to preach and speak, and in addition to sharing my sermons, I was eager to experience all the iconic British landmarks, foods, places, and personalities that make the capital of the United Kingdom one of the largest and most diverse cities in the world. While I knew my hosts would probably be happy to arrange for a guide to take me sightseeing, I wanted to play tourist without having to reveal my status as an American unaware of the differences and distinctions between the English, the Welsh, the Scottish, and the Irish—not to mention all the various cultures and countries represented as part of the Commonwealth of Nations.

Buckingham Palace was on my list, along with the Tower of London, the British Museum, Westminster Abbey, the London Eye, Big Ben, Hyde Park, Covent Garden, the West End, Trafalgar Square, and Harrods Department Store. After years of watching James Bond movies and Sherlock Holmes adaptations, I wanted to see what the city was really like. Did it really rain as much as I'd heard? Or get as foggy as I'd been led to believe? Would I be able to understand the accents easily enough, and would they be able to understand me? Regardless of how many sites I longed to take in, I knew I wanted an authentic experience but wasn't exactly sure how to make that happen. Maybe I'd simply stroll and people-watch or pop into an authentic pub for fish and chips.

After considering various tour companies, I chose the one that was apparently the most popular, with overwhelmingly positive reviews from various international visitors. On the day of the tour, I bought my ticket and stood in a queue with several dozen other visitors waiting to ride one of the large, open-air double-decker buses that would take us throughout the bustling London streets. A female voice in what I later learned would be considered a posh accent finally announced that it was time to board. I took my place up top, grateful for the few faint patches of blue sky and my dry seat after an early morning shower.

The bus pulled away with every seat filled. I sensed everyone else was as excited as I was to take in the best of this ancient, yet modern, metropolis. We had gone less than a block when a thick, staticky voice crackled on the intercom and introduced himself as our tour guide for the next four hours. The man's accent was British—at least, I think it was—but I struggled to understand him. It wasn't only the chatter of other passengers and the traffic and city noises making it challenging, because from the bits and pieces I did comprehend as we proceeded, I quickly realized he was reading from a script.

I was thoroughly surprised, or as my British friends later taught me, "gobsmacked," at the generic, impersonal quality of information the guide presented. It was a collection of facts and bland descriptions that I had already read in most tour books and travel sites. At the end of the first hour, we stopped for a quick survey of the British Museum, but I had had enough. It was time to scrap the script! I lingered and let the tour bus leave without me, and I noticed I was not the only passenger to do so. I took my time and eventually hailed a cab and headed back to my hotel.

I considered booking another tour but feared my experience would be the same. I hated to waste my time on information available to me in most travelogues. But what I didn't know then was that I needed a tour guide who was a docent, not a dilettante!

Docent or Dilettante

Feeling a bit foolish after my misadventure, I nonetheless confessed my disappointment to my hosts that evening at dinner. They chuckled and said, "Oh, you poor dear! That's dreadful! Just leave it to us and we'll get you sorted out, okay?" I politely asked them not to go to any trouble or inconvenience themselves, but they were determined for me to experience more of the charm, grit, depth, beauty, and history of their beloved London before I returned to the States.

So the next morning after breakfast, I was greeted by a tall, stately British gentleman of South African descent. He was dressed impeccably and introduced himself as a docent from the Centre for Modern History at the City, University of London. Recruited by my hosts to show me the heart of British culture and history, this gentleman asked me numerous questions and assessed my areas of interest. He then proposed a tour that would allow me to experience most of my desired sites with ample time to walk, browse, people-watch, and enjoy a pub lunch. When I confessed that I didn't exactly know what a docent was, he explained both the general meaning as well as how it applied specifically to him.

In the broadest sense, a docent is an expert willing to teach, tutor, and guide others in specific areas of interest. They typically serve on a voluntary basis and have direct experience related to the museum, park, gallery, or zoo they're showing to groups or individuals. "A docent may be seen as the opposite of a dilettante, someone with a passing surface knowledge of many subjects but expertise in none," my new British friend explained. He then informed me that docent is also a rank just below professor at many colleges and universities around the world. So being a docent reflected his role as well as his rank at the center for higher education where he served. He had a keen knowledge of British history and specialized in how the UK had colonized in Africa and India.

My time with this gentleman more than made up for the deflated touristy experience of the previous day. We enjoyed an ongoing conversation in which he described the significance of various sites and spotlighted various points that would be of personal interest to me. He seemed delighted whenever I asked questions, which only made me appreciate this unique opportunity all the more. Upon returning home and reflecting on my experience, I appreciated the difference between a dilettante, who might do just fine as a tour guide reading a script, and the personalized knowledge and depth of insight of a docent.

Many times I've heard pastors and speakers who fall into the same categories. Some play it too safe and stick to familiar scripts and well-known topics. Others, however, find a different angle and reveal new insight, often because of their own passionate interest and expertise. They're covering a familiar passage of Scripture perhaps, but they bring it alive in a way that feels custom tailored to their audience. These are the kind of communicators to emulate because they engage their listeners in ways that someone merely going over talking points never can achieve. So when you're doing research, studying various aspects of your topic, and putting together your message, find a way to delight your audience by becoming their docent.

Pioneering a New Path

If my visit to London informed how I view the expertise of the best tour guides, then a trip out West for a vacation with my family at a dude ranch illustrated the risks and rewards of pioneering a new path. I mean this literally, of course, because as the ranch foreman began describing our options for horseback riding that week, I looked forward to advancing my equestrian skills, which were next to zero, and at least feeling comfortable in the saddle.

I soon realized, however, the challenge was more daunting than expected. After growing up watching *The Lone Ranger*, *Bonanza*, and *Gunsmoke*, my vision of the Wild West entailed looking the part without appreciating the skill required to fulfill it. Yoked shirts with pearl-snap buttons, faded jeans, and cowboy boots look great on TV and in catalogs, but as I managed to step into the stirrup and swing into the saddle of a magnificent chestnut stallion named Sunset, I knew riding a horse would not be as easy as Kevin Costner made it look in some of his films. Sunset proved to be a wonderful match for my trepidation, strong and sturdy with an unflappable disposition.

That first day our little newbie group learned the

basics and got comfortable with our assigned horses. We plodded along a well-worn, familiar trail close to the ranch house, a rustic lodge-style structure bordering woods at the edge of the Rocky Mountains. The next day, after a quick review, we learned to trot and canter, finding a rhythm with our horses that displayed the same mutual trust required between formal dance partners on the ballroom floor. As my confidence grew, something in me longed to break free of the staid conformity of our group and send Sunset galloping across the hillside at full speed.

About that time, I heard a stampede of thundering hooves coming toward us and watched in astonishment as a half-dozen riders flew past. I felt like I was in the center of the track for the Kentucky Derby! The speed, grace, and control amazed me. The foreman, an indigenous, middle-aged man of the Navajo tribe, explained that these were expert riders, both ranch hands along with experienced guests, who were going into the woods to bushwhack. Unfamiliar with this ranch expression or colloquial cowboy-ism, I took the opportunity to ask him about it as we headed back to the corral to dismount for the day.

Bushwhacking, he explained, was simply what it sounded like. Riders would go off trail in order to create a new path, to locate and map a natural resource such as a stream or river, or traverse terrain that offered no other safe passage. "It's a catch-all word for what people have been doing in these lands for hundreds of years," he said. "Various native peoples as well as European settlers and American colonists had to create their own trails in order to navigate the vast wilderness. Over time, certain routes became well known and featured established paths, trails, and later roads."

Basically, bushwhacking is what trailblazers did to clear a new way forward.

It's what trailblazing communicators still do today!

The Truth of Trailblazers

I love learning new information, particularly about history and other cultures, and the foreman's explanation fascinated me. It resonated in part because I've always considered myself an entrepreneur at heart with a pioneering spirit to try new endeavors and explore new possibilities. While I'm not going to be taking Sunset for a hard ride to bushwhack through the mountains anytime soon, I nonetheless aspire to be a kind of trailblazer.

This is the role of all successful communicators, I

believe. Whether they're addressing previously taboo topics and unacknowledged issues or setting new standards in their style and delivery, communication trailblazers never shrink from risks. They know that anytime one communicates, there's the inherent risk for potential misunderstanding or miscommunication. Greater still, especially in today's cancel climate, trailblazers know that their message will upset, unsettle, and upend some of their listeners.

Jesus knew this result and considered it not only unavoidable but a positive indicator of the gospel message in a hostile world. He told his followers, "If the world hates you, keep in mind it hated me first. If you belonged to the world, it would love you as its own. As it is, you do not belong to the world, but I have chosen you out of the world. That is why the world hates you" (John 15:18–19 NIV). This dynamic has certainly emerged throughout history, whether you consider the messages of Martin Luther or Martin Luther King Jr. Anyone who dares to speak against the status quo, to question the prevailing authority, or to propose something revolutionary can count on opposition.

Delivering your best message may upset members of your church, your support group, your homeowners' association, your classroom, your country club, or your labor union. Your motives may be called into question and your methods denounced or dismissed. In our insatiable sound bite world of tweets, memes, and likes, your message may be chopped, diced, and sprinkled in ways you never imagined. Some will try to take your words out of their original context while others will compare you unfavorably with someone they support.

Even if you're not preaching a sermon or delivering a spiritual message, you will likely experience dissonance and discord from a few in your audience who will always work to find fault. In other words, haters are indeed always going to hate! Some may feel threatened because of how they interpret your message and assume you want them to respond. Others may chafe at being confronted with the truth. Because no matter how apparent or self-evident the truth of your message, someone in your audience is likely in denial and determined to stay there.

The truth of trailblazers often terrifies those trying to hide.

Preaching to the Choir

You may also face the temptation to resist taking risks. If you allow fear of criticism, rejection, or negative consequences to shape your message, then you will likely dilute your message into a benign offering with the appeal of a generic greeting card. Those in attendance may smile and nod (or nod off to sleep), but few if any will find your message memorable or relevant. Nothing distresses me more than to hear a preacher preach a dry, boring sermon! Or to sit and listen to a speaker working too hard to appease rather than to appeal!

Yes, you want to be aware of unnecessarily upsetting those in your audience just as there are times when common sense and sensitivity dictate diplomacy over directness. You may recall that Jesus also told his followers, "I am sending you out like sheep among wolves. Therefore be as shrewd as snakes and as innocent as doves" (Matthew 10:16 NIV). Many people today often mistake simply being considerate and respectful as political correctness. Savvy communicators live in the tension Jesus describes here. They understand how to tread carefully among the land mines of controversy within certain topics, issues, and truths.

If you seek to avoid any offense or disturbance in delivering your message, then you're doing nothing more than preaching to the choir. This euphemistic cliché captures the perfect picture of what happens when you play it safe and keep your message mediocre. Preachers who preach only to the choir risk virtually nothing because the choir is already required to be there as part of the service, often backing up the one in the pulpit, literally, in the choir loft. Presumably, they may have heard the sermons before and find them familiar and predictable if not bland and stale. I suspect it's the same reason we watch reruns on TV or repeat viewings of our favorite films; there's comfort in the certainty of the storyline.

The best stories, regardless of the media in which they're expressed, keep audiences enthralled by balancing some expected conventions and tropes with some twists and turns no one saw coming. A fairy tale includes magic beans, ominous giants, and beanstalks reaching to the clouds, but if those familiar elements are updated and transformed, say, into prescription medications, pharmaceutical conglomerates, and climbing the rungs to FDA approval, then suddenly the story evolves. If a romantic comedy includes a "meet-cute," opposites who attract, and a proposal at the end, no one's surprised. If the storyteller rearranges these elements, however, by beginning with an engagement party in which opposites clash with disastrous results that leaves them apart, then readers or viewers become intrigued.

The best speakers delight their audiences in this same way. They shift and glide with the serpent-to-dove dexterity necessary to meet the full range of colors and textures in their audience's world. Not only do they hold their listeners' attention by building suspense, creating surprise, and exceeding expectations, but their message resonates in ways that matter to their audience. They take the assumptions, givens, and old stories and reinterpret them to create epiphanies, surprises, and new tales that transcend what has gone before.

Instead of preaching to the choir, these communicators are like evangelists taking their good news, in whatever form, to the ends of the earth!

A Million-Dollar Voice

In fact, one of the best practitioners of communication that infused past traditions with new life is the Reverend Clarence LaVaughn (C. L.) Franklin. Until the advent of YouTube and social media, he was likely the most imitated and celebrated African American preacher in history, as Dr. Thomas reminded me. Born in Mississippi shortly after the turn of the twentieth century to parents who were sharecroppers,

C. L. Franklin was sixteen when he answered God's call to preach. He began traveling throughout the Southeast before accepting the pastorate of a Baptist church in Memphis, Tennessee. A few years later, he moved to another church in Buffalo, New York, before settling into the pulpit where he would serve the rest of his ministry at New Bethel Baptist Church in Detroit, Michigan.

From his home base in Detroit, the Reverend Franklin began preaching around the country, sharing his unique preaching style that combined his profound insight into Scripture with charismatic emotional power delivered by the silky, smooth textures of his rich baritone voice. With his sermons frequently broadcast on radio and recorded on vinyl records, by the 1950s he became known as the man with the "Million-Dollar Voice."

His powerful melodic voice wasn't limited to preaching because the Reverend Franklin was also a gifted singer. In fact, he was one of the first preachers I ever heard who would be talking and preaching in the pulpit and then segue into singing, usually from a known song or hymn directly pertaining to his message. His talent and passion for music led to the formation of his own Gospel group, C. L. Franklin's Gospel Caravan, which featured the Clara Ward

Singers as well as his young daughter, who would later be known as the iconic superstar and First Lady of Soul, Aretha Franklin.

In 1963, the Reverend Franklin organized the Walk to Freedom down Woodward Avenue in Detroit, attracting more than 125,000 marchers and featuring his friend and fellow pastor Dr. Martin Luther King, Jr., who debuted a speech declaring "I Have a Dream." Although the Reverend Franklin's life was not without controversy, particularly for aspects of his personal life, he used the microphone he was given to amplify the messages God placed on his heart.

As a preacher and voice of the community, the Reverend Franklin honed his gifts to perfection, making his messages all the more meaningful. He exuded confidence, courage, and creativity in his unique style while maintaining respect, reverence, and responsibility for the sanctity of his call to the ministry. As we're about to see, his best sermons transformed the pain of the past into the hope of the future.

From the Eagle's Nest

Perhaps the best example of the Reverend Franklin's unique form of alchemy transforming old into new is also his most famous. Entitled "The Eagle Stirreth Her Nest," it's based on a dynamic exposition of Deuteronomy 32:11–12: "As an eagle stirreth up her nest, fluttereth over her young, spreadeth abroad her wings, taketh them, beareth them on her wings: So the Lord alone did lead him, and there was no strange god with him" (KJV). The "him" referenced in the second verse refers to Jacob, the patriarch whose name God changed to Israel after an all-night wrestling match, and also represented the nation of God's chosen people also known by this same new name. "For the Lord's portion is his people; Jacob is the lot of his inheritance. He found him in a desert land, and in the waste howling wilderness; he led him about, he instructed him, he kept him as the apple of his eye" (Deuteronomy 32:9–10 KJV).

The main point of the sermon is that, just as the eagle has to disturb the comfort of the nest to get the eaglet out of there to fly, God likewise has to make the nest uncomfortable to stir the children of God such that they might fly.[1] During a time of national civil unrest and violence, this message asked listeners to reconsider the turmoil of the times as labor pains for something new that God was birthing.

What you must understand is that this sermon had been in the corpus of the black preaching cannon, the historical body of sermon material, messages, and methodology, for more than one hundred years by the time the Reverend Franklin developed his version.[2] While we have countless sources for sermon material today thanks to online technology, Franklin, as well as many other black preachers, often knew and preached popular sermons from the canon.

Of unknown origin, the sermon was passed on in the tradition until a celebrated version surfaced in the 1920s in the preaching of the Reverend Calvin P. Dixon.[3] In the 1950s and '60s, the tradition passed the sermon to Franklin, to which he added his personal style, gifts, and uniqueness, and the community responded by proclaiming that Franklin's version and performance of the sermon was genius. His version combined the best of what he had inherited while making the material fresh and the message more salient and relevant to his audience at the time. This is the art of communication.

While some critics might be tempted to ask if this sort of appropriation spills into plagiarism, I can assure you, and have confirmed with Dr. Thomas, that it doesn't. Every preacher, and I daresay every communicator, takes everything he or she has been given and transforms it into a new version. Consequently, this is not plagiarism in the classic sense of the academic community, which usually involves stealing expressions of ideas and copying someone else's language, but a fresh adaptation or remix of the sermon to meet present communal circumstances.

By the community's standards, very few of us could bring the level of virtuosity that Franklin brought to the sermon, and as a result, he changed the game. The Reverend Franklin exemplifies how preachers create sermons out of the raw materials of the tradition and offer a new version to the community to meet present circumstances that moves the tradition forward. He was both a wise guide and a gifted guardian of the legacy entrusted to him as well as a passionate pioneer blazing his own trail.

The Reverend Franklin's most famous sermon reminds us that we do not have to reinvent the wheel when communicating—but we can make it roll smoother and faster for our respective audiences!

Bless as You Address

No matter when the mic is placed in front of you or what kind of communication you're compelled to share, you have a new opportunity each time you speak, preach, talk, or teach before an audience.

Whether your audience is ten people or ten thousand, you have the power to build upon the legacy of linguistic longing that remains the impetus for public speaking. The desire to inform and educate, to challenge and persuade, to enlighten and inspire, is the heartbeat of every woman and man who dares to stand before a microphone or behind a podium and open his or her mouth.

You have a responsibility when communicating to use the conventions of language and the seasoning of oratory eloquence to the best of your ability. Because at the very least you will be fulfilling the dual roles of tour guide and trailblazer, imparting known truths and stirring curiosity in some while creating new methods and sparking hope in others. The torch has been passed to you even as you illuminate each audience you bless with your address.

Don't be afraid to take what has been entrusted to you—your education, your experience, your gifts and talents—and maximize God's return on his investment in you. Whether you're honing your use of social media, improving your speaking skills in your community, or delivering God's Word to your flock, or all of those and more, it's time to find your voice!

Don't drop the mic!

Be the communicator that only you can be.

CHAPTER 11

Sound Check

Getting an audience is hard. Sustaining an audience is hard. It demands a consistency of thought, of purpose, and of action over a long period of time.

—Bruce Springsteen

"Testing—one, two, three, testing!"

I stood onstage before an empty auditorium, well aware that within a couple of hours, thousands of faces would be looking back at me. Shrill electronic feedback shrieked, and the woman in the sound booth mouthed "Sorry!" and held up her hand for me to wait. After a few seconds, and presumably an adjustment in the sound control booth, she motioned for me to say something else, which I did. This time my voice echoed throughout the spacious venue without any glitches, and the sound engineer gave me the thumbs-up. We were good to go for that evening's event, at which I would speak.

Sound check has become a common practice for most communicators prior to delivering their speech, address, or sermon. There's not much to it, really. It's simply a quick test to make sure the technology works properly and, depending on the venue and the event, to allow the sound engineer an opportunity to adjust levels, effects, and frequencies as needed for maximum sound quality of your voice's transmission and amplification.

After decades of speaking and preaching, sound check has become a familiar part of the ritual of my public communication at conferences, churches, and leadership events. It's often my last chance to make any final adjustments, corrections, or additions to enhance my message. But it's also more than just a quick assurance that I will be heard—it's a reminder to make sure I have something worth saying.

Stay with Me

Having something worth saying and being able to hold your audience's attention for the duration of your delivery is always daunting. I want to connect with them and then have them stay with me, tracking as we engage in our rather unique one-sided conversation. But as we've seen, the best communication goes in both directions, even if your audience is not audibly participating. And since the speaker is the one with the opportunity to say the most, he or she carries more responsibility—at least when speaking.

The best communicators command the attention of their audiences without any show of force. They don't verbally bully, berate, or browbeat those collected individuals assembled before them for whatever reason or occasion. Especially for those of us who preach, a gentle force always has more power than any kind of verbal assault, fire and brimstone, or emotional manipulation. Because what preachers know that other communicators often overlook is that you want to keep your audience with you longer than just the present time you're speaking to them.

Preachers want their members and regular attenders to want to keep coming back and visitors to return. They want their congregation to grow to expand and extend the ministry of the church. But often viewed as the face of their church, pastors and preachers know that what and how they communicate during services has a direct impact on the community's perception.

If their message arrived dry as stale toast during this week's service, then some churchgoers may be reluctant to return next week. If a pattern begins to develop, then it emerges as the pastor's—and often the church's—brand message.

While we can argue about whether or not sermons, classroom lessons, political speeches, and educational lectures should be entertaining, the reality remains that you want your audience fully engaged. I believe both the message itself as well as how it's delivered should intrigue, compel, and delight those experiencing the speaker's delivery. Obviously, there are boundaries regarding what's appropriate for events, venues, occasions, and audiences, but I fear that we often place more restrictions on ourselves than anyone else. We assume that we must maintain a certain tone, style, or vibe just because it's a holiday or a memorial service or a baccalaureate address.

For example, I've never laughed harder than at a funeral I preached a few years ago. While using humor almost always includes risk, particularly in some situations more than others, I knew there was no better way to convey the message that both honored the deceased and reflected his personality and spirit than to laugh together with the community gathered to mourn him. As inappropriate, irreverent, or disrespectful as that may sound, I had known the deceased for many years if not most of my life. He was like family to me, a brother and partner in crime, and we had lived many of life's highs and lows together, cheering one another on, sharing the joys of our triumphs and the burdens of our trials. And I knew one of the things I would miss most about him was his quick-witted, outrageous sense of humor. Laughter punctuated our conversations almost every time we were together.

So at his funeral, I felt strongly that the best way to express my love and grief as well as to celebrate his life and heavenly homecoming was to share a personal story. Instead of a traditional eulogy or sermon, I told what's often called a shaggy-dog story, a series of events that kept going from bad to worse with comical results. By the time I'd finished, I couldn't distinguish the tears of my sorrow from the tears of mirth at the memory of my friend's zest for living and contagious humor. As best I recall, those in attendance laughed harder than I did, even as the funeral director raised his eyebrows and struggled to suppress a smile.

I could've let decorum, formality, and social etiquette prevent me from telling such a raucous, silly tale at a funeral.

Or I could toss aside those traditional elements, which I did, in favor of sharing what I knew in my heart would best honor and celebrate the passing of this dear friend.

Trendy or Timeless

There is another tension that can directly affect the loyalty and longevity of your audience beyond any one specific event. Do they perceive you as being current, relevant, and hip? Or as being more traditional, old-fashioned, and outdated? No one wants to be labeled the latter, and yet it can also be embarrassing to try to use street slang if you've never been in the 'hood!

The solution is creating your communication style to be timeless.

Yes, it's important to be up-to-date in your research, use of technology, and awareness of global and cultural events in a world, where headlines change online each minute. Regardless of your topic and setting, your audience may be tempted to view you as out-of-touch and irrelevant to their postmodern twenty-first-century lives. The general millennial response to dismiss their elders—"Okay, Boomer"—distills their disregard into a verbal eye roll. Once they label you, it doesn't matter whether their criticism is accurate or deserved. It only matters that they're no longer listening or considering you credible. So you want to be plugged in enough to the age and stage of your audience in order to connect.

On the other hand, trying too hard can easily backfire, leaving your attempt looking foolish and naïve. Name dropping rappers no older than your grandchildren who you've never heard but found online will not impress most audiences of young adults. Ditto with sites, posts, blogs, memes, clips, pics, and vids.

In between not caring or trying and working too hard is simply being real. From my experience, the key to an engaging, exceptional communication style is often directly addressing your fears. Using humor about your ignorance of the latest and coolest shows that you're aware of what you don't know *and* you're willing to laugh at yourself. Both disclosures will usually appeal to any audience.

Or consider it this way: In the world of fashion, the battle between trendy and timeless has also always existed. While some people love to keep up with the latest trends and try new fads, others develop a distinct personal style that remains consistent no matter what changes on the runway or on the racks. "Fashion changes, but style endures," said the legendary Coco Chanel, and this is the mantra of those who want more than what everyone else is doing.

With YouTube and social media, I've noticed a similar phenomenon in the ways participants communicate. Some are well aware of competing for views, clicks, and advertisers and willing to do whatever it takes to grow their platform and extend their online audience. They may use daily references to the latest headlines or current events, costumes and props, or attitudes taken to extremes.

Others, however, find a way to rise above the millions of other messengers online simply by being themselves. Whether they're giving a TED Talk, introducing someone at an awards show, or being interviewed, they exude an authenticity and confidence, a sense of being comfortable in their own skin. These are the online communicators who usually engage me most frequently and consistently. Because I respect who they are and not just their social media persona, I'm eager to hear what they have to say.

These are the voices, neither too trendy nor too traditional, that remain timeless.

Paralyzed by Perfection

Another barrier to keeping your audience with you, both in the moment and beyond, is perfectionism.

Whether you're teaching in a classroom, litigating in a courtroom, or telling scary stories to kids around a campfire, you have all eyes and ears on you during your moment at the mic. You not only want to make the most of your opportunity, but also want to make it memorable in the best way for the recipients of your message.

Depending on the venue and context, you may know whether or not your communication is successfully received right away. If your students grasp the concepts and demonstrate mastery, then you've succeeded. If the judge or jury returns the verdict in favor of your client, then you've succeeded. If wide-eyed children are shivering in fear one moment and giggling in delight by firelight at the conclusion of your tale, then you've succeeded.

More challenging in most cases is not knowing how your message has been received. I've preached many sermons in which I poured everything I had into the sermon and left my heart in the pulpit only to sense that somewhere I had lost my audience. Any emotional response in the congregation seemed to fizzle. Afterward, people would tell me how much they enjoyed my sermon in a way that was obligatory and polite.

A few times when I've felt this way, I've asked my wife, my children, and members of my team how they experienced the sermon. They know me well enough to understand that I'm not wanting compliments so they usually try to provide honest feedback. Most of the time, they will comment on what they found most engaging but struggle to identify where the sermon may have lost them or failed to sustain their undivided attention. Because of the volume of my preaching and speaking, I learned over the years not to ruminate too long or too intensely in order to avoid paralyzing myself through perfectionism.

Many times silencing my internal critic and letting go of his critique are harder than I want to admit. I replay the sermon or speech in my mind and look for flaws or things I wish I'd done differently. Occasionally, there's value in this exercise as I determine to make changes or take different risks the next time I'm at the mic. Like an athlete watching videos of their past game performances, I can improve my serve, delete a redundant point, or insert a needed moment of silence.

Other times, however, I have to come to terms with and accept the requisite imperfections of a given message. Especially when I was younger and still formulating and honing my unique style, I would be hard on myself for not sounding like my favorite preacher or speaker at the time. I knew better than to try and imitate them outright, but I longed to have the confidence and charisma, that sense of comfortability in one's own skin, that I experienced when listening to the communicators whom I most admired. What I didn't realize then, of course, is how each of them had already battled the same insecurities and uncertainties that I was facing. They had become experienced enough to recognize what they brought to their message that no one else could bring.

Now after more than four decades as a communicator, I've learned to let my imperfections articulate my authenticity. From my experience, that's the secret to overcoming the paralysis of perfectionism. Accept that no matter how polished, accomplished, articulate, or eloquent you may be, there will always be moments you might wish to change in any given sermon, speech, address, or talk. Whether it's a tendency to drop the dreaded "uh" as a momentary filler in between your expressions, difficulty controlling your speed as your speech seemingly accelerates of its own accord, or a proclivity for ditching your outline, we all have areas we hope to improve as we mature in our message methodology.

After all, you may have already discovered that if your delivery is too perfect, then your audience may not connect with you. If you seem too put together, they may perceive you as beyond them and therefore deem your message irrelevant to their own imperfect lives. Yes, most audiences want someone who provides both inspirational and aspirational delivery of their message, but they also need ways to relate, to connect, and to identify. They need to know that you're just as human as they are, regardless of whatever differences, ostensible or not, exist between you.

So if you struggle with perfectionism, learn to glean what is truly constructive and jettison the rest. Look for ways to improve but don't hold yourself to an impossible standard. Leave room for the dynamic creation of an experience that transcends what you're able to control!

Focus Your Feelings

Knowing how to focus your feelings may be the most important factor in creating and sustaining a bond with your audience. The emotional connection you experience with them enriches the communication process for almost everyone. People want to feel you and tap into the depth and sincerity of the feelings you're expressing. Sometimes I even wonder if what comes out of our mouths matters as much as our hearts. The Bible reinforces this belief, stating that "the things that come out of a person's mouth come from the heart" (Matthew 15:18 NIV), with the capacity to defile them or serve as "a fountain of life" (Proverbs 10:11 NIV).

Over the years, many people have complimented me on the emotional intensity of my preaching and speaking. While I appreciate their willingness to find my heart-based style appealing and remain grateful for their kind words, I sometimes wonder if I know any other way to communicate. My brain and my heart both meet in my voice. It's only when one tried to silence the other that I got into trouble or delivered less than my best.

I've heard numerous communicators in my lifetime who executed their message flawlessly and held my attention with their fresh perspectives on the latest findings in their field. I've attended concerts and shows in which the players and performers didn't miss a step and hit every note with perfect pitch. But unless I experienced their emotional engagement, their heart connection to their message, I left unsatisfied.

On the other end of the spectrum, I've also encountered plenty of people with a platform and a microphone with very little to offer other than a rant, a tirade, a lament, a scathing critique, an obsequious soliloquy, or some other expression of emotional entitlement. They open the floodgates of their feelings and let them pour out but with very little control over how they flood their listeners. Consequently, their audiences may quickly run for higher ground! Those subjected to extreme emotional expressions rarely share the same blend being distilled. Even rarer still are listeners who identify not only with the feelings being shared but also with their same intensity.

When a communicator loses control of their emotions at the mic, many listeners may check out. Even if they share those same or similar feelings, the experience may be too much for them. So instead of igniting passion in their audiences, these emotionally overwrought speakers face distant stares and defensive expressions. Others don't want to hear and feel what's being said because it's too painful, too intense, too troubling, too uncontrollable, and too powerful.

Our feelings, particularly in the heat of the moment, can certainly get us in trouble. If we allow ourselves to boil over and unleash uncensored emotions, we may likely regret it by saying things we don't mean or truly believe. In those moments of pure emotion, however, everything feels extreme, which often results in communication that is equally hyperbolic. Like a toddler throwing a tantrum, we lose control of all the strands of communication except the primal one. Consequently, we cry out from the depths of our souls, often unaware that our cries fall on tone-deaf hearts.

Because in those moments we've compromised our control and allowed our feelings to supersede our audience and our intended message. We're no longer engaged with our listeners in a kind of dialogue as much as we're forcing them to experience the volcanic intensity that's been building inside us. They want to get out of our way and avoid being torched or scorched.

Knowingly or unknowingly, when we unleash too much unfiltered emotion, we risk losing more than we can ever gain. Particularly when topics and issues are controversial, divisive, and emotionally charged already, how we handle them usually determines whether anyone wants to listen. They may dismiss us as too biased, invested, or emotionally driven, meaning that even if we pull ourselves together and deliver a brilliant message, we've already lost them.

Whether true or not, they assume that if we can't control how we feel then we can't control the message we're presenting.

Heat of the Moment

Many years ago I found myself in a unique situation that required me to consider how I use—and sometimes choose not to use—my feelings when communicating before a crowd. In this particular instance I was not preaching but rather had been invited to deliver the keynote address at that year's convention for a national nonprofit organization. This organization, although predominantly white, consisted of several thousand members across the country who often worked closely with local pastors and churches in their communities. I won't say any more about the specifics of their mission in order to protect the innocent—and the guilty!

This group's invitation surprised me in itself, and I couldn't help but wonder about ulterior motives or hidden agendas. I was fairly well acquainted with a couple of this group's executives and knew others on their leadership team by reputation. As if anticipating my unspoken curiosity, one of my acquaintances assured me that this group deliberately invited me in order to understand more clearly how they could be more inclusive of African Americans and people of color in both their membership and those they purposed to serve.

So I accepted the invitation, which was several months away, and didn't consider it again until the time approached for the convention. The week before the event, one of the leaders I knew reached out and invited me and my team to dinner with their board of directors and other executives involved in the organization. I accepted and proceeded to develop my talk, focusing it indirectly on exclusivity by looking at the way Jesus related to outsiders, outcasts, and other people, such as Samaritans, prostitutes, and tax collectors, held in contempt by many Jewish people at that time.

After flying from Dallas to the host city for this convention, I arrived at the venue with a couple of my staff who typically assist me when I travel to speak. As it so happened, however, I also had someone else with us, a relatively new friend and colleague who was assisting me with one of my new ventures. He lived close to the host city so it was a natural opportunity for us to meet and go over plans in development prior to my speaking engagement.

Now this friend, I'll call him Timothy, and I had much in common. Fairly close in age, we had each grown up in small towns in the rural Southeast, where we attended similar Protestant Christian churches. We were both married and had several children, both of us committed to being faithful husbands and devoted fathers. While he was not in full-time, vocational ministry, he was well acquainted with its demands. In fact, the most ostensible difference was our race, because he was white. But so far this difference had never been an issue in how we related and successfully worked together.

When I invited Timothy to join me at this dinner with the organization's leadership team, he gladly accepted. Although I didn't mention it to him at the time, I also liked the idea of seeing how he would engage and react with this group, which turned out to be about eight or nine individuals, mostly men and a couple of women, all white, middle-aged, educated professionals. Timothy's emotional intelligence and sensitivity had already impressed me so I was curious how he would read this racially mixed dinner meeting.

During the actual dinner, naturally around a rather large table due to the size of our party, the conversation was mostly polite as we broke the ice and got acquainted. As the meal progressed, several of the group's leaders began to ask me questions focused on how their group could be more inclusive of blacks and other people of color. If I'm generous and give them the benefit of the doubt, they didn't mean to sound patronizing and systemically prejudiced, but they did. Rather than conversing with other human beings, they sounded like a group of scientists visiting another species, eager to take notes and glean data about life on our foreign planet!

Their interests and attitudes didn't surprise me at all, and I offered honest answers as graciously as possible. Even while doing so, though, I couldn't help but notice Timothy, who was mostly keeping quiet since he was not directly involved in the evening's agenda. That man was no longer white but red! He looked like one of those cartoon characters with steam coming out their ears. His jaw was set, his eyes like lasers scanning the speakers. I could feel the heat of his anger at these people along with his shame and embarrassment that he shared their race but not their rhetoric. I could hardly contain my amusement, appreciation, and affection for his reaction in the moment, but said nothing as the meal drew to a close.

Once the organization's team departed, I invited Timothy to join me and my associates for a quick debrief. As we stepped on the elevator taking us down to the lobby, I started chuckling. My two staff members, younger black men, also began smiling and nodding in my direction. Timothy, with his face still flushed and jaw clenched, looked at me as if to ask what was going on.

"You okay?" I asked once the elevator doors closed. "You're steaming mad, aren't you?"

"How could you tell?" he stammered. "I tried not to betray my feelings, but that—that *way* they treated you was unbelievable! I'm so angry! And ashamed!"

"I know you are. I was worried you were going to burst back there! Do we need to get a doctor?"

My friend shook his head. "The worst part is that they have no clue. Right now they're probably patting themselves on the back for doing such a great job of connecting. It just infuriates me!" He took a deep breath. "I'm so sorry. I hope I haven't spoken out of place."

"Just the opposite," I said. "It's very heartening, actually. You notice what I live with every second of every day. Most people don't. Especially the people in that organization, which is why I agreed to speak here. I want to dispel their stereotypes and shake up their expectations. I want them to see that our similarities as human beings far outweigh our differences—including the color of our skin."

The next day I delivered my speech and, if you'll forgive me for mentioning it, received a standing ovation from the several thousand people filling the auditorium. Afterward, I chatted briefly with Timothy before saying our good-byes. He asked me, "How are you able to reveal your heart so passionately without letting your justifiable anger and rage get in the way?"

His question is timelier today than it was even then. I suspect it's one of the million-dollar questions every communicator, leader, and speaker must answer—regardless of their race or the issues at hand affecting their emotions. Because learning how to tap into your true feelings without allowing those emotions to overwhelm you and take over is often the key to communication that ignites, empowers, and unites.

Small Audience, Big Impact

Finally, if you want to increase your platform and expand your audience, then you must also consider the big picture and not just your next speaking engagement. What is your brand as a communicator? What are the key components of your speaking style? What compels others to listen and follow your messaging? These questions may seem relevant only for those whose communication is essential to their career, to those who speak for thousands of people on a regular basis, but I assure you it extends to anyone wishing to be heard.

Whether your platform spans social media in efforts to show your expertise with cosmetics to millions of viewers or reveals your plans for revitalizing your community to a dozen neighbors, you must never underestimate the impact you can have because of the size of your audience. No matter how large or small, people are still people. They want to know you, but they also want to be known. If you make a positive difference in only one person's life, then you have succeeded in delivering your message.

Remember, every movement starts with one person. So pay attention to the pulse points and feedback you get without letting a handful of comments crush your spirit or catapult you too high. Risk letting others see your heart and know what you believe. It may always seem expedient in the moment to capitulate to crowds and jump on the largest bandwidth bandwagon. Ultimately, though, people want to know if you're real, if what you say matters to you before it matters to them, and if you care about them beyond the handshakes, likes, and retweets.

The next time you perform a sound check prior to speaking before an audience, stop and take a moment to consider what sounds you will be delivering and why it matters to those about to be assembled before you. If your communication is smaller in scale and no sound check necessary, don't diminish the impact you can have based on the size of your audience. Jesus chose only twelve key followers to work closely with him during his ministry on earth. They were certainly not the most polished, popular, or progressive people he could have chosen either! Because they had passion and compassion, because they were willing to lead by serving, and because they trusted him for the impossible, they changed the world.

You need not be in the ministry or preaching from a pulpit to make a positive difference. You must only be willing to grasp the mic when your moment comes and share what you know to be true. You may assume it makes little difference how you communicate because you're *only* making announcements at your civic club, addressing a classroom of children, leading a neighborhood social activism group, or presenting a PowerPoint on third-quarter sales in your workplace. But for those hearing the sound of your voice, you have the power to inform, to inspire, to eradicate injustice, and to innovate.

No matter the size of your audience, accept the mic and maximize your message.

Never overlook the impact you can have on just one person's life.

Because that's all it takes to be a successful communicator!

CHAPTER 12

Keep Your Cool When the Mic Is Hot

In the last analysis, what we are communicates far more eloquently than anything we say or do.

—Stephen Covey

With camera phones, recorders, and live streaming, it happens more and more often: live mics catching communication the speaker didn't intend for broadcast! It might be an emotional outburst, a word of profanity, a vulgar slang expression, or spiteful criticism, but once the words leave the speaker's mouth and the hot mic catches them, they cannot be unsaid. For pastors, clergy, public officials, and politicians, hot mic accidents often reveal an all-too-human side that seems to counter the wholesome, spiritual moralist of their public personas. For news anchors, interviewers, and professional journalists, mics left on accidentally often reveal their personal opinions or incidental chatter rather than their carefully curated cadence.

Perhaps in times past, hot mic slips were more scandalous because public figures maintained greater control over their private lives. They crafted a persona that may or may not have reflected the reality of who they were without an audience. Today, online connectivity and social media permit many people to live their entire lives before an unlimited audience with no holds barred. They may value authenticity above all else and don't mind letting the world see their flaws, foibles, and accidental f-bombs. Or they may enjoy the attention from their attempts to shock, knock, and rock their viewers and listeners. Their mics are left on indefinitely and always assumed to be broadcasting every syllable uttered.

Perhaps you're comfortable with such unveiled, ubiquitous transparency, but I suspect most communicators still need healthy boundaries. While they may have nothing to hide, they value their privacy and the sacred intimacy that comes from exclusively personal time with family and friends. As they become more experienced, they learn how to keep their cool when the mic gets hot—a skill I highly recommend cultivating if you want to maximize your impact!

Don't Fake Authenticity

I've had my share of mishaps before live audiences, including spilling the water left at the podium for me to sip, mispronouncing someone's name without realizing it, and losing my train of thought in a mental fog caused by exhaustion. I've also experienced a few hot mic moments, but fortunately, and to the disappointment of my detractors, I could only be heard asking for more coffee or bantering with my interviewer.

When I experimented with having my own syndicated talk show, I was especially aware of the power of the mic as well as the camera to convey more than I could control. When the light on the camera in front of me went red, which I found ironic since usually green means go while red means stop, I was on. I had the advantage of knowing any misstatements or mistakes would be edited out, but I also knew that once I faltered, it could be difficult to regain my focus and composure.

On rare occasions when segments or interviews were live, then I had no choice but to make the most of it by acknowledging and, if possible, correcting my flubs. Sometimes I would get the giggles, the hiccups, or be momentarily caught off guard by a guest's unexpected response. I like to think such instances not only kept me humble but allowed my audience to identify with my humanity. To pretend otherwise or blame others may insulate my ego temporarily, but it misses an opportunity to be present with my audience in the moment and connect my life with theirs.

In fact, one of the greatest lessons I learned from that foray was about conveying authenticity on camera. While I had been filmed in the pulpit and had my sermons broadcast as well as live-streamed, I discovered it was more challenging being myself as a talk show host. Although I had certainly interviewed many others in my career, especially at conferences, panel discussions, and broadcasts of *The Potter's Touch*, I nonetheless felt a bit uncomfortable. I didn't feel the need to be anyone other than myself, but I knew I was a newbie in a role that tends to require everything at once from those wielding the mic.

I learned those who are most successful, the greats like Oprah and Steve Harvey or even Barbara Walters and Johnny Carson back in the day, quickly realize there can be little distinction between who they are on camera and who they are when filming stops and the mics go silent. Only a thin line, if any, separates the way they hold conversations on their shows rather than their living rooms. This quality is, in fact, one of the traits I most admire about Oprah as I've become better acquainted with her over the years: *What you see is what you get!* The same enthusiasm, compassion, intensity, intelligence, and creativity she revealed in various facets on her show are genuine parts of who she is.

There's no substitute for the connection that comes from sharing your authentic self with others. Keep in mind, most people can tell if you're faking authenticity even if nothing in your message betrays your pretense to be genuine. Attempting to do so eventually has the opposite result and creates greater distance between you and your audience. They not only wonder what your motive is for such deception but also doubt your credibility. When your credibility is in question, then you've compromised your authority and given your audience reason to distrust you and your message.

Authenticity is ultimately worth the risks. You may feel naked and exposed in the moment, but in removing layers from the veneer of your vernacular, you give your audience an opportunity to know you. You close the distance between the stage and their seats, between the pulpit and the pews. Everyone may not like what you reveal, but if you share yourself with dignity, they will always respect you. And if they do like what you're sharing and draw closer to you, then your message will stay with them long after you've spoken the last word.

Plan for Spontaneity

One of the primary ways communicators convey their authenticity and vulnerability is through spontaneity. It may involve asking a member of the audience to come onstage with you for a brief chat, seizing an organic opportunity to deliver a zinger, or stopping to adjust the sound quality. You might decide to forgo the slides you'd planned to show or to do a live search online that's projected for your audience to see.

Some speech experts and communication coaches discourage spontaneity because of the risks involved in loosening your control. And there are definitely risks worth considering before you decide to call an audible play and wing it! Numerous people have realized the dangers of involving children or animals in their presentations. Instead of supplying the response you hoped to solicit, the child bursts into tears or takes off their shoes. Rather than being the unexpected visual aid for your Christmas sermon, the donkey decides the manger makes a convenient bathroom.

I've seen mishaps like these happen and have been the cause of a few of them. And after one thing seems to go wrong, it can shake your confidence and make it difficult to recover. You may feel rattled and disconnected from the audience you've worked so hard to bond with. So always weigh the risks and consider as many potential consequences and contingencies as you can imagine. I realize planning ahead negates the very definition of spontaneity, but I hope you understand my point. Most times you will need to make your decision in a matter of seconds while on the fly, but this doesn't mean you haven't considered possible options beforehand.

Spontaneity can also work in your favor and provide the parachute you need for a graceful delivery after a rocky start. Your instincts may compel you to go with your gut and change the tone of your message based on the unexpected emotional atmosphere you're sensing from your audience. It's not only challenging but often futile to try and uplift an audience that's clearly quiet, contemplative, and grieving. Similarly, you may lose your audience's engagement if the sober gravity of your message disrupts their lighthearted, buoyant mood.

As you become more experienced as a communicator, you may also grow more comfortable with spontaneity. Like starting a fire, spontaneous moments can warm up the chilly mood of an audience or ignite a wildfire consuming your momentum. The key to using it successfully is discernment, mental preparation, and hedging your risk with a quick recovery. Like many of the arrows in a communicator's quiver, spontaneity requires practice, including a few misses, before you learn how to use it effectively and hit your target.

Voicing Validation

Authenticity and spontaneity must also be balanced, at least a little, by self-discipline and a willingness to put your audience before your attitude. Because accidentally leaving one's mic on is not the only way to heat up a speaking situation and feel the pressure to perform. Sometimes there's an elephant in the room that you didn't anticipate. It might be something as simple as a broken furnace that leaves the venue cold and drafty, or it could be something more complex such as a national tragedy or a just-released news bulletin. While there are exceptions, I usually recommend naming the elephant and letting your audience know that your experience matches their own, at least in part.

Because my metabolism kicks into overdrive when I speak or preach, I would probably welcome colder temps more than any member of my audience or congregation. Nonetheless, I've learned to acknowledge something that has the potential to distract them from my message. If accurate and appropriate, I take responsibility and apologize for their discomfort or inconvenience. If it's beyond my control, then I place myself alongside my audience as we endure less-than-ideal conditions together.

On larger scales and with matters of greater importance, I almost always feel compelled to acknowledge what's weighing on all our minds and grieving our spirits. Perhaps I wear my heart on my sleeve or no longer have the energy for suppressing my emotional reaction to calamities, but I see little to no value in suppressing onstage what I see in faces staring back at me that cannot contain the pain. Part of my responsibility as the one holding the mic in those moments is to be the voice of the audience, the messenger for the community, and the megaphone for a message often muffled by the noise of the world.

Voicing the pain of your audience provides validation and often vindication.

This is the reason I knew I had to at least mention what has recently been going on in the world around us. Not only the COVID-19 pandemic of 2020 but the virus of violence and plague of systemic racism allowed to run rampant for too long. To ignore the vital importance of communication in the process of seeking solutions and effecting change would be a grievous mistake and a missed opportunity. We continue to see firsthand how using the mic we've been given can start conversations, request and grant forgiveness, and sustain ongoing dialogues. Words remain our greatest hope for humankind.

There's also the real danger of losing your mic if you fail to express the full truth. In other words, ignoring the elephants wandering around in the midst of your message leaves you vulnerable to being trampled! Unspoken tensions, unaddressed issues, undeniable truths, and unimaginable losses can pile up quickly and bury your message by what you failed to say. As we've explored in previous chapters, remaining silent in the midst of suffering usually perpetuates the pain and makes you complicit in censuring what needs to be said.

With your moment at the mic comes great responsibility!

Change the Menu

Sometimes your mic feels hotter because you suddenly feel more pressure. In fact, you can assume some unexpected ingredients will usually find their way into most communicators' colloquial kitchen. You may be asked at the last minute to change your topic or address an urgent issue that's just come up. You might have to change locations, forgo the use of technology, or embrace an audience twice the size of what was initially anticipated. You could be asked to fill in for someone, substitute for a no-show, or improvise for an impromptu audience.

The key to success in such stressful moments is to be creative. While added pressure can often stifle your creativity and leave you longing to play it safe, finding a way to make the most of unexpected ingredients increases your skill and dexterity with language. In those moments when your communication opportunity goes wrong, changes, or evolves, trust that you can always rise to the occasion. You simply have to change your menu!

Just as the best cooks plan meals well ahead of time, they also grow accustomed to working with what they have when it comes to serving their meal. I love to cook and bake, and this is true from my experience. Not only do I find the process therapeutic, but I also love to eat delicious food! When the holidays roll around, especially Thanksgiving and Christmas, I will spend up to a full week before our family dinners preparing menus, gathering ingredients, and starting to cook items easily made ahead of time. I like to take my time and not feel rushed to ensure that every dish receives ample attention and execution. Over the years I've spent in the kitchen, I've learned that inevitably some dishes will not turn out as expected. Others will "accidentally" get eaten by my children or grandchildren before they reach the table. Accidents can happen, whether they involve spilling the gravy, dropping the casserole, or leaving the turkey within paws' reach of your pet pooch!

When these unplanned moments arrive, I have a choice about how I respond and move forward toward the meal I originally envisioned. I can allow my anger, disappointment, frustration, or fatigue to dampen my enthusiasm and derail our dinner. Or I can go with the flow, let go of my original vision for our meal in exchange for the one before me, and change the menu accordingly. This means I may substitute cherries for cranberries or thaw frozen vegetables in the microwave rather than use the fresh ones now spilled on the dining room floor. I may have to bake a pecan pie instead of the coconut cream I'd planned. The Christmas ham may have to be replaced by the beef tenderloin!

The best communicators learn to operate with similar receptivity, resilience, and resourcefulness. They accept the new constraints and operate within them. They use different recipes that utilize what's available rather than risk paralysis by fixating on the loss of their initial vision. You may always get nervous, feel disappointed, and freak out when things go sideways at the last minute before you're scheduled to communicate. Such reactions are only human. How you respond to them, however, is your choice!

Tilt Your Mirror

Sometimes you will experience heat from your mic because you need to convey a message you know your audience really doesn't want to hear. It may be relaying disappointing news, conceding the loss of an important client, or confronting issues that make most members of your audience uncomfortable. Communicating anything that can be construed as criticism is also challenging.

In such situations, the best communicators find ways to approach their audience and deliver their message as clearly, gently, and respectfully as possible. Sometimes this entails a direct approach that rips the Band-Aid off the audience's wound as quickly and efficiently as possible. Many times, however, ingenuity must be employed to make sure your message is received rather than eclipsed by the emotional reaction of its recipients.

I can think of no better example than a scene described in the Old Testament in which a reluctant prophet confronts a defensive monarch. In a classic case of the messenger fearing he will be punished—and in this case, likely killed—for his message, the prophet Nathan has to confront King David about his scandalous double secret, the king's affair with Bathsheba and the subsequent murder of her husband, Uriah the Hittite. Knowing the lengths David has gone to in order to hide his crimes and dull his conscience to avoid exposure, Nathan anticipates that a direct approach will not work. Not if he wants any chance not only at living but also having David repent, which is the reason God sent Nathan for the confrontation.

Out of either desperation or brilliance, Nathan chooses an unexpected approach. He knows that no one likes to have their secrets exposed or to be called out for sins they're still struggling to own, and surely David, as King of Israel, is no different. So Nathan comes up with a way into this delicate matter by finding another angle, one I call "tilting the mirror." He knows he cannot hold up a mirror straight-on and expose David's sins because David does not want to look. And as king, he doesn't want anyone to tell him what to do or judge his actions—not even a messenger sent by God. Therefore, instead of risking an ugly, failed confrontation, Nathan simply tells David a story:

> The LORD sent Nathan to David. When he came to him, he said, "There were two men in a certain town, one rich and the other poor. The rich man had a very large number of sheep and cattle, but the poor man had nothing except one little ewe lamb he had bought. He raised it, and it grew up with him and his children. It shared his food, drank from his cup and even slept in his arms. It was like a daughter to him.
>
> "Now a traveler came to the rich man, but the rich man refrained from taking one of his own sheep or cattle to prepare a meal for the traveler who had come to him. Instead,

> he took the ewe lamb that belonged to the poor man and prepared it for the one who had come to him."
>
> David burned with anger against the man and said to Nathan, "As surely as the LORD lives, the man who did this must die! He must pay for that lamb four times over, because he did such a thing and had no pity."
>
> Then Nathan said to David, "You are the man!" (2 Samuel 12:1–7 NIV)

Don't you love Nathan's brilliant strategy here? He has to feel stressed about delivering an impossible message to someone who has enough power to quiet the messenger permanently. But Nathan reports to God and has to comply with his assigned mission. Which leaves the prophet between a rock and a hard place, but not before he finds a solution by tilting the mirror he holds up to the king.

Because David can't handle hearing the unvarnished truth of his own crimes, Nathan shows him what they look like from a more objective perspective. The heinous injustice slaps the king in the face when he hears it described as a parable. The story leaves David outraged and burning with indignation that the powerful rich man should be so brazen in violation of not only

God's law but also the principles of human decency. How could someone so rich and powerful, who clearly had everything in the world, steal and kill the *only* thing belonging to the poor man?

David unknowingly judges himself and issues the severest penalty possible, death, while also paying fourfold restitution to the poor man he so egregiously offended. Only then, once the king has tightened the noose around his own neck, does Nathan reveal the shocking twist to the story! David has no defense, no excuse, and no recourse. The unfamiliar glimpse of himself in the tilted mirror of Nathan's parable catches David off guard. Then all at once, the king realizes he's staring at himself, convicted by his own response.

Nathan's example reminds us that even in seemingly impossible situations, we can still find a means to communicate the truth in a way that's undeniably received. We may not have as much at stake as the prophet and the king, but we may be able to bypass the defenses, excuses, and justifications of others all the same. In our world today, when so many divisions and differences can distance us, we must not give up on communicating truth even when it's painful to accept.

Speak Freely

Studying the way expert communicators like the prophet Nathan handle controversial issues and polarizing personalities often provides a master class in how to keep your cool when the mic gets hot. They find a way to moderate their emotions, focus on their purpose, create new approaches, and keep their connection to their audience intact. Their ability to communicate may be divinely inspired, but so can yours!

And heaven knows we need new voices willing to speak out and speak up right now. Presently, I believe we are at a juncture in our history with truly epic consequences. I'm not talking about the issues and idiosyncrasies on the surface of our world today but on the deep tectonic plates of troubled humanity shifting beneath our feet. People need hope that transcends the trauma surrounding them due to pandemics and partisan politics, natural disasters and unnatural crimes against one another. You don't have to know all the answers but merely be willing to ask the question. To have conversations in which you're as willing to listen as much as you're heard.

Today, thanks to technology, you have more opportunities to communicate and make a positive difference than ever before. You don't have to push your way to the podium or wait to be invited to the stage. With social media and the many facets of expression it provides, you have a mic within reach to address millions of people around the world. Many of the rules of rhetoric and talking points of tradition no longer apply and you can look countless others in the eye of your camera phone.

While you have a pantheon of polished communicators to draw on, ultimately you only need to communicate what you alone can speak into life. Just as each one of us has our own unique, God-given purpose, I believe we each also carry our own distinct dialect and discourse.

As I mentioned earlier, according to the Linguistic Society of America, nearly seven thousand languages are currently being spoken by the diverse peoples populating our world, with many times that number of different dialects in usage.[1] Some sociologists, anthropologists, and linguistic experts believe if taken to an extreme, each human being on the planet could be considered an originator of his or her own language dialect. Considering this perspective, I'm grateful we can understand one another at all!

Fortunately, we can resist the chaotic cacophony that erupted when our ancestors attempted to build the Tower of Babel, before the complex multiplicity of different tongues brought communication to a halt (Genesis 11:1–9). Instead we can use the structural and linguistic conventions shared by others speaking our languages to express ourselves and to understand one another. We can share the vivid texture of poetic imagery as well as the powerful persuasion of debate. Stories can be exchanged and common themes compared.

You and I can listen and reflect the messages we've received even as we transmit our own. Practicing the Golden Rule of treating others as we want to be treated, we can also listen to our neighbors as we ourselves want to be heard. Our shared language can be shaped to serve us with more precision, power, and purpose.

And while shared language is necessary for communication, this doesn't mean we conform to generic scripts and tired templates—in fact, just the opposite, as we've seen repeatedly throughout these pages. You have unlimited opportunities to collect your thoughts, clear your throat, and speak into the microphone you've been handed. Right now, diversity and originality are celebrated more than they were when I was growing up, which liberates you to say your piece within the prism of your personality, displaying all the shades of your colors shining through.

So as your voice reverberates across the space between your lips and your audience members' ears, speak freely. Don't try to be younger than you are or older than you are. Don't try to be white if you're black or black if you're white. Don't try to be who you think your audience wants you to be, needs you to be, or hopes you will be. If you can't be yourself, you will never successfully communicate the missional message unique to you, your life, and your experiences. Learn from those who have spoken, written, and recorded their messages before you. Use the linguistic legacy you've inherited to spread your wealth—of words, wisdom, and wonder—to others waiting to hear what you have to say.

Your mic is hot. But you're keeping your cool!

It's time to grow where your talent leads you.

And whatever you do, my friend, don't drop the mic!

PART 5

The Meal in the Message

As I shared with you at the beginning of this book, the prompting of Dr. Frank Thomas served as the catalyst for this book. The more he and I discussed its creation, the more I realized that maximum impact would be achieved with the rhetorical analysis only Frank could provide. If I considered my preaching to be like my grandmother's cooking without a recipe, then Dr. Thomas was determined not only to record my recipes but also to season them with his insight, acumen, and vast historical knowledge.

As we considered how this process would unfold, we both agreed that the cooking metaphor aptly parallels and expresses the different parts and processes of preaching. I've always loved to cook and have continued to try new dishes as well as traditional family recipes, particularly during the holidays. In recent years, I started curating my recipes by using online software that automatically sorts all dishes by *ingredients* as well as *directions*. This allows me the luxury of typing in a few main ingredients I have on hand to see what recipes come up or to input the amount of time available or apparatus required for preparation to see what's feasible.

This system makes great sense to me. When cooking, you must have both the ingredients and the directions in order to produce a finished dish to serve. You can't have one without the other. You may have a list of ingredients, but without knowing how much and in what order, assembly would be guesswork at best. Or if you had directions, no matter how explicit and detailed they may be, without ingredients, your dinner guests will go hungry!

These two categories, *ingredients* and *directions*, also reflect what Dr. Thomas and I bring to this book you're now reading. He's masterful at giving voice to the oral tradition of our ancestors and showing both the relevance and practical applications for his insights. Though he's primarily looking at examples and critical evaluations centered on African oral traditions and their evolution in African American preaching, the benefits transcend his specificity. Just as you don't have to be of Italian descent to enjoy Italian food, you don't have to be a black preacher to partake and enjoy the culturally seasoned directions shared by Dr. Thomas.

Similarly, the ingredients, flavors, textures, and tastes I've shared with you are diverse and flexible enough to apply to virtually all forms of oral, and sometimes written, communication. Dr. Thomas and I have borrowed from each other and discovered the intersectionality between academics and anointing, artistry and chemistry, throughout these pages. My preceding chapters have been directly and indirectly informed and influenced by his friendship, fellowship, and scholarship. I'm so grateful for everything he has contributed to help this book be the best it could be.

Now, in order to provide you with some of the same benefits of Dr. Thomas's expertise, at my request he has authored the following chapters, along with an example of his analytical methods applied to one of my sermons in the appendix, which I'm delighted to include. I know you will be intrigued, enlightened, and inspired by all he has to share! My hope is that our combined ingredients and directions will make you a better communicator regardless of your calling.

Bon appétit!

CHAPTER 13

The Recipe

By Dr. Frank Thomas

The recipe for creating flavorful communication requires following the directions—and knowing when not to!

—T. D. Jakes

Many people may not know that Bishop T. D. Jakes is a marvelous cook. On a major holiday recently, I received a picture of him situated behind an assortment of well-adorned cakes, pies, and desserts. "Did you bake all of these?" I asked.

"Sure, I cook every major holiday!" he replied. "Tomorrow, we're expecting thirty-five people." I was stunned and impressed by the cascading cakes, perfect pies, and decorous sweets that stood so prodigiously before him. My curiosity got the better of me, and I asked if he used recipes.

"I cook both with and without recipes—but always from scratch."

His comment struck me because we had been discussing the concept of recipe as a metaphor for the preaching method. Some sermons are from written recipes and others from the deep, mysterious, and spacious caverns of memory and experience. But whether from recipe or memory—or as is most often the case, some combination of both—all high-quality sermons are made from scratch.

The term *scratch* means that a cake or pie, for example, is made from basic, individual ingredients (flour, butter, sugar, etc.) at home rather than from the preassembled and prepackaged boxes or mixes bought in a store. When my family gathers for annual holiday meals, I usually tease several family members and affectionately jest that whatever they prepared was not made from scratch at home, but "store-bought." They sometimes claim that you can't tell the two apart, but I beg to differ.

The same is true of sermons. The best sermons are always homemade, original creations, not mixed and stirred from preassembled and prepackaged ingredients, such as someone else's sermon from the Internet or a chapter from another author's book. Because of this distinction, the use of recipes makes a wonderful metaphor for the analysis of the preaching method.

Grandma's Recipes

The idea of recipe as preaching metaphor emerged from a conversation Bishop and I had about the possibility of trying to understand his system from an academic perspective. He said that approaching his preaching this way was like "asking your grandmother to create a recipe."

If you're near your grandma, you can watch her cook and study how she creates luscious food and delectable desserts. You get the opportunity to talk to Grandma about her cooking and ask her questions. You notice that Grandma does not use written recipes and normal measuring cups and such; it is a pinch of this and a dash of that or a big cup of this and a little spoon of that. Grandma does not need a written recipe because she is remembering, enacting, and replicating the family rituals she learned by watching her mother, grandmother, and grandfather.

Grandma does not create dishes and desserts strictly from her own imagination. The recipes have been passed down in the family tradition, which she carries on while adding her own touch of flair and originality. If you ask her how many tablespoons or other measurements to use in a specific dish, she may tell you, "Just use half a stick of butter, or a little spoon of vanilla extract." And after all the conversation, Grandma lets you stir the batter and then lick the bowl—which is almost better than the dessert itself!

But what if you're not near Grandma? If you can't observe her and learn hands-on, you need some kind of recipe that lists ingredients and instructs you on their assembly, preparation, and cooking. Now, this is not to suggest that because the recipe is not written down, there is not an intentional and intricate system of culinary art in Grandma's head and heart as she cooks and bakes. Similarly, you could not say that the preaching of Bishop Jakes, or any gifted preacher for that matter, lacks a planned and elaborate preaching method and system just because it is not written down. The evidence of Grandma's culinary system is not whether it is written down, but in the taste and consistency of her cooking.

The very same is true with preaching. The intricacy of a manner of preaching is not exclusively bound up in explanations and definitions, but in taste, efficacy, and the transformative power of the sermon to touch and move the human heart. The best preachers in the heavily oral tradition of African American preaching know how to allow God to use them to touch the hearts and lives of those in attendance. Often, these divine messengers simply have not written down the recipe for others to follow. They are so busy cooking up great sermons that they may not take time to write the recipe down. It is for those of us who are scribes, those who seek to archive and write the tradition down, to ask questions, record, and translate the creation of the cake or pie into a recipe for succeeding generations.

This is why Bishop graciously asked me to assist in this endeavor. If we inherit, imitate, and mimic Grandma, we do not necessarily need a recipe, because we have her presence, example, demonstration, and conversation ever before us. But what happens to those who do not get the opportunity to be close to her? Or what if she dies and nothing is written down? In most cases, the farther away you get from Grandma generationally, the more you need the recipe. Someone in the family needs to ensure that the recipe gets written down. That is my goal in the following chapters.

Made from Scratch

Bishop puts together sermons in forms and shapes based on remembering, enacting, and reproducing the tradition his ancestors passed down while adding his own personality, gifts, and originality. Bishop is not producing sermons that come out of nothing and nowhere. The raw material and substance have been passed down in the tradition (Christian and African American) that he masterfully shapes and molds with his own creativity and gifts.

It is important to remember this: *No cook or preacher is greater than the tradition from which they were birthed.* The tradition came before us and will carry on after us. The tradition inspires us and envelops us. We make our contribution to the tradition, birth the next generation of the tradition, and release them to make their contribution such that the tradition and those who have gone before live on.

Just as Grandma's cooking is imitated, the best preachers are imitated. The best exemplars of a preaching tradition are celebrated and held up and broadly emulated, and if a recipe is not produced, then all that preachers are securing and are left with is a pinch of this and a dash of that. And then one day the celebrated preacher dies, and if we are not careful, the recipe goes to the grave with the preacher.

Sadly, we have a long history of many geniuses of the African American preaching tradition going to the grave with nothing written down. Families have boxes of sermons or tapes in church basements or children's and grandchildren's homes, and now, even though there are video and digital formats, there is no recipe left behind. We are left with a pinch of this and a dash of that. Many great preachers have, as the old folks say, "slipped away from us," before we could get the recipe.

During the age of the phonograph and before the age of video and YouTube, the Reverend Jesse Louis Jackson said that the most imitated preacher in the history of the African American preaching tradition was the Rev. C. L. Franklin, the father of Aretha Franklin.[1] Franklin died more than twenty-five years ago, and yet far too few resources share his recipe. I hope to prevent such a loss by my endeavors here. Undeniably, one of the most nationally and globally imitated preachers in the digital age is Bishop T. D. Jakes, and my contribution to each part of this book is intended to help others make their best homiletical cakes, pies, and desserts.

The Cultural Context of Recipes

Recipes emerge from a heritage and the indigenous customs of a group of people who—based upon their culture, context, and beliefs—marshal their knowledge into preparation of distinct foods and unique dishes. When Grandma is cooking, she brings her particular people, culture, context, belief, and region with her. Grandma's food is based in a cultural history, memory, heritage, and experience—the story of a people. Far too often, ethnic food is eaten, but not enough attention is paid to the story, one might even say the backstory, that is behind the food. Behind every bite of the food is context, folklore, history—the story and experience of a people.

Far too often we may culturally appropriate the food of a people without regard to their story and context; similarly, we may culturally and spiritually appropriate the preaching of Bishop Jakes but fail to grasp his culture, context, region, and belief. The preacher does not emerge out of nothing and nowhere. Borrowing from preaching professor Andre Resner:

> Every preacher has a constellation of cultural, family of origin, and ecclesiastical

> systems that raise and develop the preacher from the earliest stages of life. Such systems include categories of gender, ethnicity, social and economic locations of neighborhood and class, as well as conditions of physical and mental health. Most preachers are heavily influenced by these systems as they... shape their theology and the sermon that flows out of that theology.[2]

The recipe and sermonic food of Bishop Jakes comes directly out of the African American preaching context and tradition. We cannot develop a recipe for his preaching and not account for the culture, context, region, and belief from which he springs forth. We must give some consideration to the African American culture and tradition that gives rise to his preaching, which has touched the world. So let's begin with a brief summary of what the great Zora Neale Hurston terms "characteristics of Negro expression" to describe the history, tradition, and context of Jakes's preaching.

Zora Neale Hurston (1901–1960) was a civil rights activist, folklorist, novelist, anthropologist, ethnographer, and "Genius of the South." She was one of the important figures of the Harlem Renaissance of the 1920s and 1930s before writing her most critically acclaimed book, *Their Eyes Were Watching God.* Based upon extensive anthropological research and compilations of Southern American black oral traditions, she became a critical interpreter of black culture and ways of black people in America.[3]

Hurston was criticized for foregrounding the beautiful, deeply moving, and poetic language of often unlettered African American preachers in the South. She chronicled and recorded the pure genius of the sermons, emphasizing their literary and rhetorical devices and oratorical dexterity. The main character of her first novel, *Jonah's Vine Gourd*, published in 1934, is a preacher so it's not surprising that her original dedication pays tribute: "To the first and only real Negro poets in America—the preachers who bring barbaric splendor of word and song in the very camp of the mockers."[4]

In response to her critics, Hurston explained that black people in America, deriving from a cultural history originating in West Africa, have a legacy of an oral tradition, that is, the spoken word and oral transmission of tales, folklore, story, music, dance, proverbs, beliefs, and sermons. This oral transmission differs from the cultural history of the Western world, which is principally preserved and transmitted based upon the written word.[5]

In *The Sanctified Church*, Hurston skillfully articulates a theory of black narration, inclusive of all oral telling, including folklore, slave narratives, street slang, "the dozens," and especially black preaching, and identifies components of this artistry by setting forth what she calls "characteristics of Negro expression." The essays in *The Sanctified Church* explore the signs that produce meaning in black churches through worship and preaching when understood from the perspective of cultural performance.

She lists these characteristics as drama, angularity, asymmetry, originality, and the will to adorn. With our focus in mind, I have adapted three of her most relevant characteristics to preaching: drama; the will to adorn; and the overarching characteristic that permeates African American communication, folklore, and the art of storytelling.

Drama

Hurston suggests that a vital sense of "drama" permeates the whole of the Negro self, that is, expressions of meaning rich in metaphor and simile are constantly duplicated in intricate and repeated interaction rituals in the course of everyday living. Every phase of Negro life is acted out and highly dramatized based in these rituals of cultural performance. It displays itself in rituals of intense social interactions that might occur among black people everywhere. For example, the kind of posing and posturing between a young female and male as they assess one another.

One of the largest and most important venues for dramatic social ritual and interaction for the masses of black people has traditionally been the black church. In particular, and for our purposes, the worship, and especially the preaching, is a dramatic social interaction and cultural performance. These are dramatic performances and ritual embellishments of social interaction between God, people, and preacher. The preacher contributes to the drama, in respect to the preaching, by freedom of body expression, movement, emotion, tone and volume of voice, hand gestures, facial expressions, humor, call and response, and silence.

The preaching moment *is* dramatic cultural performance.

The Will to Adorn

According to Hurston, this desire for beauty, at its core, arises out of the same impulse in every person, for example, to wear jewelry, shape a sculpture, or decorate a house—the human urge, in even the most degrading and demeaning circumstances and treatment, to create and express beauty. Hurston commented that the walls of the home of the average Negro were adorned, even to the extent to sometimes be gaudy—the equivalent of the over-the-top decoration. This desire expresses the fact that in Negro life there is the will to adorn and create beauty, and according to Hurston for black people, given the most degrading circumstances, "there can never be enough of beauty, let alone too much."[6]

We find this same desire in the sermons of black preachers. They decorate, adorn, and embroider words and narration with the figurative language of metaphor and simile with the intent to satisfy "the desire for beauty" in the congregation's and preacher's soul. Bishop Jakes has said that the preacher must have enough substance to justify their style, not merely imitating others but adding their own descriptive, decorative flair.

The preacher—in language dripping with picturesque imagery, poetry, hyperbole, and alliteration, all based in the five senses of the audience—creates beauty for themselves and their audience. The sermon is adorned to create beauty in the human soul.

Without question, the African American preacher is a master of adornment.

Folklore and Storytelling

This final characteristic of Negro expression is not listed in *The Sanctified Church*, but Hurston talks about it often and practices it in her entire body of research, writing, and work—folklore and storytelling. Storytelling is the overarching method of Negro expression and black preaching; it is the envelope in which most communication in the African American community is mailed.

Storytelling is the ability to take abstract truth and place it in images of everyday life. Storytelling is the container by which truth is delivered into the hearts, homes, and community of African American people, and it is especially evident in preaching. Truth is most often not told in textual language, but in picture and story. Black preachers learn quickly that we usually take in more by experiencing truth in narrative form than conceptual, expositional delivery.

Bishop pointed out that Jesus was a storyteller and the parables are Jesus simply telling stories. In the twenty-first century, Jesus would have made movies.

Jesus would have made movies because he told stories that produced truth.

Pain into Power

Cultural context and the characteristics of Negro expression most definitely inform the recipe of Bishop Jakes's preaching. His sermon creation and delivery result from the African American preaching tradition involving cultural performance and memory, rituals of metaphor and simile, drama, the will to adorn, and storytelling and folklore. Bishop told me that he considers himself a storyteller from the lineage of storytellers of African descent.

Bishop Jakes told his family that he would be talking to a scribe about his preaching, and the question arose, "What is black preaching?" Was it the style, or the preacher himself? The race of the preacher? The demographics of the congregation? Or something else completely? I suggested to Bishop Jakes my adaptation of a definition:

> Black preaching has (1) origins in an oral tradition of transmission of tales, folklore, story, proverbs, beliefs, holy words, sermons,

> prayers, and the like; (2) the experience of slavery, racism, hatred, lynching, Jim Crow, mass incarceration, voter suppression, and the like; and (3) the message of hope, initially expressed in the folklore of High John de Conqueror and the like, and subsequently in the Christian gospel of Jesus Christ.

Some identify this hope, born out of the African American experience, in culture, music, and religious life and preaching, as "soul."

Bishop Jakes clarifies the term *soul* by suggesting that African Americans have mastered the art of turning pain into power. Black preaching is the ability of the preacher to make sense out of the nonsensical history black people have endured and to demystify the pain in such a way that suffering makes sense in the creative moment of preaching. Black preaching takes groaning, moaning, disorientation, doubt, fear, and the nonsense of life and provides order and structure to the pain such that a person can find hope, victory, and vindication. Bishop speaks to this transformative power in black preaching and regards it as the gift of black folk to the world:

> We do not want the people to feel our pain when we are preaching. We want to take

> our pain and combust it into that message in such a way that it become the engine that drives the intensity and the urgency [of healing], and we as [an African American] people have given that as a gift to the world. That is not to say that white people, brown people, or any other people could not do it, but based in the history of African roots and our journey in America, it is our gift to church, culture, and world.

Black preaching is, then, not exclusively about the emotions of style, whooping, changing keys, or exaggerated and stylized emotional performance. At its core, it is the art of turning despair into hope. Black preaching is a cultural performance filled with metaphor and simile, including drama, the will to adorn, and storytelling to turn pain into purpose. Black people had to learn to turn ashes into beauty, mourning into joy, because there was no choice if black people were to survive. Black people brought suffering to the biblical text and found a response. As Bishop Jakes explained:

> When you look at a people who have literally been beaten and a God who has been

> laid on a whipping post, when you look at a people who have been unjustly arrested and you look at a Jesus that they found no fault in, and yet crucified—he is kin to my history. He fits well at the family table. This notion of a suffering savior fits well with a suffering people of any group of people, a suffering woman, a suffering gender, a suffering generation. The suffering savior reflects us in such a way that we can be kin to him though he's two thousand years away. We are kin to the story. And to hear that he is hidden and then risen gives me hope that, if I can withstand the turbulence of Friday, Sunday's coming.... The fact that he would rise again is not strange to me because every day I have to have a resurrection, because every night before it I had a crucifixion.... I identify with the Christ story, with the Bible story. I find my face in its pages.

Bishop Jakes told an audience in South Africa that they had come through apartheid, and he, as an African American, had come through slavery, "and I will meet you at the cross." The ability to be broken and shattered and turn that into something that's usable to catapult a person forward, that is black preaching. And then any preacher, regardless of race, color, and creed, can take black preaching and emulate it if they have cried enough, suffered long enough, and done without long enough, that is, if their suffering has reached their soul, and they desire hope. This is the gift of black preaching to the world.

The recipe is called black preaching. It is a particular kind of spiritual food rising from the culture, context, region, and belief of African American people. To describe it as black preaching is not to belittle the preaching or delimit it, but to celebrate the context of its origins and remember those who forged it in the most degrading circumstance and situation. To miss, ignore, dismiss, or disregard the cultural heritage and context of black culture is to miss the major vitality and force of the recipe and settle for a pinch of this and a dash of that. I offer the words of Bishop Jakes:

> What makes us unique is that we have hung so long from the cross that we have become masterful at getting beauty out of agony. In the absence of generational wealth, strategic cultural advantage, in the absence of the things of this world, we have instead been awarded with a glory that is unique to

anybody that has been denied. Wherever I have ever been where there were people of color, there were always great churches—in the deepest parts of Africa where there is no running water and they have no building, with fabric flapping in the wind up under sticks, thousands and thousands, sometimes a million people will be gathered together to worship God in some way or form or other. And whether you go to the Caribbean, to the Aborigines, throughout America, or East Africa, West Africa, or South Africa it doesn't matter. There is something that we have mastered about church because it has become the substratum of the fact that we are not forgotten; that redemption is nigh; that we can escape; that we can endure; that we can go forward. And in some way or another like Noah, who preached the same message for one hundred and twenty years, some way or another every Sunday we preach the same message. The title changes, the Scripture changes, but the story is still the same and every Sunday morning you find a different way to say the same thing: "And still I rise."

The best of the African American preaching tradition offers hope to a forgotten, silenced, and in many ways mistreated, yet courageous, creative, and triumphant people. Black preaching has sustained African American people for four hundred years in this beautiful place of diaspora.

Lord willing, it will continue for many centuries more.

Enhancing Your Own Recipe

Ultimately, our goal in this book is to pass the torch and help you improve as a communicator and, for many readers, as a preacher. Whatever your intention for effective communication, we have offered Bishop Jakes's recipe in the hopes it will help you discover and enhance your own. We believe that the discovery and enhancement of your recipe will make you more compelling in your delivery of the message and facilitate "winning moments" for you and your audience. With this goal in mind, here are four suggestions for discovering and enhancing your awareness of your recipe and how you follow it.

First, become a student of communication and

connect it to the preaching gifts and strengths in your own culture and ancestry. No preacher emerges out of nothing and nowhere. Every preacher comes out of a tradition, and every tradition has gifts. In far too many cases, preachers are ignorant of the tradition from which they were fashioned. Being in touch with your tradition allows you to name, own, and utilize the indigenous story of your ancestors as fuel that brings the two-thousand-year-old biblical story to life in the twenty-first-century speaking moment. This familiarity changes the understanding of tenor and tone of your preaching life. The preacher more easily sees their own story in the biblical story, and that causes the preacher to be more fully invested in the biblical narrative and offer contemporary translation in a fresh and unusual way.

Second, become a student of preaching and connect with and have more awareness of the genius in other preaching traditions outside of your own. I've barely scratched the proverbial surface here of the genius of African American preaching. Look for similar explanations of other preaching traditions. This might involve building your reading, listening, and viewing libraries of preaching in other cultures. Be a sponge, ask questions, make visits, build relationships, take classes, go to school, or enroll in continuing education offerings in preaching with preachers of another tradition. Preachers who want to improve their preaching seek out and are in conversation with high-quality preachers of every culture and tradition.

Third, you must find and articulate the sources of hope in your own soul. A teacher cannot teach something he has not learned. A leader cannot convincingly communicate something she fails to practice. A preacher cannot give the people a hope that the preacher does not have. Virtually every person, as part of the human condition, has groaned and struggled in the night with pain, doubt, fear, and disappointment.

The preacher who would improve their preaching must have experienced this groaning and, as the Bible says in 2 Corinthians 1:4, offer people the comfort that they themselves have received. While many prove their fidelity to biblical principles by cogent and insightful explanation, the best preachers demonstrate an ability to emote from a deeper place what they are explaining as well. Most people come to church not just for explanation, but explanation grounded in hope and inspiration. To be able to improve one's preaching, one must be able to fundamentally answer this question off and on the stage, behind or away from the pulpit: What is the ground of my hope?

Finally, remember that the best recipes carefully

blend substance and style to create a unique communication that educates and inspires and teaches and encourages. Total intellectual substance and analysis alone is too technical to deliver the spirit behind the narrative. Consequently, the audience is informed, but not inspired. Flamboyant style without substance, however, may titillate the senses, but it leaves the intellect famished. Much like the blending of butter and sugar with eggs and flour that makes a cake delicious, the blending of substance and style yields the reception of information and inspiration.

As you ponder how the recipe for the preaching of Bishop Jakes can help you be a better communicator, start by considering all you have inherited by those before you. How much of yourself will you bring to their blend to create winning moments in your delivery? How will you take the recipes you have inherited and sustain the legacy of others even as you make yours uniquely your own? Before finalizing your answers, reflect upon all that Bishop Jakes has shared in the previous chapters about his own secret ingredients!

CHAPTER 14

The Ingredients

By Dr. Frank Thomas

Ingredients for a good sermon come from what the recipe requires as well as what you decide to add or subtract.

—T. D. Jakes

Recently, my marvelous wife of more than forty years announced we were moving to a "plant-based diet" to improve our health. She's always been an advocate for nutrition and exercise so I wasn't surprised. This time, however, I learned our new diet focused only on vegetables, whole grains, nuts, seeds, and legumes—in other words, no animal products. Meat, bone, milk, eggs, or anything derived from those items, such as butter or gelatin, did not make the cut. As much as I appreciate her efforts and culinary expertise, I silenced my reluctance to give up my favorite cuts of steak, not to mention milkshakes, omelets, and butter on my bread.

One of the first meals she prepared after making the plant-based transition made me forget what I was missing. Veggie fajitas with salsa and avocado, all from scratch, featured fresh Portobello mushrooms, red and green bell peppers, red onion, garlic cloves, and fresh ginger. For spices, the recipe called for cumin, Liquid Aminos, pure maple syrup, lime juice, cilantro, and black pepper. The dish was delicious, and when I complimented her cooking, she told me that freshness made all the difference in the quality of ingredients and, therefore, the end result.

Her comment stirred my curiosity.

As I was looking over the list of ingredients, my mind wandered to my writing of the recipe of Bishop Jakes's preaching. If the best recipes had fresh ingredients, what would be the fresh ingredients that would make for the best preaching? Just as the cook has to mix the fresh ingredients to prepare the dish, the preacher has to mix the fresh ingredients of sermon preparation to prepare the sermon. Let's consider what it means to select ingredients—some from the legacy of recipes one receives and others from new gardens—in order to cook up the best sermons possible.

Inherit and Innovate

I unapologetically believe that preachers create out of preexistent spiritual matter and substance. Sermons are developed out of the raw materials or the ingredients of a tradition. In rhetorical terms, tradition is embedded in the audience's collective memory, a set of experiences, beliefs, and assumptions rooted in audience remembrance. These are the ingredients and raw materials from which the orator/preacher is free to develop the sermon. The audience both frees and/or constrains the preacher in the preacher's practice of the tradition.

In the broadest sense, the tradition is a meaningful part of the history of the community and affords the community opportunities to perform new versions of itself without losing a sense of identity."[1] Moral values of a community, such as God, freedom, justice, or love, are never absolute and unalterable, but are debated in every generation, and these values ultimately function to sustain the identity of the community. In order to meet the evolving needs of the community, religious and political oratory functions to reframe and rearticulate community values. Oratory is both freed and constrained by communal collective memory. The tradition needs new expressions of itself to continue into the future, but there are limits to what can be promoted or offered by orators. The preacher receives the tradition and adds their own expression of uniqueness, personality, and gifts. The community accepts, rejects, or incorporates the new version of the tradition based upon the preacher's ability to persuade the community to expand its identity. Just as a speaker's energy level often reflects as well as determines his audience's response, a preacher's use of both inherited as well as innovated ingredients shapes his identity as well as the community he speaks to, speaks from, and speaks for. This symbiotic relationship means that the stories told flow in both directions, which means that preachers must know the legacy of storytelling as well as refresh and revise and reinvent those stories.

How does this process work? Let's take a look.

The Stories We Tell

I'm convinced that storytelling remains at the heart of black preaching. It is one of the primary forms in which the tradition is embedded in the audience.

Bishop Jakes talks about his mother as a major bearer and transporter of the tradition, a channel of the voice of collective memory and identity of the community that was passed to him.

I recall discussing with Bishop his mother's role in helping him adjust to his increased platform and popularity. He relates that he was just being himself and woke up one day, and the world was taking pictures of him, wanting to cast him in movies, and some saying that they had never heard anything like his preaching. He said it was confusing, scary, horrifying, and intimidating—and all at the same time. In response to all the notoriety, he consistently said, "I've always been like this." He had not changed; he had always been a storyteller. He then recounts the story of how, when he was a little boy, his mother dressed the children up and they had to do talent shows. His mother imparted the form and substance of the tradition through setting the example for the talent show by storytelling like this:

> One day I was sitting out there on the front porch watching, and I watched Mr. Richardson move up and park his car behind Miss Anna May's house. I don't think they meant for me to see it, but I declare I did. I couldn't wait for Willie Joe to get home so I could tell

> him what I saw. But he was so tired when he got home, all he wanted was a dinner, a little corn bread and buttermilk, and he went on to bed. But not me. Every now and then, in the middle of the night, I would peek out the window and see what was going on at that house. About 4:00 in the morning, I heard the sound of gravel because he had started that truck and eased out from that yard. And didn't even turn the ignition. He got to the corner, but I heard it. I don't know why it was I felt led to get up at 6:00 a.m. and take some tea cakes down to her house, but I did.

Jakes says that his mother would tell stories like this, and then they would take turns telling stories, writing scripts, and coming up with ideas in their heads. They did so much of this growing up that Jakes says he can do it now at will. When he is composing a sermon, he is right there on his mother's porch telling stories, writing scripts, and coming up with ideas in his head. The tradition was passed to him by his mother and the community. Jakes says:

> I've never been to school for it [storytelling], but I'm right there on that porch and I can

> see the red clay of Alabama. I can smell the air and the smell of cows. The sweet smell of cows off in the distance, mixed with the husk from the corn that's growing behind my grandmother's house. I can see it so clearly, as clear as the gravel being moved by the tires before you start the ignition because you don't want anybody to wake up in the middle of the night.

Bishop's mother gave him an amazing gift. She was the bearer of this rich tradition into his life. Not everyone receives this level of imagination, creativity, and storytelling passed to them in such a magnificent form. The tradition was thoroughly embedded in him, and as a result, his storytelling in preaching was unconscious, natural, rooted, practiced, and refined; it needed and sought no explanation until there was a desire to pass the recipe on to the next generation.

The Bible and Hope

Bishop grew up in the Baptist church on his mother's side and was "deeply Baptist," he says, emphasizing it with the bass tone shift in voice. He entered the Pentecostal church at age fifteen, and his father died when Bishop was sixteen. As his father exited, a void was created and a search initiated for an awareness of a father bigger than what religion itself could afford. Bishop was looking for something more to God than what he had found in the tradition of the Baptist church. For Bishop, at the age of sixteen, the Bible became very meaningful:

> When I was around sixteen years old, suddenly I could not put my Bible down. I hid my Bible in my science book at school and was reading my Bible while I was supposed to be reading my science book. I could not put it down. It made sense to me. My father had died the year before and I opened this book and it talked to me. It talked to me in the most amazing way and I could understand it.... And I liked it. And it liked me and there was something between me and it that was like a nut coming out of a shell.

Most of the Baptist churches in Charleston [West Virginia] were large and beautiful, and in comparison, Pentecostal churches were small and dank. Initially, his mother thought Pentecostal churches were beneath him, saying, "You going over there to that sanctified church?" The Pentecostal emphasis, though sometimes a bit extreme, was to study the Bible and practice the presence of the Holy Spirit. These appealed to Bishop Jakes's search for a bigger God. He says:

> The emphasis was on the Scriptures. The old men (bearers of the tradition) who taught me were not famous, were not well known, and were not renowned. I'm always intimidated when people ask me who influenced you because I want to give them these big names that they're expecting, but the people who influenced me were never seeking popularity. It's not just that they didn't have it. They didn't seek it. What I love about it is, it's shaped my priorities. I didn't have huge icons and one day I'm going to get to preach at such and such a place. No, no, it wasn't like that. It wasn't quantity, it was quality. It wasn't width, it was depth. It was being able to get the power of the Holy Spirit's expression to come out of your mouth.

Along with his mother, the aforementioned old men imparted, as part of the tradition, the meaning of the Holy Spirit and the Bible to Jakes.

Along with the Baptist roots and fervor and fire for the Bible and the Holy Spirit, I felt led to ask Bishop this question: What is the ground of your hope? With level gaze, simplicity, depth, and calm honesty, he said, "On a personal level, I know God is with me." He then offered this reflection:

> Kari Jobe wrote the song "You Are for Me," and the first time I heard it, I started crying and I couldn't quit.[2] Because all of my life I knew that God was for me, I never could understand why. I disappointed God at every turn. But from that little boy screaming at the top of the steps at the very top of his lungs with my father breaking up everything downstairs with an ax and my mother screaming her head off, God has always proven that God was for me.

Based upon God being for him, Jakes admittedly is an optimist by nature. He believes that any human being can get up if they fight hard and long enough because God is with them. Jakes shares, "I know what it is to have nothing but hope. Sometimes when I was losing my job and had no money, hope was the only thing in our refrigerator! I would go gather fallen apples, which were free, to feed my family. My story epitomizes hope. Hope in the amazing, bodacious soul-invading grace of God." The heart of his message to people is that God is for them and they can make it and can get back up. Bishop sums up his hope and ministry with this poignant story from his childhood:

> I'm coming around the road from passing papers, a mountain road in Charleston, West Virginia, and all these puppies were trying to nurse. They were newborn puppies and the German shepherd mother was dead. And they were trying to nurse at the breast of a dead mother. I put all the puppies in a box and I brought them home. I guess I'm about 7 or 8 years old. I decided I was going to make them live. So, I poured out Momma's Palmolive dishwashing liquid and put some warm milk in the bottle and a little bit of oatmeal and—I don't know why [laughter]—don't ask me why, but that seemed like it would be good. And I put it in there and warmed it up a little bit and I nursed the puppies. Well, two things I learned that is if the right person picks you up and they fight hard enough, they make you live, because the puppies all

lived. I didn't lose any of them. And I learned that oatmeal gives puppies diarrhea. Really bad diarrhea. I think I'm still that little boy gathering up puppies. At my core I still am that guy who will pick you up where you're at and feed you whatever I got to get you up on your feet so you can fulfill your destiny. And that's my blessed hope.

Align Your Assets

As the parts and pieces fall into place, a preacher creates a sermon similar to the way a composer creates a song. The comparison is apt because there is indeed a kind of music to preaching. There is a melody to the sermon that has moments of crescendos and moments of silence, a kind of symphony that has a vocal typography that goes up and down to maintain the interest of the listener. There are some who have a profound intellect but whose delivery is in a monotone. They seemingly have little ability to orchestrate the intellectual content in such a way that it connects with the audience. They miss the fact that oration is musical regardless of the intellectual content one delivers. Many orators make the mistake of paying exclusive attention to intellectual content and giving little attention to the music of delivery.

In conjunction with the voice, the body is also an instrument. Bishop acknowledges that he is an animated person. His hands are in the message. His walk, his stomp, and even his stance are in the message. He tells the story of a friend in Caracas, Venezuela, who would watch him preach and touch the screen and cry. He didn't know what Bishop was saying because he spoke Spanish and Bishop speaks English. He invited Bishop to Caracas based upon how his spirit felt hearing the sound of Bishop's voice and looking at the stance of his posture. He received the message that he could not obtain through speech and auditory channels. Bishop used the story to make the point that communication reaches people on different levels.

Communication is much more than the words that we speak. In our roles as preachers, when we mount the pulpit or stage, everything about us communicates. The question is, are the body, voice, and mouth harmonious and communicating the same message? Bishop encourages preachers to look at how much communication goes beyond the mouth and wrestle with this question: Is my mouth out-talking the rest of me? If the preacher has the confidence in God so as not to be so worried about personal inhibitions, they might be willing to sacrifice their self-image such that God can use everything, the total person of the preacher, to communicate the message.

Bishop suggests that this does not mean that the preacher should not be authentic to who the preacher is. Bishop realizes that his broad breadth of communication is a Pentecostal idea. Pentecostals tend to utilize the whole person in their preaching and communication. Bishop says he uses his size as an asset, but even if a person is small, that can be an asset because there are some things that a small person can do that big people cannot do. Bishop speaks to seeing one's own person and gifts as an asset:

> If you see it as an attribute and not a liability, anything is an asset...anything is a tool. I've seen preachers preach with no arms at all. And they used it as an asset and not a liability. [The preacher says:] "You know one day my arms will be back....I can't shake your hand right now, but one day..." That's what I mean about having confidence enough to walk up on the stage and be certain enough to use everything as an attribute to deliver, including stance, pitch, and demeanor. All of these abstract individual nuances collectively create

> a brand called you. And being true to that brand makes you legitimate and authentic.

Bishop Jakes is a master at call and response, the audible dialogue between a preacher and the audience. Bishop never wants to create an atmosphere where people come and watch because, as he says, "This place we're trying to go is so sacred that I can't get there without them." He invites listeners by his voice and body into the moment of God's presence that can only happen if they build and enjoy it together. As a result, preaching is a sacred dialogue between the preacher and the audience.

Like an experienced doctor diagnosing a patient, when the preacher says something that the people feel, but do not have words for, the audience will respond and endorse what was said. When the preacher hits the spot, the audience will let the preacher know. This helps the preacher know to help. The preacher is trying to help the people, and people supply the necessary information for the preacher to help.

The Closer

In every preaching/oratorical tradition, there is a focus on the close of the sermon. The closing expressions as summary and closure are critical to the remembrance and living out of the message. I have yet to encounter a tradition with as much emphasis and pressure on the close of the sermon as in the African American preaching tradition.

In much of the African American tradition, there is an emphasis and expectation of celebration, which often looks like seeking to leave people standing and "shouting" as principally the singularly and most effective close. This is considered evidence of the Holy Spirit, and many preachers will tear up a wonderful sermon trying to have this specific kind of close.

Although known for dynamic and soul-stirring closes to the sermon, Bishop advocates that no one style of close is appropriate for every sermon. He says that people do not shout and celebrate through correction or coercion. In other words, there are many kinds of sermons and closes, and the preacher must strive, without inhibition, to deliver the close that is natural and organic to the specific kind of sermon that the preacher is preaching. Bishop advises to stay true to the sermon just preached rather than veering dramatically or shifting tone or style suddenly at the end. He encourages us to find a cohesive way to end the delivery so that people know where they are and how they've been changed by what they just heard and experienced.

If cooks believe that "the proof is in the pudding," then preachers like Bishop Jakes know that quality ingredients, both inherited and invented, are essential for success!

CHAPTER 15

The Taste

By Dr. Frank Thomas

The taste of a sizzling sermon satisfies the soul like nothing else!

—T. D. Jakes

When you take the first bite of a scrumptious meal or a rich, decadent dessert, you savor the experience slowly and deliberately. You allow the blended flavors to emerge even as you experience and identify each separate ingredient's unique contribution to the finished dish. Whether sweet or savory, spicy or barely seasoned, the bite of food lifted by your fork and landing in your mouth deserves culinary appreciation as well as pleasurable consumption. You allow the taste to linger on your palate as the flavors fade and you begin to anticipate the next bite.

As your meal progresses, you not only enjoy the distinct taste of all the diverse flavors involved in your food's preparation, but you relish the overall flavor of how they come together for a more singular, comprehensive effect. Your taste buds notice each bite while your mind and body record the overall sensory impressions accompanying your dining experience. Taste and flavor work in tandem to tantalize your mouth even as digestion immediately commences to signal your sublime satisfaction.

Communication, particularly with sermons served from the expertise of preachers such as Bishop Jakes, often provide the same flavors, textures, and satisfaction as a delicious home-cooked meal. If the proof is in the pudding, as the old saying goes, then the test of taste determines your assessment. Similarly, the flavor of your experience while receiving a scintillating sermon determines the taste that lingers as you leave the church service and go on with your life. Like the memory of an exceptional feast, however, you are forever changed by the taste you enjoyed and the spiritual food nourishing your soul.

Spiritual Seasoning

The classic definition of rhetoric, derived from Aristotle, is defined as "the ability to discover the available means of persuasion." The ancient Greeks were critically concerned with language and spoken word because, in a democracy that demanded participation and that citizens speak to make a claim for their interests, persuasion was a critical skill. The political skill of the age was the ability to speak effectively for one's interests. Therefore, rhetoric was established as the means to teach rules of argument and persuasion.

Within the field of rhetorical studies, rhetorical criticism is the study of the various persuasive options available to speakers in the creation of speech texts (for our purposes, sermons) and how those options work together to create effects in the preacher and the audience. Rhetorical criticism allows us to see with greater clarity the persuasive choices the preacher made, and potentially other choices that were *not* selected, all in the effort to ascertain how the speaker is attempting to persuade the audience. In other words, you can compare the recipe used, the ingredients included, and the process of cooking with the flavors and tastes of the sermon.

In Chapter 13, "The Recipe," you may recall my assertion that the intricacy of a homiletical system is not exclusively bound up in explanations and definitions, but in the "taste," efficacy, and transformative power of the sermon to touch and move the human heart. Much of the efficacy and transformative power of a sermon is the domain of the Holy Spirit; therefore, it is the work of the Holy Spirit that I am defining as the "taste" of the sermon in the mouth, heart, and soul of the hearers.

While taste is primarily the work of the Holy Spirit, the preacher plays a significant role by what the preacher gives the Spirit of God and the audience to work with. The sermon is not just a compilation of spoken words, sentences, and paragraphs, but rather an organized system of ideas, images, and rhetorical arguments intentionally designed by the preacher to persuade the audience and assist the Holy Spirit in creating the taste of God in the mouths, hearts, and souls of the audience. Therefore, a sermon has a rhetorical topography, a kind of persuasive geography and terrain of intent that can be charted like the charting of landscape on a physical map. With close inspection, we can chart a preacher's intention and tools of persuasion.

When one charts this persuasive geography, it is clear that the sermon is living art. The sermon is every bit as much of an art form or art piece as a picture on a wall. The artist paints the picture, and when placed in exhibition, the art piece is interpreted by those who view it. Not everyone interprets the picture in the same manner. There is often discussion, especially among art critics, as to what the artist meant and the techniques and processes used to produce the effects that viewers perceive in the art. Art often does not have a standard, correct, or right interpretation because what we see is often influenced by our social location and life experience.

I believe that enlightened discussion of many and various interpretations, from different life experiences and perspectives, helps us to approach the "meaning" of the art piece, hence the term *living art*. Any art that is still being interpreted and discussed is indeed living art. Therefore, my goal herein is, in the best sense of the word, to serve as a sermon critic and rhetorical topographer of Bishop Jakes's sermon and homiletical system. Rhetorical criticism allows us to peer deeply into the inner world of the preacher by analyzing the speaker's persuasive choices that expose the preacher's mind, heart, and belief system as represented in ideas, images, and arguments that the preacher offers to the Holy Spirit and audience to work with.

There are various persuasive options available to preachers in the creation and delivery of messages, such as choice of text(s), abstract truth, stories, metaphors, images, and similes, as well as breath, creativity, articulation, body movement, and intensity of expression. Preachers make rhetorical choices to both include and exclude material based upon the intention to persuade. My goal is to critically analyze the choices and how those choices work together to create effects in the preacher and audience as an offering to the Holy Spirit, who creates taste in the mouth, heart, and soul of the hearers.

The preacher formed by the tradition offers the recipe and ingredients, preacher and people stir the batter in delivery through call and response, then God bakes the sermon cake in the oven of heavenly fire. Preacher and audience then receive the taste, or the "moment of presence," that is, the evidence of the Spirit's efficacy and power to move the human heart. God is present in the human mouth, heart, soul, and the very room of the preaching event.

Please understand that I am not the kind of critic who seeks to find something wrong with Bishop's preaching, or what is missing, and offer instruction and correction. Bernard Devoto, an important literary critic of the 1940s, said, "The ultimate test of any form of criticism is not its insightfulness into a few plays but the standards it establishes for future creativity."[1] The goal of my being a sermon critic is to establish methods and standards from Bishop's preaching to inspire future creativity in readers' preaching. My greater purpose is that the reader might examine and carefully critique the recipe and ingredients they offer the Holy Spirit and the audience. The goal is to evoke new forms and standards of creativity in preaching and oratory.

Principles behind the Preaching

Much of what we have discussed herein came out of the experience of wonderful conversations with Bishop about preaching. I heard several important concepts and principles that shape his preaching that I would be remiss not to share. The principles are:

1. Broad thinking galvanizes people,
2. Preach to the people whom you see in your spirit, and
3. How bad do you want it?

Broad Thinking Galvanizes People

In our interviews, I continued to ask Bishop about his experience of preaching in diverse settings and what he had learned given such extensive preaching exposure that would help other preachers improve their preaching. Bishop talked first about the weight and transformative power of global leadership:

> I have been in the White House in the middle of some of the most volatile, turbulent times in the history of this country. I was about eight feet away from Bill Clinton when he announced his guilt with Monica Lewinsky.... I was with President Bush in Katrina, met Air Force One when it landed in Baton Rouge. I rode in the car with the governor and the mayor.... I spoke for President Obama for his Easter service. I spoke for him for his inauguration, which was probably the most nervous I've ever been in my life, incidentally. Those moments, the weight of the world rests on you. It's not about being an excellent orator. It's about the huge responsibility that you have to say something

> meaningful that galvanizes a body of people who are shattered and angry or hurt.

He mentioned that, as an orator, he would go in seeking to change the situation, but found that the situation most often would change him. Then he named the change: "You leave the room a little bit larger in your thinking and understanding of what it takes to lead a diverse group of people."

It is one thing when preachers lead a church or a group of people who think what the preacher thinks, who by and large agree with what the preacher thinks. But when we get outside of that bubble into a diverse set of ideas and feelings that has to be managed with sensitivity, one has to consider more than one's own perspective to be effective. These experiences explain one of the key principles underneath Bishop's preaching: to approach preaching from a broader perspective that allows the preacher to encompass the various and many experiences of diverse people in an audience.

Bishop says that this global perspective is his responsibility every Sunday because his audience is made up of everyone from homeless people coming out of shelters to teachers at university whose expertise is Greek and Hebrew; from chemists, doctors, and lawyers to people making beds and people who just got off work and come to church wearing a Walmart or Kmart uniform. On a regular basis, he speaks to diverse Americans whether they are black, white, Latinx, Nigerian, Ghanaian, Barbadian, Bahamian, or Jamaican. Bishop speaks to people who have translation systems in worship because they don't even speak English, but only, for example, Portuguese, Spanish, or French. There is signing for the hearing impaired. And we could add to this an international audience of many nations and people streaming the service through the Internet. Bishop says it makes him careful about what he says because he is speaking virtually to every generation, ethnicity, or political persuasion in America, and not only in America, but in the world. It forces him to be broader in his approach.

These broad experiences and situations taught Bishop that we are more alike than different, and the moment a preacher realizes this, they become a bridge builder. Again, Bishop relates his experience:

> I did a three-day revival in San Quentin. I ministered to Erica Sheppard on death row. I've been with parents about to bury a [Down syndrome] baby or who just disconnected [a loved one] from life support. When you are

> with people in trouble, you get to see who they really are. All the shades come down when the bleeding starts. And we are more alike than we are different, and knowing that I'm a centrist in my thinking, I tend to be a bridge builder and a unifier wherever possible. And if I can't build a bridge, I leave you alone.

Bishop Jakes sees himself as a bridge builder and unifier. That is powerful.

He believes that our country is polarized by a system designed to feed information and make money. Sometimes those two ideas, giving information and making money, conflict because the media can do a story for ratings rather than relevance. When it is necessary to satisfy the numbers in order to charge the advertisers, sometimes the "punch gets spiked" with division to get ratings. The country is being separated and divided because ratings and profit have ruled more than reality. If we ignored the divisive rhetoric, we might notice that our villains are not as bad as we think, and our heroes are not as holy as we think. A more realistic perspective might be that people are in the middle and can be both at some time or another. This approach broadens thinking in one's leadership and preaching. This also shapes the way that Bishop approaches the text, because he cannot be broad everywhere else and narrow when it comes to the text.

What this broad thinking amounts to is that a great orator must be a great listener. Bishop thinks that you cannot speak if you cannot hear. Ministry is born out of the ability to listen to people, to find out where they are, and to understand how to connect and relate to them. All of us want to be loved; want the best for our children; want to give love; want to be appreciated; want clean air, safe water, and healthy children; and want an opportunity to get up and become somebody. All people want to withstand the vicissitudes of life and see progress in their lives. Bishop argues that there are more things that unite us than divide us. Whether we are in rust belt states or the inner city, if you listen closely, the complaints are pretty much the same. America has started talking so loud that people can't hear each other. If people could back up a moment and hear each other, there's more to unite than there is to divide. And Bishop thinks this is true of all groups of people.

How Bad Do You Want It?

Bishop mentions that he has heard many fabulous preachers of all races and persuasions who were great orators, with immense ability to communicate and reach people. Whenever he hears this caliber of preacher, he asks himself, what made them good? What made them effective? What made them extraordinary? He finally concluded that each of them "wanted it," and if you wanted to be really good at preaching, you had to want it. It is only fitting that we go to storytelling rather than intellectual propositions to explain the meaning of this truth:

> There's an old story where a young preacher came to an old preacher. Old preacher was retired and gone fishing. Young preacher came down to old preacher and says, "I can't believe I caught you by yourself. I love everything you preach. I've heard everything you preached." The old man kept fishing because he didn't want to be bothered. He came out there to get away from all this.... The young boy kept bothering him, bothering him, bothering him. Old man wouldn't say anything to him, thinking maybe if I don't say anything, he'll go away.... Finally, old man put down the rod and reel, grabbed the boy, snatched him, and threw him in the lake. The boy couldn't swim. And he's [gurgling

> noise] going under the water, drinking water, and all he could drink. And about the third time he's going down about to die, the old man reached in and snatched him out of the water. "Why'd you do that? Why'd you do that? I was just trying to talk to you. Why'd you do that?" the young preacher asked. He said, "Shut up. Listen to me." He said, "You remember when you took that last breath and how bad you wanted it? That's how bad you have to want it." And he went back to fishing.

Bishop says the truth of the matter is most people don't want it like that. They want it, if God does it, or if it happens, or if it's supposed to be. They want it, but they don't want it like that. People who are truly great at what they do—whether that's culinary mastery, masonry, intellectualism, or preaching—they want it like that. If you don't want it like oxygen, you'll never be great at what you do. If you don't stay up when others fall asleep, if you don't listen to every sermon and interview and evaluate how well stated it was and, every now and then, jot down a word you didn't know to add to the arsenal to better articulate the wondrous grace of God, then you don't want it bad enough. And if you do not want it bad enough, it will never happen for you.

Enhancing Your Recipe

Ultimately, our goal is to help you improve as a preacher, and as a result, we have offered the ingredients of Bishop's sermon preparation process to help you discover and enhance your own preaching. We believe that the discovery of the ingredients of Bishop's sermon preparation process will make you more compelling in your delivery of the message and facilitate "winning moments" for you and your audience. Here are four suggestions for what you can do to discover and enhance your awareness of the ingredients of your sermon preparation process.

First, Bishop articulated his overall sermon preparation method as study yourself full, think yourself clear, pray yourself hot, and let yourself go. Please reflect on your sermon preparation process and organize your process in these four categories. What do you do that you would categorize as "study yourself full"? "Think yourself clear"? and so on? Or maybe you have other or different categories you might add. It is perfectly fine to revise Bishop's categories or even invent your own. The goal here is to have you intentionally identify and reflect upon your sermon preparation process such that you can critically evaluate its effectiveness. Perhaps you might add to your sermon preparation process or take something away. What is the relationship between prayer and preaching in your sermons? How consistent are you with your sermon preparation process? How would you improve your sermon preparation process after reading this chapter?

Second, Bishop explained that in our roles as preachers, when we mount the pulpit or stage, everything about us communicates. Bishop encourages preachers to look at how much communication goes beyond the mouth and wrestle with this question: Is my mouth out-talking the rest of me? It might be good to get a notebook or a diary and, across a few weeks, take notice of the parts of your delivery. Is your voice contributing to the music of preaching, or is it just an instrument of speech? Is your body inhibited? Are you self-conscious or God-conscious? How do you engage call and response? If you do, is it vocal only or does your body call the audience to respond? Are you a good doctor? Do people tell you where it hurts? In your preaching, do you let yourself go?

Next, I suggested two principles of Bishop's

preaching that you might want to carefully reflect upon. How broad is your preaching? Do you only preach to the people who agree with you? How diverse are the audiences to which you preach? Do you desire to preach to broad audiences? Do you think broad thinking galvanizes audiences? How well do you listen? Do you preach to the people whom you see in your spirit? Do you need a big crowd to preach well? How do you handle it when God puts you in small places or gives you a small crowd? Do you have a standard of preaching that you do not fall below regardless of the crowd?

Finally, Bishop challenged us to engage in self-reflection and a tremendous amount of self-honesty when he asked how much do we really want it? With all the honesty that you can muster before God, what do you say when you ask yourself how much do you really want to be an effective preacher? Am I willing to stay up late at night? Am I willing to put the necessary hours in to hone my craft? Do I believe that it is up to God and not to me? How bad do I really want to improve?

The art of preaching reflects the recipes inherited, the ingredients chosen, the process of blending and cooking—all in order to serve sermons as soul food with exquisite flavor. If you wish to create cravings in those that hear you preach so that they savor each of your sermons until the next one, then you cannot overlook any part of the process. No matter how much work went into the preparation and process, ultimately, the taste is what will be remembered.

APPENDIX

Analysis of Bishop Jakes's Sermon "I Didn't Know I Was Me"

By Dr. Frank Thomas

After multiple interviews with Bishop Jakes, I offer a close reading of "I Didn't Know I Was Me."[1] I have chosen this sermon because I believe it to be, in its purest form, an excellent example of the oratory and preaching of Bishop Jakes. There are many messages that could have been chosen, given that Bishop has spoken in diverse venues and settings across the globe—including at Microsoft and Toyota; before the king of Swaziland, the president of Uganda, and the president of Namibia; at Hillsong in Australia; on various talk shows, interviews with Larry King, Oprah, Dr. Phil, and the Breakfast Club; and at *Essence* events. He graced the covers of *Time*, *Ebony*, and the *Wall Street Journal*. This speaks to the depth and breadth of his oratory and preaching and its impact on the church, culture, and world. "I Didn't Know I Was Me" was preached on September 29, 2019, at the regular Sunday morning worship service of the Potter's House, Dallas, Texas, where Bishop serves as senior pastor.

The discovery of Bishop Jakes's rhetorical choices helps us to ascertain what makes him such a persuasive preacher. We must understand seven concepts critical to his persuasive strategy:

1. Call and divine authority
2. Balance of intellectualism and spiritual demonstration
3. Bonal structure of the sermon
4. Flesh on the bones: defining the formula for balance
5. Embodiment of the message
6. The Daddy persona, and finally:
7. The empowerment homiletic

Let's begin with Bishop's understanding of call and divine authority.

Call and Divine Authority

Without any question or hesitation, for Bishop Jakes, preaching is a divine call from God. The preacher does not just decide, based upon any of a myriad of human reasons, to become a preacher of the Word of God. There is a divine unction, a heavenly urge, and a spiritual call. Bishop explained his sense of the call in "I Didn't Know I Was Me," based in one of the main biblical texts of sermon, Jeremiah 1:4–5: "The word of the Lord came to me saying, before I formed you in your mother's womb, I knew you and I set you apart." For Bishop, being set apart means that God knows us and ordains us. God formed every person with a divine destiny before they were ever shaped in their mother's womb, and for preachers, that divine destiny is a call to preach the gospel.

Those whom God sets apart and calls, God also imbues with divine authority to speak. Bishop created great anticipation for a "word" from God in the congregation when he said, in announcing the sermon "I Didn't Know I Was Me," "God has been dealing with me about this message all week. I'm excited to be able to share it with you. I believe God is going to do great things." Bishop claimed and relayed a divine unction and authority given him by God to give the sermon to the people, to which the congregation, upon hearing that God had been "dealing" with him, responded with anticipation and enthusiasm by shouting and clapping. Divine authority is critical to Bishop's preaching. The reception and effectiveness of any preacher are based in their sense of call, unction, and divine authority that creates enthusiasm and anticipation in the people.

Balance of Intellectualism and Spiritual Demonstration

Although we emphasized the rhetorical force of the African American sermon in Chapter 13, "The Recipe," one feature that we did not adequately explain was the balance of intellectualism with spiritual demonstration, that is, abstract ideas of thought and substance combined with emotional freedom in interpretation and delivery. The best preaching combines the discovery and communication of the abstract ideas of the text with the feelings and moods that the text creates in the human heart. Although it is not the only form of preaching, the art of storytelling seems most often to accomplish the balance of both of these essential dimensions in preaching.

Bishop Jakes believes that preachers today do not put enough significance into the artistry of preaching. Many are fascinated with the stage or platform without the critical understanding that preaching is a calling and an art form. We have already discussed preaching as a calling, and Bishop now comments on preaching as an art form:

> It [preaching] is such an art form that I can tell a true master orator in two minutes of listening. I can tell the depth of the preacher because the artistry with which a preacher paints a picture in front of an audience causes them to see the abstract idea that was born in the preacher's head, prayer life, or consecration. It is then the preacher's responsibility to paint until the audience sees it without contamination, pollution, or dilution.

Preaching is the delivery of an abstract idea, born out of the preacher's personal, spiritual, intellectual, and emotional integration with the biblical text and its context. The artistry of preaching is to paint the picture such that the audience can see clearly the abstract truth or idea as relevant to their lives and context. Bishop admonishes preachers:

> We don't want to hear how the preacher feels; we want to hear how the preacher thinks. And if we hear how you think long enough, you can bring in how you feel. I do not want to come Sunday morning to hear you think me down because the sermon is all intellectualism, and I am taking notes and in class. What spurs the soul to keep on living is not always the dispersion of facts and wise quotes from intellectuals. There is nothing wrong with facts and wise quotes, but it is the passion with which the narrative is discussed, the balance of intellectualism and spiritual demonstration. Sometimes, it's more valuable than the content itself. Sometimes it is how you said it, and it isn't even what you said. You have to blend them together, thinking and feeling. When I work on a sermon, I feel like I am weaving study and intellectualism with passion and creativity. I am trying to get the mix right. I vacillate from that which is descriptive to that which is factual, from that which is intellectual to that which is experiential.

The sermonic message is a balance between intellectualism and spiritual demonstration of intellectualism with the addition of passion and creativity. Before I explain how Bishop achieves this critical balance, I would like to describe the skeletal system of his sermon. A skeletal system is the bonal frame that holds up and undergirds the human body. Without the skeletal system, the human body would be a shapeless sack of flesh. Likewise, the sermon has a skeletal system that provides the bonal structure of the sermon. Without it, the sermon disintegrates into a shapeless and formless mass of thought.

Bonal Structure of the Sermon

"Structure" is my word for the skeletal and bonal system of the sermon that allows the overall movement, organization, and logic and flow of the sermon based in idea development of one central thought. I remember being a kid and singing the old spiritual "Dem Bones."[2] Maybe you sang it, too:

The toe bone's connected to the foot bone,
The foot bone's connected to the ankle bone,
The ankle bone's connected to the leg bone,
Now shake dem skeleton bones!

We would sing all the way through the body: "The hip bone's connected to the back bone; the back bone's connected to the neck bone." The point is that all the bones have to be connected and working together for the body to carry out simple tasks such as walking or running. The same is true of the bonal system of the sermon; all of the parts have to work together.

Structure is what allows the bones of the skeletal system of the sermon to work together. H. Grady Davis says that a sermon is "an audible movement of thought across time."[3] If the bones are not connected and thought moves too slowly, then the sermon bogs down and is considered boring or not worthy of attention by the audience. If thought moves too quickly, then the audience cannot apprehend and listens passively overwhelmed, confused, and unable to keep up with the speed of the thoughts of the preacher. Thoughts have to be organized, developed, timed, connected, and "structured" to be effectively understood.

Based in the existential angst of African American life in America, in many African American sermons, and particularly Bishop's sermons, the overall bonal movement of the sermon is in the storytelling form of from trouble to grace, trouble in the text and life to the gospel that overcomes the trouble with grace, love, hope, and truth.[4] Grace is stronger, and as Paul Scott Wilson says, "trouble to grace re-enforces the overall movement of faith: *from* the exodus *to* the promised land, *from* crucifixion *to* the resurrection and glory.[5] My own basic method for trouble and grace is situation, complication, resolution, and celebration.[6] Bishop Jakes's "I Didn't Know I Was Me" sermon easily flows into an adaptation of this bonal structure:

Life Situation: God created us in eternity, knows us intimately and personally, called us, and sent us to earth with a divine purpose and destiny.

Life Complication: We came to earth and forgot our purpose and divine destiny, forgot who we were, and got lost, distracted, and fearful.

Situation in the Text: God put the Israelites into bondage and oppression at the hands of the Amalekites and Midianites because they chased idols (forgot who they were).

Complication in the Text: Gideon is threshing wheat in the wine vat to hide the harvest. An angel of the Lord appears to Gideon and says, "The Lord is with you, mighty warrior." Gideon retorts that if the Lord is with us why has all this happened to us? Why has the Lord abandoned us and handed us over to our enemies?

Resolution in the Text: The Lord then says to Gideon, "Go in the strength that you have and deliver Israel from the hand of the enemies." Gideon still hesitates, saying that he is of the smallest tribe and he is the youngest of that tribe. The angel says, "Go!"

Resolution in Life: We must remember that God knew us, fellowshipped with us, and sent us to earth with our divine destiny. Though we might think that we are small, we are mighty warriors with the assurance that God is with us to deliver us from the hand of the enemy. God wants us to go and win the battle.

Life Celebration: God knows you intimately and personally, called and sent you to a divine destiny. Arise to your divine destiny. Praise God, because you already have the victory. Praise God, because you know who you really are.

In some preaching circles, the central thought, as we said in the last chapter, is known as the theme sentence or the purpose statement, in effect, the bonal structure of the sermon. Here is what I would suggest is the theme sentence for the "I Didn't Know I Was Me" sermon, though Bishop never identifies it in the sermon itself: *God sent Israel and Gideon to earth with a divine destiny. Israel and Gideon forgot who they were, and were placed in bondage. God, in Judges 6, restores Gideon's and Israel's divine purpose, and though, like Gideon, we hearers forget who we are, God calls us to be mighty warriors and know that there is no enemy that we cannot defeat.* Bishop carries this central thought, this DNA, all the way through the sermon.

Flesh on the Bones: Defining the Formula for Balance

Now that we have defined the bonal structure, we must put the flesh on the bones for the sermon to come to life. When we use the phrase, for example, "putting flesh on the bones," we mean that in the human body on top of the bones is the soft tissue of the body, consisting mainly of skeletal muscle covering the bone. Likewise, Bishop places soft tissue on the bonal structure of the muscle. The flesh on the bones is Bishop's technique and process for balancing intellectualism and spiritual demonstration. Bishop's formula for the balance of intellectualism and spiritual demonstration is this: The preacher:

1. Develops the abstract principle from the biblical text and life experience into what might be called a contemporary proverb.

2. Moves to ensure the beauty of the proverb for the hearer (adornment).
3. Illustrates said proverb in the life of the hearer and their relationships (drama).
4. Directs, prompts, and requests call and response from the audience.
5. Receives the "moment of presence" from God.
6. Leads the people to connect with God and live out the biblically contextualized proverb.

Please allow me to explain each of these stages.

Abstract Principle to Proverb

The biblical text, based upon the story of God's interaction with human beings, is the primary venue to distill abstractions of divine truth into human experience. Sometimes the abstraction comes by looking deeply at the biblical text, and then approaching life, and other times one observes life, and then approaches the biblical text. Either way, *the divine truth of the text intersects with human life and is distilled by the preacher into the wisdom of human experience.*

Preaching professor Alyce M. McKenzie suggests that "wisdom is of God and signals God's presence" and principally comes in three forms: (1) a wise person—which is the personification of an aspect of the character of God (Jesus, for example, is God's wisdom in person); (2) a body of proverbs and teachings from the Bible, such as the books of Proverbs, Job, Ecclesiastes, Psalms, sayings and parables of Jesus, prologue to the Gospel of John, James, etc.; and (3) the path—the "art of steering a life" or walking in the way of wisdom.[7]

What makes one a wise person is to receive and act on wisdom that is revealed by another wise person based in teachings from the Bible, which steers one on the right path of the best way to live. Many would argue this is one of the main reasons and motivations as to why people come to church: to receive from the personification of an aspect of the character of God (the preacher) teaching from God's Word to steer the hearer in the way of wisdom.

After Bishop uncovers the abstract truth from the text, he delivers it to the people in the form of a contemporary proverb, much like a biblical proverb, a short phrase of practical wisdom long on meaning and experience that connects immediately to a person's life. The wisdom from the text that was born in the head, prayer life, or consecration of the preacher forms, crystallizes, and is brought into the listener's context, story, and personal life by the preacher's distilling the abstract idea into a contemporary proverb.

Allow me to offer an example from "I Didn't Know I Was Me" of a proverb from the biblical text. Bishop says, "So putting the text in context requires that I start from an unusual place. I want to begin with God, God himself, the notion of God, not church, not religion, God." The proverb is "God is not the church or religion, but God is God." Bishop wants to directly introduce the hearer to God. Bishop usually starts the sermon with an experience, fact, or piece of information that directly connects with the hearer's life, but in this message he is starting with the abstract concept of God.[8] Bishop is trying to help the hearer understand that people have mistaken God for church. God is bigger than church, religion, doctrine, theology, and all the rules and understanding that we as human beings have of God. Bishop's goal is to bring the notion of God into the reach and experience of the congregation. To make this happen, Bishop quickly moves to make the contemporary proverb beautiful by adorning it.

Adornment of the Proverb

After announcing that God is God, Bishop then says: "The One who rules and super rules and reigns, has absolute control, the Auspicious One, the Omnipotent One, the All Sufficient One, the El Shaddai, the

Consolation of Israel, the Mighty God, the Prince of Peace, God." The goal of adornment is the creation of beauty, wonder, awe, and adoration of God in the soul of the hearer. By the attribution of long-standing biblical names, descriptors, metaphors, and similes to describe God, Bishop creates an emotional attachment to the abstract thought. He adds passion and creativity to the abstract thought to help the audience see, feel, and hear God, even though there is no adequate human language that can describe God.

Many in the audience are familiar with these biblical descriptors for God and have an emotional history with Bishop's biblical recitation. If one is not familiar, the passion, conviction, and emotional commitment of Bishop and the audience are contagious. It is the passion with which the abstract thought is discussed that speaks to the audience. The rhetorical ability to add emotional intensity, spectacle, and beauty to abstract thought opens up another dimension of reception in the human mind, heart, and soul. Rhetorical devices such as alliteration (e.g., the *p*raise, *p*urpose, and *p*ower of God) move audiences because this level of attention to adorning language adds beauty, artistry, and emotional connection.[9]

Another classic example of adornment—adding beauty, intensity, and spectacle to language—is Martin

Luther King Jr.'s use of anaphora in "I've Been to the Mountaintop," the classic and ageless sermon the last night of his life, April 3, 1968, in Memphis, Tennessee.[10] King tells the story of being stabbed in New York City while signing books. He recounts that the blade was so close to his aorta that if he had sneezed, he would have died. He then mentions that he got a letter from a little white girl in White Plains High School that said she was so "happy" that he did not sneeze. King uses anaphora to raise the emotional intensity, "I, too, am happy that I did not sneeze. *If I had sneezed*, I would not have been around here in 1960 when students all over the south started sitting in at lunch counters." King traverses the civil rights movement by offering six anaphoric occurrences of "*If I had sneezed*," and with every "*If I had sneezed*," King raises the emotional intensity and pitch, and the audience enthusiastically responds, going higher and higher into the dimensions of passion, beauty, and conviction. Adornment moves beyond the rational dimension of abstract thought and allows abstract thought to reach the head, heart, body, and soul of the hearer. Bishop goes from abstract truth expressed in a proverb to the creation of beauty in the heart and soul of the hearer.[11] Let's now turn to the next step in the formula: illustration of the proverb.

Illustration of the Proverb

In Chapter 13, I said that, historically, every phase of Negro life was acted out and highly dramatized based in rituals of cultural performance. Jakes now places the proverb in the social relationships and demonstrates how the proverb might play out in cultural performance among family, friends, coworkers, and especially "haters." In "I Didn't Know I Was Me," he says:

> Jeremiah 1:4–5:... [shouts]... Before I formed you in the womb I knew you. *Before, before* I formed you. *Before* you had your first birthday. *Before* you were one week old. *Before* you were one day old. *Before* your momma was pregnant, I knew you. *Before* you were born. *Before* you were born. *Before* you were born I set you apart; [applause] I set you apart. I meant for you to be different. *Before* you ever even got here, I meant for you to be different. And you spent the first twenty years of your life trying to fit in. But the reason you never fit in is that I set you apart before you ever even got here. You didn't even fit in with your neighbors. You didn't fit in with your friends.

> Uh-oh. You don't even fit in your family. [Shouting] You are the only one in your family who thinks like you think because I set you apart before I formed you in the belly.... I knew you. I ordained you. I set you apart.

The abstract concept of God is adorned in the last section, and then illustrated and personalized in this one. The biblical proverb or abstract thought in Jeremiah 1:4–5 is that God knows us and sets us apart.

According to the formula, Bishop adorns the abstract thought, dramatizes it, that is, he pictures the abstract thought in cultural performance in social relationships. He adorns the proverb by the repetition of *before*. Repetition, in this instance, is repeating the same word *before* and *before you were born* many times for emphasis and raising the emotional intensity. God knew us and set us apart to be different, and because we are different, many people do not fit in with their families, friends, or neighbors. While this feeling of being different can be painful, Bishop reorients the feeling by suggesting that God knew the hearer and formed them in their mother's womb to be different or set apart. Set apart is dramatized, that is, pictured and placed within social relationships.

The proverb is placed in the personal life and social

relationships of the hearers with action words that can be pictures, by examples and not abstractions, and thus emotional intensity is evoked. Bishop repeats this process over and over again in the sermon. He takes the abstract thought from the biblical proverb, shapes it into a contemporary proverb, adorns it, and dramatizes it in the cultural performances of the hearer. Bishop moves through the entire text with this same process: abstract thought and proverb, adornment, then illustration in the social relationships of the listener. Each time he employs the formula, it connects to the last time he performed the formula, and each time builds upon the last time, rising in emotional intensity and effect. Let's look at the next step in the process, the prompting, directing, and engagement of call and response.

Call and Response

Now that an abstract truth expressed as proverb is adorned and dramatized, Bishop then calls for, directs, or elicits call and response from the audience. I mentioned call and response in the last chapter, and herein I would like to explicitly demonstrate how call and response functions in a sermon and how Bishop Jakes uses it as a persuasive strategy. As I suggested, the simplest definition of call and response is that the preacher says, and the people speak back, and the dialogue forms the pace, pitch, tempo, movement, and content of the message.

Some believe that the preacher shapes the message alone in the study. The preacher *prepares* the message alone in the study with God, and then offers it to the congregation. The audience is not passive in its acceptance of the message. Either the audience responds enthusiastically, which tells the preacher to continue on, or demurs and limits the preacher by lack of response, which, in effect, tells the preacher they are heading in the wrong direction. The audience constrains the preacher by their response or frees the preacher to rhetorically symbolize what is in the preacher's soul. Preacher and people partner to make the message happen. Bishop says:

> ...while I am preaching, I'm composing it right in front of you. And the weird thing is my television director is doing the same thing backstage that I'm doing onstage. Camera number one, zoom in. Camera number two, back up. I'm doing the same thing while I'm preaching, more of that, less of this, move this over here, move that over there. Because some of preaching is spontaneous for me. And

> in that moment of preaching there is that relationship between the pulpit and the pews and the cadence that exists in how we minister that to the congregation almost directs you to the spot. And you can feel all of that like a surgeon feeling for a knot. And so, I'll say more of this and sometimes, the other day, half my message didn't get out because I didn't need it.

Call and response is the rhythm and cadence between preacher and pew. The preacher, in the rhythm of preaching, makes space for the response, and the people fill the space with their response to what the preacher is saying. Call and response is a rhetorical device between pulpit and pew and functions best when it is playful, indicative of a positive and affirming relationship between preacher and audience.

There are several forms of call and response evident in "I Didn't Know I Was Me." The first is Bishop's check and register of what is going on in his own soul as he delivers the sermon. In several places, he checks, appraises, and bears his own witness to the material that he is preaching by saying several times, "Oh, my God, this is good!" He announces at the beginning of the message that he is dedicating five to ten minutes to set the context and put a frame around the picture (the heart of the message), but in checking with his own soul temperature, and the temperature of the audience based in call and response, he feels permission to go further. The announced five to ten minutes becomes thirty minutes because in the conversation with himself, the audience, and God, he felt the freedom to extrapolate. In another instance, he says, "This is so good!" or "Oh, my God!" "I feel like I am supposed to preach this today." He is checking the temperature of his own soul based upon what is being preached, and in these kinds of remarks, he is bearing witness that the spiritual temperature is high in his own soul.

Second, similar to the doctor probing for a knot or a lump, he checks on the spiritual temperature of the audience and ascertains it by their response. In this instance, he prompts, elicits, and directs their response.[12] Throughout the sermon, he says: "Are you hearing what I am saying?" "Come on, Potter's House, do what you do!" "Are you following me?" "I'm going to prove this to you. Can I prove this to you!" "You got me?" "Where my blessed people? Holla' at your boy!" "Isn't that good?" "Where my real people at?" "Who am I preaching to in here?" "Give me thirty seconds of crazy praise!" "I feel the power of God in this room." "Somebody shout 'YES'!" "Yes! Yes! Yes! Yes! Yes!" "Open your mouth and shout unto God." "Can I preach this thing? Should I preach this thing?" "Everybody who is tracking this word with me this morning, touch your neighbor and say, 'I think there's something on the inside of me'" "I'm talking to someone." "High-five somebody and say, 'Watch this!'" Who am I preaching to this morning?" "If I am preaching to you, make some noise in this place." These are the questions/instructions that the preacher offers to direct and discern the temperature of the audience, because that temperature shapes the direction of the message.

Third, the audience offers unsolicited feedback based upon abstract truth as proverb, the adornment of the proverb, and its dramatization. In the last chapter we said that when the preacher says something that the people feel, but do not have words for, the audience will respond and endorse what was said. People voluntarily and without direct solicitation from the preacher offer their own feedback, such as shouting, clapping, nodding their heads, laughing, and standing up at points in the message. The audience audibly says, "Go ahead, preacher," "Paint the picture," "You preachin' now!" "Bishop!!!" "Stay right there!" "Preach!" "Yes!" "I see!" The preacher does not control this. What has become popular since the 1990s is that people will stand up as physical affirmation of the truth of the message. The feedback is freely offered from the hearts, mouths, and bodies of the audience. They have been touched and want to respond, and again, their response solicited or unsolicited helps to shape the direction of the message.

All of this process—contemporary proverb from the biblical text, adornment, drama, and call and response—is combustible material baked by the Holy Spirit in the oven of heavenly fire. All of a sudden, because of the grace of God, God's presence is demonstrably available to the room. In Bishop's terms, God ushers in "the moment," what I label as the "moment of the presence." Having experienced "the moment," all I can say as preacher and congregant is that God is merciful. God puts heavenly treasure into broken earthly vessels. God is merciful to the human family. Thanks be unto God!

The Moment of Presence

Many of you know that Bishop has both Baptist and Pentecostal roots. Usually, in African American Baptist and Pentecostal circles, there is a "moment" when the presence of the Holy Spirit fills the room, and there is tangible and visceral demonstration of the Spirit's presence—dancing, shouting, hand-clapping, foot-patting, waving of the hands, crying, running up and down the aisles, jumping up and down, physical healings, and the like. There is also the aspect of inner healing of old hurts and wounds, the overcoming of fear, disappointment, and heartache, and the experience of joy and peace. Traditionally, in the Baptist church, the celebration, the last stage of the sermon, is the highest expression of the visible and demonstrable presence of the Holy Spirit.

In Pentecostal churches, there is an even greater focus and emphasis on celebration such that the moment of presence is evidenced by a "baptism" in the Holy Spirit, usually accompanied by all of the above in the Baptist church and also evidence of "speaking in tongues."[13] Pentecostals and neo-Pentecostals emphasize the demonstration and work of the Holy Spirit by baptism into the Holy Spirit. I believe it is principally the movement of the Spirit in the moment of presence in Bishop's preaching that has led to such increased exposure and fame across the globe. This joining of African American Baptist and Pentecostal traditions in preaching has resulted in dramatic and spontaneous eruptions of the Holy Spirit in the moment of presence that are, for many, the trademark of Bishop's preaching.

This moment of presence is the result of the process that we have heretofore outlined in Bishop's preaching. This does not mean that we can control the Spirit or any human processes can demand the presence and agency of the Spirit, but we can say that Bishop offers his very best in the formula, and then prays that the Spirit would come. And when the Spirit comes, there is shouting, dancing, hand-waving and hand-raising, etc. The call and response is now with the Holy Spirit. It is intensified and operative in the moment of presence at a fever pitch. The preacher and people are caught up in a fervor from God that opens up and reveals deliverance and new possibilities in the lives of the audience. In recognition of this moment of the presence in "I Didn't Know I Was Me," Bishop pulls back to explain and identify the "moment of presence:"

> [Shouting/applause] So this is where we are right now. The anointing of God is in this place. The Lord has you here for a reason. There is something that God is getting ready to do with your life. There is something that God has for you that is important. And I'm telling you, not knowing is a problem. Not knowing who you are is a real problem. Living your life based on your net worth is a real problem. The message is called "I did not know I was me." Lord have mercy. I feel like I'm supposed to preach this today! [Applause/shouts]

It is to this moment that everything in the sermon, the formula, and the persuasive process directly leads. Everything is subservient to the moment that God is front and center stage. Bishop talks about his own subservience to the moment of presence:

> And you have to love the moment more than you love the message. Once God has accomplished what he's trying to do, he doesn't necessarily have to use everything you have planned. And you have to know when to give up because if you don't, you will sacrifice the moment to get in the final three points of the message and lose the moment. So, you can't love what you prepared more than you love who you prepared it for. This is not about me, and it's not about my formula and my method and what I imagined. That's how Jesus becomes Lord when we submit to whatever he wants to do in the moment. I don't try to be God.... I do everything I can to study and pray and read.... So, never be more committed to the formula than you are to the Presence.

As a sermon critic, I, too, am more committed to the presence than I am to the formula, but the formula is a way to help preachers understand the presence of God in Bishop's preaching and get to the presence of God in their own preaching. Admittedly, formulas can be artificial and an overly technical explanation for spiritual phenomena. Like Bishop trying to explain who God is in human terms, I am trying to describe what cannot be described in human terms, the coming of the Holy Spirit in a sermon, and how and what techniques the preacher used to get there, how the people and preacher got there together, and this is very difficult to do. All of this labeling and naming almost feels artificial. Scribes find formulas in the effort to write the recipe and ingredients down so that contemporary preachers, as well as preachers in succeeding generations, will learn to help facilitate the taste of God in the mouth, body, heart, and souls of the people. If it is going to be passed down, it must be placed in a recipe, made up of formulas. I am never more committed to the formula than the moment of presence, because the Holy Spirit is helping me to understand and write the formula right now. This is not all of my intellect and homiletical acumen; it is some of that, but I feel the Holy Spirit leading me in this process. Thanks be to God!!

Allow me to further illustrate this point. I had a preaching mentor once to whom I said this: "You do an amazing job of preaching and you break every formula and rule that I teach my students." He looked me squarely in the face and said in good humor, "I stopped painting by numbers a long time ago." I had to laugh because, as we are learning, we paint by numbers until we no longer need them. All of this labeling and description in this chapter is a bit like painting by numbers. Necessary, but numbers *can* be guided by the Holy Spirit until we no longer need them.

And when the moment of the Holy Spirit's presence arrives, it presents an opportunity for profound transparency and honesty, where hearers and preachers can go inside themselves and confront fear, disappointment, pain, heartbreak, and anguish and make a decision to trust and follow God. Sometimes people come to the physical altar, and sometimes the altar is in their heart in their seat, or even, based upon livestreaming, in one's living room. Not in every sermon, but certainly in this sermon, Bishop utilizes altar call as the response to the moment of the presence.

The Altar Call

When I say the "altar call," I do not mean the altar call as the "invitation to discipleship," or what some would know as the opening of the "doors" of the church to receive new persons into the Christian family. That could be one kind of altar call, but in the instance of "I Didn't Know I Was Me," the altar call is a collective and communal prayer. The moment of presence presents a space where, based upon apprehension of the DNA or the central idea of the text, people can be honest before God and admit that, for example in this sermon, they forgot who they were. In the moment of presence, they reaffirm, reconnect, and make a profound commitment to walk in the way of the wisdom and blessing that they have received from the preacher and God.

In "I Didn't Know I Was Me," after the moment of presence, the altar call starts with the transparency of Bishop Jakes:

> I was the last person to know I was T. D. Jakes. I didn't know that. Books were being translated into different languages. I didn't know that. I saw it, but I didn't see it. The stadiums were full, people fighting outside to get in. I didn't know I was me. I don't like saying it because it makes me sound stupid. I was on the *New York Times* bestseller list; it still did not add up that I was me. I think sometimes grace puts blinders on your eyes. I could see all of you, but I could not see me. But there was a voice in my head, correcting

> damaged thinking. Honestly...I am telling you that I was playing the piano for people and driving people around. I didn't know I was me. That does not mean it should have happened any sooner because I think it is the menial things that develop you. [Applause] I think it is the blind spots that give you focus. I'm not trying to rush the process. I'm just trying to describe a place that you might be now. All I knew is that whenever I got around something that had my destiny, I was drawn to it. [Applause/shouts]

This transparency leads to the people being transparent before God and the pastor leads the people in prayer where new commitments are made and lives are reinvigorated. The process of the balance of intellectualism and spiritual demonstration is complete. The Holy Spirit has come and done the work that only the Spirit can do.

However feebly, I have attempted to define the formula as flesh on the bones and as part of the persuasive strategy of Bishop Jakes, given the context of the sermon "I Didn't Know I Was Me." The process of persuasion includes abstract principle to proverb, adornment of the proverb, illustration of the proverb, call and response, the moment of presence, and the altar call. It is also difficult to understand why Bishop Jakes is so persuasive without a discussion of the performative nature of his preaching, which we labeled in the last chapter as delivery and using the body as an instrument. In the last chapter, it was abstract theory, and herein, I want to show how it functions in the actual sermonic process that helps to generate the taste of God. I specifically want to talk about Bishop's use of space and walking across the stage and down into the audience. I have labeled the body as instrument in this chapter as embodiment.

Embodiment of the Message

In the African American preaching tradition, the Word of God has to be "embodied," that is, grounded in the total person: head (rationality), heart (emotions), and, for our purposes in this chapter, the body (physicality) of the preacher. The Word must be incarnated in the preacher's body and, in the best sense of the word, performed. Relative to Bishop's preaching, his bodily performance of the Word of God is the backdrop, undergirding, and foundational scaffolding upon which all of the concepts that we have discussed thus far are built: call and divine authority, balance of intellectualism and spiritual demonstration, defining the formula for balance, and structure and synchronization. Performing the Word means full and free inclusion of the body in preaching, including body movement, voice inflections, hand gestures, walking across the stage, coming down and walking among the congregation, facial expressions, head bobbing, and even timing and syncopation with the organ. Again, in the last chapter, I talked about delivery, but specifically I want to look at Bishop's utilization of space and his walking across the stage and down into the audience.

Bishop is credited with a new movement in preaching in the 1990s that Martha Simmons labeled as "from a pulpit to the stage."[14] Preaching moved from standing directly behind the pulpit to free movement and walking back and forth across the stage. Though he can preach from behind a pulpit, for Bishop, there is a relationship between space, walking, and preaching because he walks most of the message. I asked him about walking and he said:

> It's so funny because I preached alone so long without a congregation, walking behind my mother's house in the woods and sometimes pacing in her basement. I have this proclivity

> between thought and walking. When I walk and preach, I am back at my mother's house.

And even though he walks up on the stage, there is always a point in the message at which he comes down the stairs into the audience and walks among the audience in the same manner he walked upon the stage. I asked him about coming down from the stage and he reflected that it was a way of connecting, building relationship, and communicating that we are all on the same level:

> Originally, in the days of Christ and the early church, there were no platforms and the whole idea of an elevated preacher in a lofted position was something of which the Scripture had disdain. The power of Jesus was to be one from among you. To understand the fact that he has come to be with us, Emanuel, God with us, the whole narcissistic Nicolaitan ideology of pulpits was to create aristocracy. So, ultimately when I come down to the ground, it's for connectivity. I want to be close to you. I want to be one from among you. I want to sit where you sit. I want to look you in the eye. I want to create

> the intimacy that this stage will not allow.... And it's about connecting with the audience on the most personal level especially if you're going to deal with the most personal subjects. If you're going to talk to me about my childhood, my marriage, my finances, and being molested when I was twelve, don't do that from some lofty position of arrogance. Come down where I'm at and be one with me and recognize that that vulnerability means something. And those tears falling from my face—it's my life, my life.

These are examples of embodiment of the word in the total person of the preachers, and especially body. Body movement and space are very important as part of the strategy of persuasion for Bishop. Much more could be said in this discussion of embodiment, but for lack of space and time, the body is fully engaged in the preaching moment. Bishop fully utilizes his body, in regard to space and walking, as part of the strategy to persuade the audience.

I want to go to a very important concept that is a critical part of the persuasion strategy of the preacher, and that is the preacher's persona.

The Daddy Persona

From the overarching perspective of how a preacher persuades an audience, every preacher adopts a persona. For Aristotle, every orator had three modes of proof that makes persuasion possible—ethos, pathos, and logos. *Logos* is the logical thought structure of the sermon, which we earlier described as structure and synchronization; *pathos* is the emotion, conviction, or passion that a speaker brings to the oratorical moment; and finally, and what Aristotle said is the most important of the proofs, is *ethos*, or character. Ethos is the credibility that the speaker has with the audience in regard to the subject matter at hand. The reason that we listen to Warren Buffett so intently when he speaks about investments is that his track record gives him a large cache of credibility. Bishop's credibility is the demonstration of the Spirit's power that has fallen around his preaching in many prior times, circumstances, and preaching opportunities. He has spiritual credibility with the audience based upon past performance. Ethos is the speaker's credibility with the audience.

As part of establishing our credibility, speakers develop a persona to aid in gaining authority with the audience. Persona is a role or identity that the preacher constructs and adopts to convey ethos or credibility as part of the strategy of persuasion. Persona is the total package of how the preacher shows up to the pulpit, including clothing and dress (from suits to robes to skinny jeans), biographical data, résumé, curriculum vitae, or social media profile, or whatever preachers or those introducing the preachers choose to highlight out of their background. I was preaching in Mississippi, and to establish my credibility with the audience, the pastor introducing me emphasized that I was one of theirs because my résumé indicated that I had been born in Mississippi. I had instant credibility with the audience. Some might call credibility the preacher's brand, but I prefer persona. Historically, the term *persona* is derived from theater, the wearing of a mask to play a part. In the best sense of the word, persona is the mask that the preacher brings to the pulpit, or the appearance one presents to the world. In contemporary pop culture, the onstage persona of Beyoncé is "Sasha Fierce," indicative of her high-octane performances. Sasha Fierce is the onstage performance persona of Beyoncé Knowles Carter.

Our persona might be embedded or unconscious because many of us have never consciously named the way that we show up to the pulpit, though consciously, one way or another, we have meticulously planned our arrival. It might be that we have never viewed our planning as a strategy of persuasion. Every preacher consciously or unconsciously constructs their persona as a strategy of persuasion to reach an audience.

In my graduate preaching classes, I present the aforementioned definition of persona in a lecture. I invite the students to take a few minutes and reflect, then write a statement that best represents their understanding of their persona. After writing their own statement, I ask them to pair off with one of their classmates and take a half hour each and describe their persona to the other student. Typically, this is a deeply moving time in class, and often there are hushed tones, quiet laughter, and even tears. At the completed time, I ask those who are willing to share their ethos with the whole group. After hearing their sharing, I then share mine. I share mine to help the reader understand the concept. I wrote my aspirational ethos as this:

> Frank A. Thomas: The Good Man Speaking Well
>
> The importance of moral character, intelligence, kindness, and deep belief in God.[15]

Based upon prayer, careful reflection, honesty, and feedback from those that know me best, this is how

I try to show up, not only in the pulpit, but in the world. Of course, I am not always this, and of course, I at times fall short, which is why I used the term *aspirational.*

Let us turn to ask this question: What is the persona of Thomas Dexter Jakes? Notice I called him Thomas Dexter Jakes because "Bishop Jakes" is part of the persona.

In regard to the discernment of Jakes's persona, he said this:

> Sometimes I will sacrifice a preaching moment to have a daddy moment to talk to you like your father should have, to challenge you.... I never sought to be a great orator. I just wanted to help people. So, one year we bought these boutonnieres for all the fathers and everybody was supposed to pin a boutonniere on their father. Then I realized that most people didn't have a father to pin it on. A little boy got up, walked up front, and pinned me while I was standing there. He said, "You're the only father I have." And one by one, grown men and women started coming till I was covered with roses.... So I am literally bleeding under my clothes and I still

> didn't stop them from pinning it because it was worth the pain to provide the moment. And being what people need is always painful. And there's always a bleeding that they don't see. And so, it wasn't strange to me that I was bleeding under my clothes because I've always been bleeding under my clothes. And it's a good illustration of what ministry is at its best. The roses they pin on you create bleeding in places they do not see, and yet we stand there and we wear the rose and when we get home we wipe the blood.

I believe this statement is a window into the persona of Bishop—wise, spiritual, and sacrificial father. He talks to the congregation and audience as a good father talks to his family, evidenced in the comment about "a daddy moment." The wisdom of God is personified in him as a father who disperses divine truth in proverbs such that people know how to steer their lives. He realizes that being a father takes great sacrifice. As a good father, he is also sacrificial for the family. He follows the example of Jesus, the wise and sacrificial savior.

Let me explore the final aspect of Bishop's persuasion strategy, empowerment preaching.

The Empowerment Homiletic

I want to suggest that, in the final analysis, Bishop Jakes—based in God's call on his life and through gifts of entrepreneurship and communication—offers to the church, nation, and world an "empowerment homiletic," that is, messages that are designed to empower people to enact fundamental change in their lives.[16] Most preachers would suggest that they seek in their preaching to empower people, so let me explain and clarify further. Bishop's empowerment homiletic is *an unequivocal message of hope and overcoming, based in the gospel of Jesus Christ, that leads to a change in consciousness as a strategy of personal and social liberation.* Empowerment preaching is a liberation strategy, often entrepreneurial and economic, that seeks to raise people and a community from poverty, lack, hopelessness, and fear, or any negative emotion or barrier that hinders people from the future God has for them.

While empowerment preaching acknowledges structural and internal barriers that limit people—such as oppression, violence, racism (personal and institutional demons), and hate—all of this can be overcome when one discovers one's purpose in God. Based in a relationship with God, the goal is to control one's own destiny, and especially one's economic future and destiny. This differs drastically from "prosperity preaching," where the crucial concern is individuals prospering financially and "sowing seeds" for blessing and miracles. This differs from social justice preaching, where the concern is to disrupt systemic and institutional systems of racism, hate, and bigotry. At this point, it is best to allow Bishop to speak in his own words:

> I see myself as an economic empowerment catalyst because I am trying to teach our people, not through magic, not through throwing $20 bills on the altar, that there is a way to get up when a person will not let you get up. I'm trying to demonstrate entrepreneurship, economic empowerment, financial literacy, and second chance opportunities. I am trying to teach them in my life, teaching, and ministry that it is possible to get up.

Empowerment preaching locates and identifies any negative attitude, place of fear, doubt, defeatism, or being hindered by internal or external oppression and vanquishes it with the challenge to be who God created one to be, or in popular parlance, to live out one's divine destiny. I apologize for quoting Bishop extensively, but he says it better than I could ever explain it:

> I feel more like a messenger, a Moses, than just a preacher. I have the weight of the gospel, but I also have the weight of our people and their struggle on me.... I want to see them achieve. I want to see them come up. I want to see us tell our own stories and build our own companies and businesses. I'm tired of begging other folks to give me a chance. I would rather make my own chance and let them beg me. I know that if we put our efforts, finances, and talents together, we can do anything. But we have been trained to think that the only way we can get up is at the mercies of some other people. I rebuke that with everything inside of me.... I do not believe that my future is in the hands of someone who hates me. I believe that I am fearfully and marvelously made; that I am gifted, bright, and talented; and I can create my own place in the world. I want my congregation to be relentless and tenacious....

> We can do anything—build neighborhoods, communities, schools, and malls. We can build anything.

Week after week, Sunday sermon after Sunday sermon, speaking engagement after speaking engagement, in movies, books, talk shows, interviews, television appearances, conferences, digital empowerment products, social media, business round table meetings, and meeting with politicians and celebrities, the message is the same: *Through an eternal relationship with God, each of us is fearfully and marvelously made, gifted, bright, and talented, and can create our own place in the world. We do not have to beg anyone to give us a place or a chance; through relationship with God, we can create our own places and chances in the world.* Bishop Jakes offers his sense of call and divine authority, balance of intellectualism and spiritual demonstration, defining the formula for balance, structure and synchronization, embodiment of the message, and the daddy persona to the Holy Spirit and the audience as an empowerment homiletic that attempts to persuade people that they can control their destiny in God. The Holy Spirit has utilized this strategy of persuasion to place the taste of God in the mouths, hearts, and souls of millions of people across the globe.

Discovering and Enhancing Taste in Your Preaching

Ultimately, our goal is to help you improve as a preacher, and as a result, we have offered this analysis of the taste of Bishop's sermon in the hopes that it will help you discover and enhance the taste of your own preaching. We believe that the discovery and enhancement of the taste of your preaching will make you more compelling in your sermons and facilitate "winning moments" for you and your audience. Here are four suggestions for what you can do to discover and enhance the taste of God in your preaching.

First, I would suggest that each preacher go back to God and reconnect to their sense of call and unction and discover or rediscover their divine authority. A certain kind of enthusiasm and anticipation comes to us and is contagious to the audience when we are anchored in our call and divine authority.

Several years ago, I went through a slump in my preaching. All of a sudden, I noticed that my preaching was not uplifting and inspiring to me, and if not uplifting and inspiring to me, in all probability it was not to anyone else either. I rationalized that we cannot always preach our best sermons, but the same feeling persisted in me for several months. My experience is that preachers, like hitters in professional baseball, can go into a slump, and I thought that I would come out of it like hitters in baseball eventually come out of their slumps. A year later, I was still in the slump.

To make a long story short, I got my Bible and went to the sanctuary and reconnected with God about my call, the unction from God that was on my life and in my preaching. I discovered again my divine authority. From that moment on, I determined I would never again allow anyone or anything, including myself, to block the free delivery of a gift that God gave me, namely preaching God's Word. I was going to freely share my gift of preaching with energy, passion, strength, confidence, insight, and clarity. Every now and then in our ministry service, we must find a place to connect or reconnect with God to discover or rediscover the call and unction from God on one's life and receive divine authority. We simply cannot effectively preach without a sense of divine authority.

Second, having heard Bishop's strategy of persuasion, including a formula, compare Bishop's formula to yours. What is your formula? What is your strategy of persuasion? Do you adorn or dramatize? What is your structure? I would suggest a careful survey of your own preaching based upon some of the techniques and processes defined herein. It is not a matter of you doing them as Bishop does them. It is about you being intentional and identifying what you do, evaluating what you do, and affirming the good of what you do and then deciding upon areas of improvement. Preaching like Bishop is not your calling. Bishop's preaching is a lifetime commitment to a method, formula, and structure of preaching, along with the desire before God for continuous improvement. Your calling is to preach *your* very best. It is about adding a level of consistent discipline and evaluation to a level of talent and gift you have such that you maximize all that God has given you.

Third, follow the directions that I shared in the section on persona. What is your persona? What is your ethos? Your credibility? What is your strategy to persuade as you show up in the preaching moment? I would suggest that you reread "The Daddy Persona" above and follow the directions that I utilize in my classrooms. Sit with yourself in prayer and meditation and write down what you perceive as your persona. Then share that perception with someone you trust and get their feedback, or share it with a couple of people that you trust and get their feedback. Gain perspectives that intentionally allow you to understand your persona, your overall strategy to persuade an audience. Gaining this insight will embolden you by allowing you to be more intentional in persuading people.

Fourth, I took the bold step of naming Bishop Jakes's homiletic, his overall strategy of preaching and persuasion. If you had to name your homiletic, how would you name it? I know that this sounds daunting, but take a stab. Have some prayer, do some reflecting, and see what God reveals to you. It will improve your preaching. It will bring to the conscious level what you have been doing unconsciously all along. Once you name it, you can own it, critique it, celebrate it—all in the effort to be more effective in preaching.

Notes

Chapter 5

1. https://americansongwriter.com/tom-waits-on-tom-waits-interview/.

Chapter 10

1. For further information on the central message of this sermon, see Martha Simmons and Frank A. Thomas, eds., *Preaching with Sacred Fire: An Anthology of African American Preaching 1750–Present* (New York: W. W. Norton, 2010), 509–14.
2. For more information on the early preaching of "The Eagle Stirreth Her Nest," see Charles Lyell's *A Second Visit to North America*, 3rd ed., vol. 1 (London: Spottiswoodes and Shaw, New-Street-Square, 1855), especially Chapter 2.
3. Lerone A. Martin, *The Phonograph and the Shaping of Modern African American Religion* (New York: New York University Press, 2014), 67–68.

Chapter 12

1. https://www.linguisticsociety.org/content/how-many-languages-are-there-world, accessed September 29, 2020.

Chapter 13

1. The Reverend Jesse Louis Jackson said this in the forward to Jeff Todd Titon's book *Give Me This Mountain: Life History and Selected Sermons* (Urbana, IL: University of Illinois Press, 1989).
2. "Do You See This Woman? A Little Exercise in Homiletical Theology," in David Schnasa Jacobsen, ed., *Theologies of the Gospel in Context: The Crux of Homiletical Theology* (Eugene, OR: Cascade Publishing, 2017).
3. Hurston's four novels, two books of folklore, an autobiography, her short stories, and her plays are an invaluable source on the rhetoric of oral cultures of African Americans. She and her work were virtually forgotten until, in 1975, *Ms. Magazine* published Alice Walker's essay "In Search of Zora Neale Hurston," which revived interest in the author. The essay was republished in Walker's book *In Search of Our Mothers' Gardens* (New York: Mariner Books; repr., 2003) as "Looking for Zora," 93–118. In 1973, the words "Novelist," "Folklorist," and "A Genius of the South" were placed on the marker erected at Zora Neale Hurston's grave in Eatonville, Florida, by Alice Walker.
4. Valerie Boyd, *Wrapped in Rainbows: The Life of Zora Neale Hurston* (New York: Scribner, 2004), 296.
5. Hurston wrote these reflections in *The Sanctified Church: The Folklore Writings of Zora Neale Hurston* (Berkeley, CA: Turtle Island Foundation, 1981), published as a posthumous

edition that assembled various essays on folklore, legend, and popular black mythology first published between the late 1920s and the early 1940s.

6. Hurston, *The Sanctified Church*, 53.

Chapter 14

1. Following Cicero and Isocrates, Michael Charles Leff makes this argument in "Tradition and Agency in Humanistic Rhetoric," in Antonio DeVelasco, John Angus Campbell, and David Henry, eds, *Rethinking Rhetorical Theory, Criticism, and Pedagogy: The Living Art of Michael Charles Leff* (East Lansing: Michigan State University, 2016), 18.
2. Kari Jobe, "You Are for Me," https://www.youtube.com/watch?v=6d9Lkgy-Nkc.

Chapter 15

1. Edwin H. Friedman, "The Play's the Thing," originally presented at Georgetown University Medical School, Match 20, 1980 as "The Therapeutic Reversal as Psychodrama."

Appendix

1. The video of the sermon "I Didn't Know I Was Me" can be viewed at https://www.youtube.com/watch?v=h2J7cqnvAOc.
2. "Dem Bones" (also called "Dry Bones" and "Dem Dry Bones") is a Negro spiritual. According to *Wikipedia*, the melody was composed by author and songwriter James Weldon Johnson (1871–1938) and his brother, J. Rosamond Johnson. It was first recorded by the Famous Myers Jubilee

Singers in 1928. Both a long and a shortened version of the song are widely known. The lyrics are inspired by Ezekiel 37:1–14, where the prophet Ezekiel visits the "Valley of Dry Bones" and prophesies that they will one day be resurrected at God's command, picturing the realization of the New Jerusalem, https://www.youtube.com/watch?v=GiLrnhcPQrU.

3. H. Grady Davis, *Design for Preaching* (Philadelphia: Fortress Press, 1958, 14th printing 1985), 165.
4. Paul Scott Wilson argues that Milton Crum originated the description of the trouble/grace school, which is the biggest school in preaching today. Wilson acknowledges African American preaching as a major force in the trouble/grace school. See Paul Scott Wilson, *Preaching and Homiletical Theory* (St. Louis: Chalice Press, 2004), 101–15.
5. Ibid., 98.
6. For more information on structure (that is, situation, complication, resolution, and celebration), see Frank A. Thomas, *They Like to Never Quit Praisin' God: The Role of Celebration in Preaching* (Cleveland: Pilgrim Press, rev. ed., 2013) and *Preaching as Celebration: Digital Lecture Series and Workbook* (Indianapolis: Hope for Life International, rev. ed., 2018).
7. Alyce M. McKenzie is a professor of homiletics at Perkins School of Theology, where she holds the George W. and Nell Ayers LeVan Endowed Chair of Preaching and Worship. Her 2018 presentation is entitled "Holy Boldness: The Four Virtues of the Wise Preacher." See also her *Preaching Proverbs: Wisdom for the Pulpit* (Louisville: John Knox Press, 1996) and *Preaching Biblical Wisdom in a Self-Help Society* (Nashville: Abingdon Press, 2002).

8. Bishop Jakes usually starts the sermon from some familiar illustration or story grounded in the experience of the listeners to build rapport with and the interest of the hearer. In this case, he starts with God, an abstract concept for many, and has to work harder to build the rapport.
9. Bishop Jakes said in an interview: "Alliteration is the occurrence of the same letter or sound at the beginning of adjacent or closely connected words. Some preachers alliterate their outlines, making all their points begin with the same letter. Sometimes just the main points are alliterated, other times the sub-points are alliterated, still other times the sub-sub-points are alliterated."
10. Anaphora is the repetition of a certain word or phrase at the beginning of successive lines of writing or speech. It can be used in novels and short stories, but it's most commonly seen in poetry, essays, and formal speeches. Anaphora appeals to the feelings or emotions of the audience. Repeating a word or phrase causes readers or listeners to start to anticipate the next line. They are drawn into your words through a sense of participation. Because they know what's coming next, they are more receptive to the emotional resonance you are trying to get across.
11. Bishop Jakes establishes the pattern of abstract thought, adornment, and then dramatic illustration, but in the middle of the sermon, what we will soon call the resolution or teaching, Bishop goes straight from textual proverb to what we will discuss next, illustration of the proverb with drama and action words and not abstractions.

12. In the period of the 1980s and 1990s, there was a shift such that the historic "call and response" of the black church was replaced by a preacher-directed response. For example, no longer were congregants starting or finishing the sentences of preachers according to their shared storehouse of worship jargon or the traditional calling for "Amens" or rhetorical devices such as "You don't hear me." Instead preachers were prompting people to "touch two people," "give the Lord a handclap of praise," "high-five a friend," "touch a neighbor," or repeat something instructed by the preacher. See also *Preaching with Sacred Fire*, 590.
13. Jakes was raised Baptist and became a Pentecostal at Greater Emmanuel Apostolic Church, where he was ordained as bishop and later resigned. Baptists and Pentecostals (and neo-Pentecostals) are two similar groups of Protestant Christianity who believe in the working of the Holy Spirit in very different ways. Pentecostals believe that glossolalia, "speaking in tongues," is the initial evidence of the baptism in the Holy Spirit and the person has not been "saved" until he or she has believed, been immersed, and received this "gift of the Holy Spirit." Baptists do not believe in the initial evidence of the baptism in the Holy Spirit. Believers receive the Holy Spirit but there is not the requirement of initial evidence.
14. See Martha Simmons, "Whooping: The Musicality of African American Preaching Past and Present," in *Preaching as Sacred Fire*, 875.
15. This statement was heavily influenced by Quintilian, who believed rhetoric was not just good speaking, but added the

ethical dimension of the character of the speaker, hence the good man speaking well. One could not be a good speaker if one was not a good person.

16. For more information on the four categories of preaching and empowerment preaching itself, see *Preaching as Sacred Fire*, 9–12.

About the Authors

T. D. Jakes—one of the most inspirational, influential, and treasured spiritual leaders of our time—is the #1 *New York Times* bestselling author of more than forty books. He is the CEO of the towering TDJ Enterprises, spanning film, television, radio, publishing, podcasts, and an award-winning music label. He is a Grammy Award–winning music producer, and his blockbuster films have achieved international success at the box office. His inspirational conferences (MegaFest; Woman Thou Art Loosed) continue to have a profound global impact. Bishop Jakes is a master communicator whose trusted voice is heard in more than 80 million homes daily and across a vast worldwide audience via social media. He resides in Dallas, Texas.

Frank A. Thomas, PhD, currently serves as the Nettie Sweeney and Hugh Th. Miller Professor of Homiletics and Director of the Academy of Preaching and Celebration at Christian Theological Seminary, Indianapolis, Indiana. Indicative of his great love of preaching, an updated and revised version of *They Like to Never Quit Praisin' God: The Role of Celebration in Preaching*, considered by many to be a homiletic classic, was released in August 2013. For many years, Thomas has also taught preaching to doctoral- and master's-level students at McCormick Theological Seminary in Chicago, Illinois, and at Memphis Theological Seminary in Memphis, Tennessee. He is the CEO of Hope For Life International, Inc., which formerly published *The African American Pulpit*. With a long history of excellence in preaching and preaching method, Thomas was inducted into the prestigious Martin Luther King Jr. Board of Preachers of Morehouse College in April 2003. Thomas also serves as a member of the International Board of *Societas Homiletica*, an international society of teachers of preaching. Thomas is the author of *American Dream 2.0: A Christian Way Out of the Great Recession*, released by Abingdon Press in August 2012. He also coedited *Preaching with Sacred Fire: An Anthology of African American Sermons, 1750 to the Present* with Martha

Simmons, published by W. W. Norton & Company in 2010. This critically acclaimed book offers a rare view of the unheralded role of the African American preacher in American history. Thomas is also the author of several other books on subjects from matters of prayer to spiritual maturity. He served with distinction as the senior pastor for two remarkable congregations: New Faith Baptist Church of Matteson, Illinois, and Mississippi Boulevard Christian Church of Memphis, Tennessee, for eighteen years and thirteen years, respectively. Thomas holds a PhD in Communications (Rhetoric) from the University of Memphis, a Doctor of Divinity from Christian Theological Seminary, Doctor of Ministry degrees from Chicago Theological Seminary and United Theological Seminary, a Master of Divinity from Chicago Theological Seminary, and a Master of Arts in African-Caribbean Studies from Northeastern Illinois University. Thomas and his wife, the Rev. Dr. Joyce Scott Thomas, each earned their Certified Professional Coaching Certificate (CPC) from the Institute for Professional Excellence in Coaching (iPEC). While they are equipped to coach in corporate, executive, business, life, personal, or group settings, they are most passionate about enabling pastors and pastors' spouses, as well as coaching in the area of preaching. Thomas's most recent book, *The Choice: Living Your Passion Inside Out*, published by Hope For Life International Press, October 2013, explains and explores the spiritual and coaching process to live your passion from the inside out. Thomas is a nationally and internationally sought-after keynote speaker and lecturer. Thomas and his wife have two adult children.